Gardening With Dwarf Trees and Shrubs

Pinus heldreichii 'Compact Gem'

THE GARDENER'S HANDBOOK: A SERIES OF USEFUL BOOKS—VOLUME I
DR. JOHN PHILIP BAUMGARDT, GENERAL EDITOR

Gardening With Dwarf Trees and Shrubs

ANDREAS BÄRTELS

Translated by
Roberta J. Cooper

John Philip Baumgardt
Technical Editor

TIMBER PRESS
Portland, Oregon

Drawings: Gisela Tambour, Göttingen, W. Germany
Color Photographs: Andreas Bärtels, Waake, W. Germany

German edition published 1983 by Eugen Ulmer GmbH & Co.
Wollgrasweg 41, 7000 Stuttgart 70(Hohenheim), W. Germany

ISBN 0-917304-93-4

Printed in Hong Kong

Timber Press
9999 SW Wilshire
Portland, Oregon 97225

Contents

Foreword

In today's small gardens, entryway gardens, roof gardens, and containers (pots, planters, window boxes) on terraces, patios, and balconies there is no room for full-sized trees and shrubs. In most cases, there is only room for trees and shrubs that grow slowly and remain small. This book will discuss dwarf trees and shrubs, their habits and needs, and how they can be optimally incorporated into small gardens.

This book does not attempt to cover the species and cultivars of dwarf trees and shrubs in their entirety. My intention is to include only those which are most suitable for gardens and are currently available on the market, if only in specialty nurseries. It is surprising how many varieties are available today. Such a wide selection is helpful to plant-lovers who only have a small area to work in, and want to cultivate a variety of plants.

A brief review of the chapters may seem to dictate that large areas are needed to accommodate the plants described. Closer reading however, will make it clear that in all cases dwarf woody plants can be used alone or integrated with standard trees and shrubs, if the garden area available is large enough. The drawings will give the reader an idea how the two types can be used together.

Using the plants correctly requires some knowledge of the ecological conditions of their natural habitats. Therefore, the encyclopedia portion of this book is arranged by the type of habitat in which the species and forms are naturally found.

Thanks to the scrupulous and precise work of Mrs. Gisela Tambour, numerous habitat drawings appear in the book. These drawings and the color photographs complement the text.

In 1951, Camillo Schneider laid the foundations of gardening in small areas with dwarf plants in *Our Important Dwarf Woody Plants,* (Pub. Eugen Ulmer). As a result, dwarf plants are now better understood. It is hoped that this book will stimulate the use of dwarf trees and shrubs and be instrumental in creating successful landscapes using them.

I would like to thank my publisher, Roland Ulmer, for his prompt and enthusiastic support of my proposal, and for his assistance in organizing the material. I would also like to thank his co-workers in the proofreading and production departments. Their contributions were important to the book's completion.

I will gladly receive criticism and feedback from my readers to help make *Dwarf Trees and Shrubs* a more comprehensive work in future editions.

Waake, Spring 1983   Andreas Bärtels

1

What Are Dwarf Trees and Shrubs?

Garden and park landscapes utilize trees and shrubs of greatly varying heights. They range from hardly taller than a hand's width, such as a carpet or mat, to trees of 30 to 40 meters. Generally, woody plants defined as dwarf should not exceed 1 meter in height. This arbitrary limit does, however, allow for natural variations.

According to their growth characteristics, we can categorize dwarf woody plants into several groups.

1. Authentic Dwarf Species
Trees and shrubs belonging to this group seldom reach 1 meter even after many years' growth. Included here are species such as *Erica herbacea* and *Vaccinium vitis-idaea,* both with a naturally prostrate or low habit, and also various garden forms of normally taller growing species including countless dwarf conifers, *Berberis thunbergii* 'Atropurpurea Nana' among others. Others are perennials which are sometimes considered to be somewhat woody (subshrubs) due to their woody base (suffruticose); for example, *Alyssum* (including *Aurinia*) and *Iberis.*

2. Trailing Shrubs
This group includes trees and shrubs whose branches lie on top of the soil and, therefore, reach only a negligible height. Representative of this group are *Vinca minor* and *Cotoneaster dammeri.* All larger-growing varieties and forms must be excluded from this group; for example, the flat but far-spreading *Cotoneaster dammeri* 'Skogholm', *Cotoneaster salicifolius* 'Park-teppich' or *Symphoricarpos* × *chenaultii* 'Hancock'.

3. Small, Summer-Blooming Shrubs
As with roses, some trees and shrubs develop blossoms in summer or early fall. *Caryopteris, Hypericum,* and *Perovskia* are typical. As a rule, these forms are pruned back each spring. They grow out during the summer, but rarely grow taller than 1 meter.

4. Bushy Broadleaf Woody Plants
Most of these shrubs grow rapidly in the early stages, reach their mature height quickly, and then branch out. Typical are the *Potentilla fruticosa* cultivars, some dwarf willows, and the *Genista* and *Berberis* species.

5. Dwarf Conifers
Save for a few exceptions like *Pinus mugo, P. pumila,* and some *Juniperus* species, conifers are all large trees in the Northern Hemisphere. Dwarf conifers are selected cultivars of otherwise arborescent species. Most of them grow very slowly, often only a few centimeters per year. Some reach a height of 2 to 3 meters only after decades. These cultivars will be discussed in detail in the encyclopedia of conifers.

The popular container grown forms from China and Japan, known as penjing or bonsai, will not be included. These forms are forced to a dwarf-like height through gardening artifices. These include continued shaping, regular pruning, gross reduction of feeder roots, and closely controlled nutrient and water supplies.

The Origin of Dwarf Trees and Shrubs

Basically there are two kinds of dwarf woody plants used in ornamental plantings: natural species and selected cultivars of otherwise larger-growing species which remain small as the result of genetic mutations. As a general rule, deciduous dwarf woody plants are natural species, whereas dwarf conifers result from mutations.

Natural species

Dwarf species are usually found growing in stress-causing climatic and soil related ecological conditions. In the Arctic and Alpine regions, certain species have adapted themselves to wind exposure, drought, and poor soil or to sites of excessive moisture. These species must contend with deep snow, high winds, insufficient supplies of water and nutrients and in some cases, they must struggle with a population density for survival, all of which causes partial reduction of their size.

Environmental requirements of dwarf woody species are revealed by their natural habitats: the northern alpine and arctic regions, gravelly and stony dry sites of the mountainous and sub-alpine regions, sub-mediterranean and high locales in the mediterranean zones, dry forested areas in the Balkan Peninsula, the steppes of Eurasia and East Asia, the arid deciduous forests and prairies of central North America, the nutrient poor sand dunes of the Atlantic heaths and the transitional moors, heaths and tundras of the Temperate and Arctic Zones. The natural distribution of each species will be discussed in the encyclopedia section of this book.

Cultivars

Dwarfed garden cultivars frequently result from spontaneously occurring branch mutations. Among conifers, an example is the "Witch's Broom". These mutations are usually identified on plants in cultivation, but are sometimes found in the wild. Dwarfism commonly expresses itself as a reduction of internodal length and stronger, thicker shoots. The strong shoots arise from a dormant bud in many cases.

The causes and mechanics of dwarfism are thus far not understood. For example, the dwarfing character of slow-growing dwarf apple rootstocks apparently derives from a relatively higher content of growth-inhibiting, and a lower content of growth-producing, hormones. But the causes are not yet scientifically certain. Other dwarf cultivars are derived from selected and cloned (vegetatively reproduced) wild species which are more or less clearly differentiated from the natural population through specific attributes (such as reduced growth, better blooming qualities, and different blossom colors or increased fruiting).

Naturally dwarf species retain their phenotypic characteristics when propagated from seed. Dwarf cultivars, on the

3

other hand, must be vegetatively propagated for two reasons: most of them either do not develop the capacity to produce fruit, or they do not produce viable seed, while the offspring of those setting viable seed quickly revert to type in succeeding germinations.

A Heath Garden; the real intent is "A moor landscape."

Various Landscape Uses of Dwarf Trees and Shrubs

For a number of reasons gardens are becoming smaller. Rows of condominium gardens are no longer an uncommon sight. According to a study done in 1981, the average size of 10-year-old or older gardens in West Germany is 4500 sq. ft. Often the only garden area available today is an entryway plot and more often than not, only small terrace gardens or window boxes are available. Under the best conditions today's gardens have but limited space for standard trees and shrubs. Confined gardens must use small woody varieties, especially terrace gardens and containers such as planters.

However, the use of dwarf woody species is not limited to small gardens. They are indispensable in larger gardens and parks as well. Some gardens are inconceivable without dwarf woody plants, particularly heath gardens, rock gardens, narrow strips at the front, back and sides of houses, on sloping areas and steep banks.

The term "dwarf trees and shrubs" should not be associated with the preconception that they are "unnatural", "ugly", or "crippled". Many of the miniature woody plants in the latter part of this book are native species which develop beautifully when used in compatible environments with carefully chosen companion plants.

Heath Gardens

No group of dwarf shrubs has ever been as popular as heathers. It does not matter whether the plant is the summer-blooming *Calluna vulgaris* or the winter-blooming *Erica herbacea*. The heath garden has become one of the most beloved kinds of gardens, even if realized only in a reduced landscape scheme. Seldom is there enough space in a garden to replicate an authentic, restful, spacious heath landscape. However, through careful site and plant selection, a very pleasing garden can be designed in a smaller area. To do this, it is necessary to understand the various species and varieties of heaths and heathers, their climate and soil requirements, and how to arrange and cultivate them in a garden.

Natural Heath Landscapes
The term "heath" varies in meaning from treeless dwarf shrub acid moors through the plant assemblages found in chalky soil in mountainous and hilly areas to sparse pine groves growing on sandy soil. In earlier times heaths were called "Commons". Commons were poor grazing lands which belonged to no one and were commonly used by all the landowners in the vicinity. "Heath" was in those days a proper term and was not used to describe landscape.

In central Europe, natural treeless dwarf shrub heaths have been influenced by mankind for centuries. During their heyday about 150 years ago, they were

A Heath Garden with *Calluna vulgaris* cultivars and *Empetrum nigrum*.

6

markedly varied. Since then, many have disappeared through controlled cultivation and reforestation.

The plains of central Europe support only three environments which still contain species such as *Calluna vulgaris, Erica tetralix* and *Empetrum nigrum:* lime-free, shifting sand dunes, bogs and marshes, and soils composed of acid mixtures of peat and minerals.

In their ecology, there is a difference between the natural treeless dwarf shrub moors of northwestern Europe, and the protected moors of the flatlands. The coastal *Erica* and swamp heaths, and the winter-hardy crowberry (*Empetrum*) moors along the northern seacoast belong to the first group, while the dry sand moors (*Calluna* heathers), the moist sand moors and the loamy moorlands belong to the second group.

Dwarf shrubby Ericas appear as bushy mountain heaths and clump grass meadows not only in the forested mountain ranges of central Europe, but also in the Scottish Highlands and high elevations in the Swabian Jura Mountains. There, basic rock formations are covered with acid loam. *Calluna vulgaris* is present only in the lower levels of the true Alpine Zone, but in the montane and sub-alpine zones *Rhododendron ferrugineum* or *Vaccinium uliginosum* populations take over.

Calluna Heaths

In western and northern Europe, *Calluna* moors are found in areas with oceanic climates. The Lüneburger heath is by far the best known. Dwarf shrub heaths stretch along the humid, constant climates of the Atlantic coastline, from Scotland and Scandinavia, to the western Atlantic Balkan Peninsula.

A major component of the *Calluna* moor is *Calluna vulgaris,* which grows best in dry, sandy situations. The only other plants likely to grow there are a few brooms (*Genista* spp.), some grasses and junipers. In central Europe, sandy heaths often overlap with neighboring plant communities. They often extend into transition moors, into sparse birch and oak forests and pine groves. There are no treeless dwarf-shrub moors in eastern Europe. Because of the inland climate, this sort of plant community can only flourish under the protection of thin forests.

In the Arctic, north of the polar timber line, dwarf shrub heaths (moors) overgrow the tundra. Tundra is a treeless community of plants adapted to nutrient-poor soil among beds of peat of varying sizes and depths in which only dwarf woody species are found. Along with shrubby heaths and heathers, other evergreen heathers grow here such as *Vaccinium uliginosum,* Bog Billberry; *Arctostaphylos uva-ursi,* Bearberry; *Phyllodoce caerulea,* Blue Mountain heath; *Rhododendron lapponicum,* Lapland Rhododendron; and *Loiseleuria procumbens,* Alpine azalea; a few dwarf willows; *Salix herbacea,* Dwarf Willow; *Salix reticulata,* Neatleaf Willow; *Salix glauca; Salix lanata,* Wooly Willow; and the dwarf birch, *Betula nana.*

In addition to the previously mentioned Coastal Ericas, there are other plants which grow well in a moor environment. Except for a few tree and shrub species such as the Sand Birch, the common Scotch Pine and various junipers; Pimpernelle Rose, Woadwaxens and Gorses, and other small shrubs are more commonly found to the west due to damper soil. Especially in sand dunes, *Genista* is often supplanted by *Empetrum nigrum,* or not uncommonly by *Arctostaphylos uva-ursi.* Other *Genista* species colonize similar soils, but unlike the dry moor Broom-Heathers, appear in prevailingly maritime-influenced zones. These include *Genista pilosa, G. tinctoria, G. anglica,* and *Ulex europaeus.* Very dry locations are often colonized by *Salix repens* ssp. *argentea.*

In addition, *Erica tetralix, E. cinerea, E. vagans* and even *E. ciliaris,* which is barely winter-hardy, all appear in the mild coastal areas in central Europe. In moister locations, frequently in the thick hummocks of the sphagnum mosses, *Vaccinium oxycoccos, V. uliginosum, Ledum palustre* and *Andromeda polifolia* are found. *Vaccinium uliginosum, Ledum palustre* and *Vaccinium myrtillus,* grow in the midst of Scotch Pine and junipers.

Sedges (*Carex arenaria*), grasses (*Cornyphorus canescens, Festuca ovina, Koeleria glauca, Nardus stricta*), and a few herbaceous perennials integrate well and they break up the carpet moorland of plants: *Thymus serpyllum, Sedum acre, Helichrysum arenarium, Campanula rotundifolia, Hieracium pilosella, Dianthus deltoides, D. arenarius, Armeria maritima, Verbascum densiflorum, Verbascum thapsus, Jasione montana* and *Antennaria dioica.*

Laying Out A Heath Garden

The *Calluna* moor, as a rule, serves as a model for designing heather gardens. If the garden is to function optimally, specific soil, climate and plant location requirements must be met.

Climatic Requirements

Calluna vulgaris is the most important ingredient in a heather garden; it is best suited to Atlantic climates, which have constant temperatures. It cannot endure extreme winter temperatures or snow, and some cultivars cannot endure dry spells in summer. Among others, 'H.E. Beale', 'Elsie Purnell', 'Peter Sparkes', 'Silver Queen' and 'Tom Thumb' are considered somewhat frost susceptible. Lack of moisture and direct sunlight damage the slow-growing species and all the yellow-leafed cultivars whose foliage quickly burns.

It is very important to protect *Calluna* from drought and cold winds beyond its natural range of distribution, especially in higher elevations.

In suitable climatic conditions, a heath garden can be laid out in an open, sunny location. In the continental climates, it should be laid out beneath the shade of high-crowned trees. In this area, the more tender *Erica* cultivars will have to be left out of the garden. If necessary, *Calluna* can be replaced with the less demanding *Erica herbacea.*

Soil Type and Soil Preparation

The soil requirements of Callunas are flexible. Their natural habitat is the damp, acid humus of sphagnum moors, but they colonize as well in dry, permeable sand, coarse rock debris and granite gravels. Their greatest expanse is attained on the acidic, nutrient poor, silica-rich sandy moors of the ice-age which are covered with a more or less heavy virgin humus layer.

A heath garden is best developed on acid, fast draining, high humus soil (sandy, moorland soil). Whenever such conditions are not present, the soil must be adjusted. According to the soil type and its condition, organic materials should be added until the soil is brought to the correct pH and texture.

In addition to the correct pH, soil must meet other requirements if a heath garden is to develop optimally. The fine roots of many species of moorland plants (including many conifers) live in symbiosis with various soil fungi, which only flourish in well-aerated, permeable soil containing a high percentage of organic matter.

Optimal pH levels are dependent upon the soil type. According to van de Laar (1976), the following levels should be created for a heath garden:

Sandy soil	4.5 to 5.0 pH
Moorland soil	4.0 to 4.5 pH
Peat-enriched moorland soil	4.0 to 5.0 pH
Sandy loam	under 5.0 pH

In strongly alkaline soil, iron and manganese are so tightly bound that the plants cannot benefit from them. This leads to leaf chlorosis which is expressed as a yellowing of the leaves.

The best material to lower the pH level is sphagnum peat. It helps to use it in all soils as a supplement to organic materials. If the pH level is not higher than 6.0, substantial additions of peat will suffice to lower it. According to Berg and Heft (1979), a pH-level between 6.0 and 7.0 will fall to 5.5 by adding 4 cu.m (5 cu. yds.) of peat for each 10 m² of the soil. The peat can be worked into the soil by hand or with a rototiller. After planting, it is advisable to mulch the bed with an additional 2 cu.m (2 cu. yds.) of peat to a depth of several inches.

Lowering the pH level in a small area can be accomplished by adding agricultural grade sulfur to the soil. Sulfur oxidizes in the earth and changes limestone, which is harmful to most heath plants, into a harmless gypsum. The Botanical Garden of Tübingen recommends the following amendment of sulfur crystals to reduce the pH level:

Sulfur kg/m²	Lower pH-level from	to
0.8	6.0	5.0
1.4	7.0	5.0
1.9	8.0	5.0

The sulphur should be spread evenly and worked into the soil, 15 to 20 cm deep. After about 4 weeks, peat and other materials can be added.

The peat, continually being broken down, can at least in part be replaced through applications of composted shredded (hardwood) bark or with a 1:6 mixture of finely chopped brush or wood chips and peat or leafmold. The comparatively coarse condition of the twigs and manure compost guarantee a long lasting soil structure stability and good aeration of the plant's substrate. To keep the pH of a naturally acid soil from becoming more acid van de Laar recommends mixing .5 kg/m³ and 1.0 kg/m³ of calcium ammonium nitrate with sphagnum peat.

As a rule, sphagnum peat is sold in pure form but fertilized peat mixtures are also available in some areas. It is important to use as coarse and fibrous peat as possible because it aerates the soil better and decomposes less quickly than fine peat. Fertilizer formulated for use with Ericaceae is often recommended. It has a high percentage of organic matter, a pH level of 3.5 to 4.0, 240 mg/l phosphorus and 360 mg/l potash and other trace elements.

When improving soil, loosen it quite deeply, especially if an impermeable hardpan is present. Aeration and drainage, in heavy, clayey soils can be improved by adding coarsely grained concrete sand (at

9

least 1 wheelbarrow full per 3m²), together with organic materials.

Although moorland plants occur on nutrient poor soil in their natural habitat, nutrients have to be carefully added to the soil in a moorland garden. Rhododendron and other fertilizer-peat mixtures (with trace elements, if available), composted manures and organic fertilizers (hoof and horn meal, blood meal, and bone meal) should be worked into the soil in small amounts before planting.

Artificial Growing Media

Clay, heavy loam, or strongly alkaline soils cannot be adjusted enough by adding peat or sand to be suitable for heath gardens. In such cases, the native soil must be replaced with an artificial growing medium. Remove at least a spade deep (10–12 in.) layer and replace it with a suitable medium.

Several different "synthetic" media formulae can be recommended. A peat-sand mixture (3 bales of peat to 1 wheelbarrow coarse sand), a mixture of peat, composted bark, and sand, consisting of equal volumes of sphagnum peat and decomposed, finely ground bark humus (0 to 8, or 0 to 16 mm) to 1 wheelbarrow coarsely grained sand.

Useful, but rarely obtainable are native moorland soils (soils which have a layer of peat 10–12 in. deep underlying decayed leaf humus and leafy litter deposits, and a pH level of 4.0 to 5.2), heath soils (dry, peaty, raw humus deposits with admixtures of fine quartz sand and a pH level of 4.0 to 5.2), conifer needle soils (having a pH level of 3.5 to 4.5), and leaf molds (having a pH level of 5.3 to 6.4). All of these soils should be mixed with an equal volume of coarse sphagnum peat.

To prepare a planting area first break up the underlying soil for fast drainage; the overlying prepared soil should be at least 10 inches deep. After removing the top soil of the bed area, the loosened bed bottom and edges should be covered with 10 to 15 cm of coniferous prunings or wood chips. By doing so, not only will the soil drain well, but the planting medium will not be exposed to calcareous subsoil. The planting medium should then be added to a depth 6–8 in. higher than the original soil, and the edges should be shored up equally as high with a border of lime-free rocks or wood (impregnated logs or rail road ties are best if wood is used).

The newly introduced planting medium will compress and in time it will be level with the surrounding soil.

Terrain Features

The restful leading line of a gently sloping terrain, as is often encountered in the middle of the Lüneburger moors, is characteristic of a heath landscape. A sloping terrain often is characteristic of a heath landscape. Such a landscape cannot be reproduced in most small, home gardens. Sculpting valleys and hills in small gardens is inadvisable. Only large gardens offer the room to include a softly sculptured landscape. In small gardens the illusion of a fluid terrain has to be created. This is done by skillfully choosing the right combination of plants.

The use of rocks in a heath garden landscape are problematic. If used, only good-sized, rounded rocks should be incorporated (the exception being the use of jagged rocks around the edges of an elevated garden to shore up the soil). These rocks should be placed in the ground, heavy side down, exactly as they are found in nature. They should be sunk

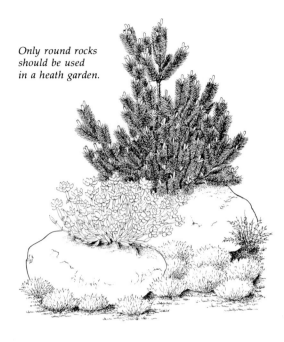

Only round rocks should be used in a heath garden.

It is important to plant in favorable weather (however, not during high summer temperatures) and with optimal soil conditions. Planting in soil which is too wet quickly leads to soil compaction, which is especially dangerous for the fine roots of the Ericaceae.

Planting holes should be no larger than is absolutely necessary in thoroughly prepared soil. In loose soil, heaths, heathers, and other moorland species may be planted a little deeper than they were in their containers or in the nursery. After planting and treading the soil around the plants, each should be thoroughly watered. They should not be squirted with a nozzle, but rather deeply soaked with a slow-running stream from a watering can or a hose. Then, the soil should be gently loosened and mulched with coarse, damp peat. Additional watering is only necessary in very dry or warm weather. It is better to underwater as it is easy to drown freshly planted shrubs.

It is very important to make sure the entangled roots of the *Calluna* and *Erica* varieties are untangled before planting. Otherwise, the roots cannot grow into the adjacent soil and so can parch even in damp soil. [Take plants from pots or unwrapped balled Ericaceous species and slosh the root ball vigorously in a tub of water to free at least the outer roots, then plant quickly before roots air dry.]

into the soil for a part of their height. Avoid using clusters of small rocks as they tend to seem unnatural in a heath garden.

Planting and Cultivation
After all weeds and their roots have been removed and the soil has been prepared, heaths, heathers and other moorland species can be planted in the fall or in the spring. Since almost all plants come in containers these days, fall planting can start as early as late summer. Early planting has the advantage that the plants will have established their roots before heavy frosts set in. Root establishment is a prerequisite for carefree overwintering. Spring planting should be undertaken as late as possible (perhaps from around April) so that late frosts will not damage the plants.

The spacing between heathers is dependent upon their growth habit and growth rate. Slower-growing varieties of *Calluna vulgaris* are planted 20 to 30 cm apart; faster-growing ones between 40 to 60 cm. *Erica herbacea* varieties are planted between 30 and 60 cm apart, depending on their rate of growth. *Erica tetralix, E. cinerea* and *E. vagans* varieties require somewhat less distance.

Most shrubs in a heath garden do not require pruning. Usually Genistas and *Daboecia cantabrica* are pruned. When planted in spring, these varieties remain tidy until the following spring, at which time they should be pruned back almost to the previous year's wood.

Subsequent cultivation of an established heath garden requires little work. Of course, weeds must be constantly controlled, since some of the slow-growing heather varieties cannot compete with rapidly growing weeds. When weeding, take care to only superficially disturb the soil as the *Calluna* and *Erica* species have shallow root systems. It is recommended that exposed soil be mulched with coarse, damp peat until the root systems have matured enough to become encrusted. Constant walking on soil compresses it and impedes root growth. Therefore, it is wise to put in walkways of rock or wood (thick boards or slices of logs, or split railroad ties) for subsequent maintenance at the time the bed is prepared.

Although *Calluna vulgaris* is rather drought resistant, a heath garden has to be irrigated during long dry periods. Obviously, it is beneficial to irrigate with water having a low degree of hardness, as the lime content of hard water must be compensated for by adding more peat to the soil.

Fertilizing is another part of regular maintenance. Even Genistas, members of the nitrogen-fixing Leguminosae which thrive on nitrogen poor soil, can tolerate small doses of fertilizer, and the other plant varieties cultivated in a heath garden require it. In addition to organic fertilizer and peat fertilizer mixtures, 20 to 30g/m^2 of chemical fertilizer should be added to the soil on a yearly basis. The chemical fertilizer used should be slow release or water soluble and in solution be pH neutral or in the acid range, preferably chlorine-free. It should contain trace elements in addition to nitrogen, phosphate and potash.

Winter precautions need only be taken when frost sensitive plants are used

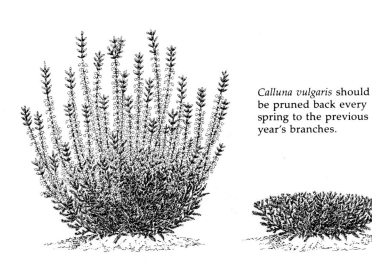

Calluna vulgaris should be pruned back every spring to the previous year's branches.

outside of their normal range of distribution. In the more continental climate zones, some varieties must be protected from parching winds and intense winter sun. These include, *Daboecia cantabrica, Erica vagans, E. tetralix, E. cinerea* and the yellow-leafed cultivars of *Calluna vulgaris* and *Erica herbacea.* In such cases, the plants should be covered lightly with well needled small branches of pine or other conifers. In the spring, the blanket of branches will gradually shed needles, allowing the plants to slowly adapt to bright light. The plants should be completly uncovered only during cloudy, rainy weather.

Precautions against frost heaving include mulching exposed soil, especially under the branches of small, frost sensitive plants, but also throughout the bed. Such small shrubs include *Caryopteris, Ceanothus,* a few *Daphne* spp.; *Elsholtzia, Fuchsia, Hebe* spp., *Perovskia,* Japanese Azaleas, *Skimmia* spp. and *Ulex* spp.

Whether heaths and heathers need to be pruned on a regular basis is widely debated. Some enthusiasts object to any pruning whatsoever. This attitude can only be maintained as long as the gardener is willing to replace plants as soon as they become unsightly. In their native habitat, Genistas do not become lank and straggly because they are pruned by grazing animals and regularly regenerate themselves by seed. In a city garden however, heath (moorland) gardens must be pruned rather than eaten away by sheep. It should be noted that once plants become lank, shaggy and begin to fall apart, they cannot be reshaped.

With the exception of the slow, mat forming *Calluna vulgaris* cultivars, all others should be pruned between mid-March and mid-April every year. They should be pruned back so that only a short, leafy piece of the previous year's growth is left. As a rule, plants growing alongside one another are uniformly pruned to the same height with hand or electric hedge-shears. Although isolated shrubs are usually pruned symmetrically, a better appearance is achieved if the branches are pruned somewhat unevenly.

Summer-blooming heaths such as *Erica vagans, E. tetralix* and *E. cinerea* are pruned back in a similar fashion. Species and cultivars such as *Erica carnea* 'Springwood White' may remain dense and compact for several years without being cut back; this is also true for species and cultivars of *Cassiope* and *Phyllodoce. Daboecia cantabrica* varieties should be pruned back at least to the previous year's inflorescence.

Plants For The Heath Garden
In designing a private heath garden, one does not have to limit oneself to enjoying the customary complement of plants of the wild, moorland heath. Numerous dwarf woody plants, grasses, and perennials selected from other plant populations enhance the character of a heath garden. This includes many dwarf garden forms of otherwise larger-growing species.

With all the conceivable variations of plant material available, the typical appearance of a heath should, however, be maintained. The garden should be carefully designed using a sparse selection of shrubs, widely spaced, and interplanted with *Calluna vulgaris* cultivars, *Erica* species and cultivars, and other mat-forming heath-type plants to create a close-knit carpet effect. Other recommended plants are: *Empetrum nigrum, Arctostaphylos uva-ursi, Vaccinium oxycoccos* and *V. macrocarpon.* It should be noted that grasses and perennials are only enriching ornamentals and should never dominate a heath garden.

Conifers and Broadleaf Trees and Shrubs

[Broadleaf rather than deciduous because many of these are broadleaf evergreens; very few are deciduous]

With the exception of those species requiring shade and alkaline soil, there are numerous conifers and broadleaf plants described in the encyclopedia portion of this book that will fit nicely into a heath garden. Among them, the Ericaceae: (*Andromeda, Gaultheria, Kalmia, Ledum, Pernettya, Pieris*), the small-leafed *Rhododendron* and *Vaccinium* species, Brooms and their relatives (*Cytisus, Genista* and *Ulex* species), *Helianthemum* spp., *Teucrium chamaedrys*, the ever-blooming *Potentilla* varieties and *Spiraea bumalda* hybrids, all of the bushy dwarf willows and dwarf birches, many summer-blooming shrubs (for example *Caryopteris, Lavandula, Perovskia* and *Santolina*), and the miniature and shrub roses, deciduous and evergreen *Berberis* spp., *Cotoneaster, Euonymus, Hypericum* and *Paxistima* spp. Of the dwarf conifers, junipers, spruces and pines are best suited for a heath garden.

In miniature heath gardens, the only appropriate woody plants are dwarf cultivars. In larger gardens, however, some standard trees and shrubs are used. Among deciduous trees, birches, especially the white-trunked birch species which thrive in sandy soils are particularly effective. (*Betula jacquemontii, B. × koehnei* and *B. papyrifera* look well.) All of the *Sorbus* species also make excellent heath garden trees. Consistent with the heath garden's character are wild roses and Polyantha Roses, all sorts of *Genista*, deciduous and evergreen *Berberis* and *Cotoneaster* species, the elegant, late winter-blooming *Corylopsis* species, the attractive, autumnal tinted *Euonymus alatus* and *Fothergilla* species, and the evergreen

Ilex aquifolium and *I. × meserveae* cultivars. As standard trees of small stature suitable for planting in or near the heath garden all species of *Sorbus* are outstanding.

When using conifers the choice is not restricted to common pines and columnar junipers. There are many slow-growing varieties which remain small and do not exceed the restrictions of a small garden. The junipers offer an indispensable addition to every heath garden. These include the especially slender cultivars of *Juniperus virginiana* and the ornamental cultivars of *J. communis*, Oblonga Pendula' and 'Horstmann' which often are regarded as a "must" for the heath gardens. Among the pines, must be mentioned pencil-thin *Pinus sylvestris* 'Fastigiata', the elegant *P. parviflora* cultivars, interesting *P. aristata*, columnar *P. wallichiana* 'Densa' and *Pinus nigra* var. *pyramidata*, slow and compact-growing *P. nigra* 'Jeddeloh', decorative *P. leucodermis* and its 'Compact Gem' cultivar, and lastly, the colorful, yellow-leafed *P. contorta* 'Frisian Gold'. Among the spruces, the omnipresent *Picea likiangensis* var. *purpurea*, native to western China, and the Japanese *P. glehnii* are valuable alternatives. The slow-growing *Picea breweriana* are especially elegant with their drooping branches.

Among the hemlocks the dwarf forms of the beautiful, silver-blue needled *Tsuga mertensiana* are very useful.

Finally, the yew should be mentioned. In a heath garden, the thin columnar forms are especially valuable; also useful is a special form such as *Taxus baccata* 'Dovastoniana', vertical but with pendent new shoots. (See also the section on Entrance Gardens.)

Perennials and Grasses for the Heath Garden

Perennials	ground covering varieties	Growing height		
		short 5 to 20 cm	medium 30 to 50 cm	tall over 50 cm
Acaena buchananii	×			
A. microphylla	×			
Achillea tomentosa		×		
Anaphalis triplinervis			×	
Antennaria dioica	×			
Armeria maritima	×			
Arnica montana			×	
Aster × frikartii				×
Campanula rotundifolia			×	
Cerastium tomentosum 'Columnae'	×			
Dianthus arenarius		×		
D. deltoides		×		
Echinops ritro				×
Eriophyllum lanatum			×	
Eryngium bourgatii			×	
E. planum 'Blauer Zwerg'			×	
E. tricuspidatum			×	
Helichrysum arenarium			×	
Hieracium pilosella 'Niveum'	×			
Hieracium × rubrum	×			
Jasione laevis			×	
Liatris spicata				×
Nepeta × faassenii			×	
Origanum vulgare 'Compactum'			×	
Potentilla verna 'Nana'	×			
Sedum acre	×			
S. album	×			
S. floriferum	×			
S. hybridum	×			
S. sexangulare	×			
Stachys byzantina	×			
Teucrium chamaedrys 'Nana'	×			
Thymus × citriodorus 'Nana'	×			
Thymus doerfleri 'Bressingham Seedling'	×			
Thymus praecox var. *pseudolanuginosus*	×			
Verbascum bombyciferum				×
V. hybrid Densiflorum'				×
V. olympicum				×
V. phoeniceum				×
Veronica prostrata		×		

Perennials and Grasses for the Heath Garden (cont.)

Grasses (Heights refer to blade tips)	Height		
	short 5 to 20 cm	medium 30 to 50 cm	tall over 50 cm
Avenela flexuosa		×	
Bouteloua gracilis	×		
Briza media		×	
Carex buchananii		×	
C. montana	×		
C. ornithopoda 'Variegata'	×		
Festuca amethystina		×	
F. glauca	×		
F. mairei			×
F. ovina	×		
F. tenuifolia	×		
F. valesiaca 'Glaucantha'	×		
Helictotrichon sempervirens			×
Hystrix patula			×
Koeleria glauca		×	
Luzula nivea	×		
Melia transistoria			×
Miscanthus sinensis 'Gracillimus'			×
Molinia caerulea			×
M. caerulea 'Variegata'		×	
Panicum virgatum			×
Pennisetum compressum 'Hameln'		×	

Perennials and Grasses

Some perennials and grasses for the *Calluna* heath garden have already been mentioned. Together with plants occurring in a "wild" association, an additional selection of blooming perennials, grasses and flower bulbs help brighten a heath garden. These should be incorporated into the garden in keeping with their natural character. With the exception of the ground covering varieties, they should be planted individually, or in small clumps.

Grasses are almost indispensable in a heath garden. They fit harmoniously with their graceful shapes and their often blue-gray color. This is true not only of indigenous species, but also the exotic species as well. Short, thin-bladed species are best planted on flat surfaces near the edges of the garden. The loose-clumped, taller species should be planted separately or in clusters.

Bulbs and Corms

Although bulbs are not found in *Calluna* heaths, ornamentals growing from bulbs, corms, and tubers (hereafter referred to as "bulbs") can be planted in a heath garden, as long as they are carefully and sparingly incorporated, and only the less conspicuous species of the smaller bulbs are chosen. Low-growing, early spring-blooming ornamentals such as *Chionodoxa luciliae, Crocus ancyrensis, C. angustifolius* and *C. tomasinianus, Eranthis hyemalis, Galanthus elwesii* and *G. nivalis, Iris danfordiae* and *I. reticulata* and *Scilla siberica*) are handsome when planted together with grasses, shrubs, or in groups among ground-covering perennials. Such early ornamentals brighten the otherwise out-of-bloom garden. Spring or early summer-blooming genera such as *Allium, Muscari, Ornithogalum, Puschkinia* and *Scilla* are often useful; so are the fall-blooming *Colchicum* species which grow in large clumps so requiring considerable space.

Prairie and Steppe Gardens

Prairies and steppes are plains with a seasonal scarcity of water, and are characterized by the almost total absence of trees and shrubs. The perennial grasses and herbaceous species which dominate the prairies and steppes are consistent in their behavior. They grow luxuriantly in the rainy, early summer, but quickly complete their cycle and die back during the dry summer or autumn. Short to medium-sized shrubs are often interspersed among the grasses and herbaceous perennials especially close to the forest edge. They even penetrate adjoining dry deciduous forests. On the other hand, some forest tree and shrub species extend into the steppes. These forest intrusions usually follow water courses or are located over underground water deposits.

As a rule we could not, nor would we want to, reproduce the prairies in a garden. It is conceivable, however, to use some trees and shrubs native to prairies and steppes in a garden to very good effect. Such plants are excellently suited to dry, inland climates.

Their outward appearance points to their natural means of survival: The number of stomata, through which the plants exchange water vapor and gases with the air in both stems and leaves, is markedly reduced as compared to plants native to more hospitable environments. The limited number of stomata help the plant survive periods of drought by conserving water internally. Associated with these organs which preserve moisture and nutrients, prairie and steppe plants also have in some cases developed spines and thorns to deter grazing by animals. In addition, their stems and leaves often are covered by a waxy coating or with hairs so their leaves are not green, but rather more of a gray or silver color.

Prairies and steppes represent one of the most difficult environments for plants. Steppe heather species share the capacity to survive with the other plants which live there. Few of the characteristic central European steppe heathers grow well in the southeastern European steppes. Southern Germany's unforested drylands are labeled steppe heaths. They are composed of grasses and herbaceous perennials, interspersed with shrubs. The soil is very rocky, calcareous, permeable and is exposed to the full intensity of the sun. The steppe heaths of the southern interior, in the Jura Alps, are confined to small areas. The European, Eurasian, Northern and Western Chinese steppes, the North American prairies and the Western and Northern European *Calluna* heaths are subjected to harsher and more extreme climatic conditions.

Stone cliff and scree heaths (rich in limey sea-creature remains, calcareous, humus-poor screes and gravel heaps), turf heaths (lacking lime-yielding components, nutrient-poor fine-textured soil), shrubby heaths (with sloes, roses and seabuckthorns, *Hippophaë* spp.) and lastly, grass heaths of patchy turf (dark green and growing only during the rainy season), all belong to the steppe heaths. In Southern Europe, the steppe heaths include the Garigue. The Garigue is an open, ankle to knee high community of small shrubs which are remarkably rich in volatile oils. Most of these varieties are not sufficiently winter-hardy to grow in central Europe or elsewhere.

A Steppe Garden

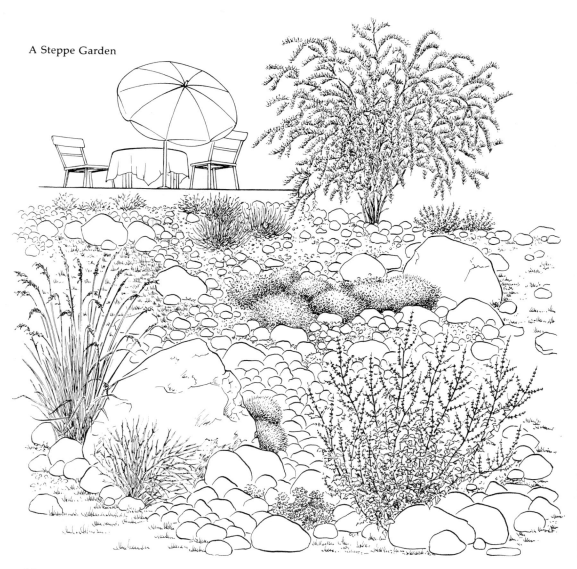

Location and Soil Preparation

To lay out a steppe or prairie garden, permeable, calcareous soil is required. The site should be inclined slightly to a southern exposure, if possible.

If the soil is not naturally well drained, then sand, gravel or stone chips should be worked in. The amounts needed are determined by the soil type. Especially dense, moist clay soil has to be amended. Dittrich recommends that a 15 to 20 cm under-layer of coarse, crushed limestone be layed over a 15 to 30 cm substratum layer. It should be enriched with structure-stabilizing ingredients such as coarse sand or pulverized lava cinders. Pelleted styrofoam, heat-expanded clay, and similar synthetics are sometimes used where weight is a consideration. These ingredients guarantee optimal aeration and drainage.

If the soil has a pH level that is too low (the trees and shrubs listed below can withstand alkaline soils with a pH-level over 7.0) it should be limed. The amount and form are determined by the soil type and the condition of the soil, which should be ascertained through a soil analysis. In light soils, crushed agricultural limestone is appropriate. In heavy soil, builder's lime or slacked lime are better. About 25 kg (50 pounds per 100 sq. ft.) per 100 m² is considered a suitable application for powdery agricultural limestone. 10 to 15 kg per 100 m² (22–30 pounds per 100 sq. ft.) is common when using builder's lime and slacked lime.

Plants For The Prairie and Steppe Garden

As in the Calluna heath, trees and shrubs should not be crowded in the steppe garden. Large woody plants should be planted singly, dwarf trees and shrubs in small, loose groups. Enough space should be left for flowering bushes and bulbs.

This book will not cover the majority of deciduous shrubs and small trees which are indigenous to the Eurasian steppes and North American prairies, all of which are relatively drought-resistant and lime-tolerant. Only those possessing ornamental qualities which are valuable in a garden will be discussed. Conifers are also a welcome addition in the steppe or prairie garden, especially the upright-growing forms of *Juniperus communis* and *J. virginiana* or the gray-leafed forms of *J. scopulorum*. Pine species which are best suited to calcareous, dry soil (*Pinus sylvestris*, *P. nigra* and *P. leucodermis*) are better replaced by their dwarfed garden forms when used in small areas.

Conifers should serve as side and background plants, as deciduous trees and shrubs predominate in the steppes or prairies themselves.

For use in a steppe or prairie garden, the following dwarf shrubs and suffruticose perennials are recommended. They are all drought-resistant and lime-tolerant but vary in frost hardiness.

Aethionema grandiflorum
Alyssum saxatile (*Aurinia saxatilis*)
Amorpha canescens
Anthyllis hermanniae
Caragana jubata
—*pygmaea*
Caryopteris species
Ceanothus species
Ceratostigma plumbaginoides
Cytisus × *beanii*
—*decumbens*
—× *kewensis*
—*purpureus*
Ephedra distachia
Genista species
Helianthemum species
Lavandula angustifolia
Lithospermum purpureocaeruleum
Lonicera albertii

19

Moltkia petraea
Ononis fruticosa
Perovskia species
Prunus prostrata
—tenella
Salix purpurea 'Nana'
—repens ssp. rosmarinifolia

Santolina chamaecyparissus
Syringa meyeri 'Palibin'
Teucrium chamaedrys
Yucca filamentosa

Perennials and Grasses for the Prairie and Steppe Garden

Perennials	Height		
	short 5 to 20 cm	medium 30 to 50 cm	tall over 50 cm
Adonis vernalis	X		
Anemone sylvestris	X		
Anthericum liliago		X	
Aster amellus		X	
A. linosyris		X	
Campanula persicifolia			X
C. sarmatica	X		
Carlina acaulis	X		
Dictamnus albus			X
Filipendula hexapetala	X		
Gentiana cruciata		X	
Inula ensifolia		X	
I. salicina		X	
Linum perenne		X	
Lychnis viscaria		X	
Potentilla alba	X		
P. arenaria	X		
Prunella grandiflora	X		
Pulsatilla vulgaris	X		
Stachys nivea		X	
Veronica spicata		X	
V. austriaca ssp. teucrium		X	
Grasses and sedges			
Carex flacca	X		
C. humilis	X		
Carex montana	X		
Festuca amethystina		X	
Stipa barbata			X
S. capillata			X
S. gigantea			X
S. pennata			X

Drought-resistant Trees and Shrubs for the Prairie and Steppe Garden

Species	Height(m)	Noteworthy Qualities
Berberis diaphana	2–3	dark yellow blossoms, scarlet autumnal tints, bright red fruit
Buddleia alternifolia	3–4	with its pendulous branches and an abundance of fragrant, violet blossoms; one of the prettiest blooming shrubs
Caragana arborescens	4–6	erect shrub, light yellow blossoms in May
Cotinus coggygria	4–5	smoke-like seed-heads, orange to scarlet fall colors, cultivars like 'Royal Purple' have summer and fall red foliage
Cotoneaster multiflorus	3–4	flowers and fruits very abundantly
Elaeagnus angustifolia	5–7	strong grower, lanceolate white-tomentose leaves
Elaeagnus commutata	3–5	suckers freely, both sides of leaves silver and glossy, fragrant blossoms
Halimodendron halodendron	2–3	gray-green evenly pinnate leaves, light violet papilionaceous plant
Hippophaë rhamnoides	5–7	shrub with wide-spreading branches, leaves scaly on both sides, yellow-orange fruit rich in vitamins (on female plants), vigorous suckers
Indigofera gerardiana	1–2	elegant, pinnate leaves, purple-pink blossoms in upright clusters
Lonicera korolkowii	2–3	gray-green leaves, whitish-pink blossoms, light red fruit
Lycium barbarum	2–3	arching, pendulous branches, gray-green, lanceolate leaves, violet blossoms
Prunus dulcis	6–10	early-blooming, small tree; both fruit and ornamental varieties
Prunus fenzliana	3–4	very thorny shrub with whitish blossoms in March
Pyrus salicifolia	5–8	more or less pendulous branches, young leaves are silver-gray on both sides, white-tomentose blossoms
Rosa foetida	1.5–2	deep yellow, 5 cm wide, blossoms smell like bedbugs
Rosa hugonis	2–2.5	light yellow blossoms in spring, fruit is deep red to blackish
Rosa oxycodon f. *haematodes*	2–3	3 to 7 dark pink blossoms, lightly fragrant red fruit, egg- to bottle-shaped
Shepherdia argentea	4–6	similar to Sea-buckthorn, narrow leaves, both sides silver
Tamarix pentandra	3–4	brown-red, pendulous branches, small scaly leaves, bright pink blossoms in large panicles, July–August
Tamarix ramosissima	2–4	gray-green, scaly leaves, light pink blossom clusters in apical panicles, July–September

Hansen and Stahl (1981) recommend the use of bulbs, corns, and tuberous flowering plants for steppe- and prairie-like flower masses; they are especially adapted to a southern slope of non-acid, sandy or loam soil which is dry through summer months.

Bulbous plants are commonly associated with shrubs and grasses in the steppe or prairie. I suggest the following:

for spring, crocus species (*Crocus ancyrensis, C. angustifolius, C. chrysanthus* and *C. tomasinianus*); Grape-Hyacinths (*Muscari armeniacum* and *M. botryoides*); and bulbous iris (*Iris danfordiae* and *I. reticulata*); for summer, *Allium* species (*A. cyaneum, A. flavum, A. karataviense,* and *A. oreophilum*) and the tall, Desert Candles (*Eremurus elwesii, E. himalaicus* and *E. robustus*); for fall, the fall-blooming crocus species (*C. pulchellus* and *C. speciosus*).

Rock Gardens

The rock garden is certainly one of the most favored forms of landscaping among gardeners. Unfortunately, far too many gardeners create gardens which are only caricatures of rock gardens. Terraced slopes or other inclined areas are too symmetrically set up. Strangely colored stones in a variety of sizes are uniformly distributed over the slopes, and finally, a few shrubs and perennials are haphazardly planted between the rocks. Their unwitting makers then label their creations "rock gardens". Such pale imitations of a rock garden need not be.

A genuine rock garden, really an alpine garden, ought to be the goal. Most botanic gardens offer excellent models of true rock garden design. These models can be adapted by the clever amateur gardener to his home situation with excellent results.

In addition to its usual character as found in nature, other forms of the rock garden are conceivable: rock garden beds, natural or constructed rockeries, dry walls and dry wall embankments. Container gardens, the most condensed form of rock garden, will be discussed in a separate section.

There are a number of reasons for constructing a rock garden: the natural desire to create a personal environment of alpine plants, the landscaping opportunity offered by the necessity to deal with sloping topography on home sites; and the opportunity to bridge differences in height in areas such as occur near the entrances to houses.

Dwarf woody ornamentals are seldom used exclusively in a rock garden. Normally, they are used to articulate and break up drifts and groups of alpine herbaceous perennials, or to complete the overall picture of the garden. Alpine perennials will not be described since a number of thorough, first-rate books quite adequately present them.

Natural Rock Gardens

In botanical gardens, the alpine landscapes are usually thematically arranged in keeping with their native habitats in Europe (particularly the Alps), Asia and America. This is done to group plants with similar ecological and hence cultural demands. The home rock garden should be organized in a similar fashion—both to assure a sound environment for the plants and also to reduce the effort on the part of the gardener.

Conditions to be considered when constructing a rock garden include the composition of the rocky subsoil (basic, neutral or acid conditions, granitic rocks, sedimentery rocks or gravel deposits), soil moisture and drainage, humidity, and exposure to light and air associated with the higher elevations preferred by most species.

Gardeners seldom design their landscapes on an accurate and scientifically-based reproduction of an ecological niche as do botanic gardens. Rather, they select the plants to be used in

A Rock Garden

their landscape on the basis of esthetic judgments or individual preoccupations with one or a limited number of genera. Given this approach the gardener must pay especial heed to creating an environment which fairly closely replicates the ecological requirements of the plants.

Never construct a rock garden as a simple hill or knoll in the middle of a level garden, standing alone like a sore thumb and unconnected to other landscape elements. Rather, some ingenuity must be employed to make it appear to be a natural part of the landscape. For example, if there are no natural height differences in the garden, an area connecting a building or a terrace to the garden can be built up. Schacht recommends that on a level site, some earth be excavated in various places and mounded in others so that the necessary contours are formed in a naturally rolling manner. If this procedure is followed, an efficient drainage system is necessary, in most cases, capable of removing water resulting from heavy rains which will pool in the excavated spots.

A rock garden is frequently constructed in the form of a richly planted mounded hill or knoll. It is important to use stone native to the area so that the rocks are of a color and form which correspond with the natural rock outcrops of the neighborhood.

Unhewn quarrystones and "foundlings" (carefully selected, weathered field stones) should be used exclusively in a natural rock garden. Further, it is advisable to use rocks found in the immediate vicinity for simple economic reasons.

Take care to use one sort of stone (gray granite, weathered dolomite, or other) in closely related sizes—which means that round foundlings should not be used with square stones, or sedimentary limestone with granitic rocks. Fewer rocks, but larger ones are more attractive. Naturally, space should be left between the rocks to accommodate the perennials and trees which will be planted. The choice of rocks used is dependent upon the type of plants to be cultivated and vice versa.

Rock Garden Beds

Gardeners who wish to avoid the expense of constructing a rock garden, or have only a confined area in which to work, can construct rock garden beds. Rock garden beds are level, raised (30 to 50 cm) beds bordered with rocks or wood (impregnated, perpendicular, partially sunken, posts, or railroad ties). A drainage bed must first be laid underneath the top soil, made of crushed rock or gravel, which ensures that all extra water will be quickly and efficiently carried off.

This 30 to 50 cm (10 to 20 in.) thick substratum should be made with crushed rock or native gravel mixed with larger broken rocks. The dwarf trees and shrubs cultivated in such beds require proximity of rocks to thrive.

In reviewing site requirements, a rock garden bed does not differ much from a steppe heath garden, save that a rock garden bed can be much smaller. Consequently, plants, including all of the alpines described in the section on steppe gardens, can be incorporated into rock garden beds.

Natural or Constructed Rock Gardens

When the site selected for a rock garden slopes, there are numerous possibilities for constructing natural rock gardens; for example, the difference in height between streets and driveways, or house entrances, or similar embankments. In level areas, an option is to construct raised beds around the edges of sitting terraces, the rim of sunken gardens, or the edge of a garden pool.

If your site is not suitable for a rock garden or you do not wish to construct one, you might consider growing dwarf plants in dry walls. Unlike the natural rock garden, dry walls generally are constructed with square-edged rocks, naturally stratified, or even cut rocks. Dry walls accommodate alpine plants very well. Today they are often made of concrete L-shaped or U-shaped blocks with smooth surfaces, or vertical wood palisades made of ties.

Creating the planting spaces in a dry wall is done in the same manner as with rock garden beds. Building the underlying soil substratum will be discussed later.

Cushion and mat-forming plants are not only intrinsically attractive in rockeries, but are vital design elements which articulate the planting. Such plants should not be planted in areas with poor drainage, as they will rapidly fall victim to disease and die. Cushion plants require a lot of energy to keep up and must often be replaced. They require sunny locations and mineral-rich, fresh soil. They thrive especially well when planted behind rocks or allowed to grow over the edge of walls.

The following list is a selection of particularly good rock garden plants. Additional plant lists can be found in good rock gardening books.

Variegated cushion and mat types for sunny locations in rockeries

Achillea ageratifolia var. *serbica*
Alyssum saxatile (= *Aurinis saxatilis*)
Arabis caucasica
A. procurrens
Armeria pseudoarmeria
Aster × *alpellus* 'Triumph'
Aubrieta hybrids

Rock Garden Beds

Campanula carpatica
C. poscharskyana
Cerastium biebersteinii
C. tomentosum
Chrysanthemum arcticum
Dianthus gratianopolitanus
D. plumarius
Dryas octopetala
Eriophyllum lanatum
Euphorbia myrsinites
E. polychroma
Gentiana septemfida var. lagodechiana
Geranium dalmaticum
Gypsophila hybrid 'Rosenschleier' ('Rosy
    Veil')
G. repens
Helianthemum hybrids
Nepeta × faassenii
Phlox douglasii
P. subulata
Phuopsis stylosa
Potentilla 'Goldrausch'
Saponaria × lempergii
S. ocymoides
Sedum floriferum 'Weihenstephaner Gold'
S. kamtschaticum
S. kamtschaticum ssp. ellacombianum
S. kamtschaticum ssp. middendorfianum
    'Diffusum'
S. spurium cultivars
S. stoloniferum
Silene maritima 'Weisskelchen'
S. schafta 'Splendens'
Stachys byzantina 'Silver Carpet'
Thymus × citriodorus 'Golden Dwarf'
T. rotundifolius 'Purpurteppich'
Trifolium repens 'Purpureum'
Veronica gentianoides
V. spicata
V. austriaca ssp. teucrium

Plants for partly-sunny, partly-shady rockeries and wall crevices

Campanula carpatica
Chiastophyllum oppositifolium
Corydalis lutea
Cymbalaria muralis

Plants for partly-sunny, partly-shady locations on rocks, between rocks and terraced surfaces

Bergenia species and cultivars
Dicentra eximia and similar species
Epimedium grandiflorum and similar species
Heuchera hybrids and cultivars
Hosta dwarf and low growing species
Polygonum affine cultivars
P. capitatum
Primula juliae
Saxifraga arendsii hybrids
S. cuneifolia
S. × geum
S. hypnoides
S. muscoides
S. umbrosa
Sedum sarmentosum
S. hybridum 'Immergrünchen'
S. kamtschaticum ssp. ellacombianum
S. spurium 'Album Superbum'
S. stoloniferum

Dry Walls and Dry Wall Embankments

Dry walls have already been addressed in the last section. Unfortunately, in modern garden designing, they are often replaced by prefabricated concrete walls. In the garden, however, we should not forego them. They offer ideal growing conditions for many alpine plants, especially for crevice inhabitants in sunny and shady locations.

Dry walls can be built with any type of rectangular rock. Especially suitable are naturally stratified and sedimentary rocks (for example, slate, limestone, and sandstone) which are easily split.

When constructing a dry wall, it is im-

27

portant not to erect it perfectly vertically. It should slope backwards, at a rate of 1:6 to 1:3. The rocks resist soil pressure better, and conduct rain and irrigation water immediately to the plant roots when tilted downward at the back. If the wall is built in a craftsman-like way, the vertical seams should not extend beyond one or two tiers of rock. To ensure lasting stability, each stone should be situated over the joint of the two rocks below. Low walls can be constructed directly on compressed soil. The first row of rocks should be sunk into the soil a bit. Higher walls require a foundation, the depth of which is calculated in relation to the height of the dry wall.

Especially important is a drainage system. Drainage has to be built into a high wall. It should be surrounded by loose material and connect with a drain.

In building a dry wall, cut stones should be laid using the narrowest possible seams between them. Irregularities in the stones are left as they will fill in naturally as the

wall is built and plants will find homes in them. When using uncut stones, the seams will be larger. Be certain to fill them carefully with alpine garden type soil. So the stones do not touch above and below, lay small stone chips of uniform size on each stone, fill around the chips with soil, then bed the next stone firmly on the prepared site.

Dry wall embankments consisting of two dry walls built parallel with a narrow soil fill between them are a common sight in England. They seldom have a structural function, but rather are constructed simply to cultivate alpine woody plants and perennials. They are comparatively narrow and usually do not exceed 1 meter in height. The outer surfaces are made of flat stones, slanted downward towards the middle. The seams between the rocks are carefully filled with rich rock garden soil. The core is made of rubble or gravel to guarantee optimal drainage. This is of great importance, especially in areas of heavy rainfall.

The decorative, robust cushion plants listed in the last section are well suited for dry walls. Dry walls provide an excellent environment for cultivating demanding and unusual alpine plants.

Building a Rock Garden

As already mentioned, when constructing natural stone structures, drainage and preliminary treatment of the subsoil need to be taken into account. In addition, before, or at the latest, immediately after establishing the size and form of the rock garden, weeds must be controlled. Nothing is more disastrous in a rock garden than using soil which is contaminated with weed plants, roots, and seeds. Since treating soil with steam for weed eradication is impossible in gardens, the only way to eradicate weeds and their

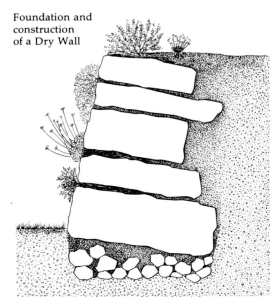

Foundation and construction of a Dry Wall

seeds is with chemicals. Only trained applicators are allowed to use the especially effective agents, but Roundup is effective enough against most weed roots and their seeds and can be used by the gardener. It should be applied 30 to 60 g/m² (1–2 oz. per sq. yd.) (the higher dose is for heavy soil), then turned under to a depth of 20 cm (8 in.); after 14 days till the soil to aerate and dissipate the chemicals. Treatment works best in the spring when the soil temperature is 10°C (50°F) or lower, but the waiting period is 3 to 4 weeks.

There are a few general rules to observe when constructing a rock garden so that on completion the garden does not seem artificial.

— Use fewer, but larger rocks.
— Always arrange rocks in groups, never singly.
— Lay the rocks so that their flattest sides are on the soil; if the rocks are rounded, set them into the soil a bit.
— Rocks in layers should be set so that they tilt back and down as in dry walls. By doing this, moisture will drain to the plant roots; also stability is assured.

A Stone Wall Niche Garden

— The face of rock should not be buried in the soil, but the sides may be embedded.
— Large rocks require a firm, graveled subsoil, which controls the flow of water, thus, allowing the rock's own weight to slowly sink it into the soil.

When designing and building a rock garden, by all means install repeated, pleasingly stepped planting terraces while developing the quietly (gently) flowing changes of elevation. If the garden is large, pre-planned walkways should be laid out as far into the rockery as necessary for viewing and maintenance. The borders of the walkways provide additional planting surfaces with different exposures. Of course, sufficient planting area must be left between the terraces and levels. Even the smallest crevices between the rocks will accomodate alpine perennials which live in natural cracks and fractures.

If a rock garden must be constructed over heavy, compacted subsoil, the soil can be made more permeable by mixing it with crushed rock, gravel, or concrete rubble. To ensure adequate drainage, however, it is more effective to lay in a 20 to 40 cm (8–15 in.) deep drainage bed connected to a drain. The soil layer is then built over it.

Laying the rocks and constructing drainage systems in rock gardens

Soil Mixtures for Alpine Plants

It is scarcely possible to reproduce a root environment which meets all the requirements of alpine plants. This is especially true with regard to the soil origin, type and condition, moisture, humus content and lime content of the soil. Luckily, it is not necessary because many alpine plants thrive quite well in "artificial" soils which scarcely duplicate natural alpine soils. Practical experience has also proved that it is not necessary to prepare different soils for alpine plants originating from different locations, with notable exceptions.

The physical properties of the soil generally are much more important than its chemical content. In stable, well-drained, and well-aerated soil, lime tolerant and lime-demanding species thrive at a pH level barely under the neutral mark of 7.0. pH-indifferent plants thrive at the same or somewhat lower pH levels, and species which require acid grow best in soil with a pH level of 5.0 to 6.0.

A standard mixture of equal parts of garden or farm loam, peat and coarse sand (or other coarse aggregate which does not decompose) is suitable for all alpine plants. Garden or farmland soils are most suitable if weedless, well drained and friable, and loamy, rich in nutrients. If such soil is not available, well decomposed compost soil (made of stacked and decayed sod) can be used. Peat buffers the soil; it mobilizes the soil's nutrients; it stimulates growth by its acidity; it contributes necessary humus; and it provides optimal texture for water movement and aeration to the soil.

Because peat disintegrates comparatively rapidly, the coarse soil components (sand, aggregate, stone chips) assume the role of the soil skeleton. They assist movement of water and aeration. Coarse concrete-sand is often used (with a grain size of 2 to 5 mm) but lava cinders have proved more useful (with a grain size of .1 to 16 mm). For years, lightweight lava cinders have taken the place of sand at the botanical garden in Tübingen. Its value is due to great porosity which provides a high water storage capacity (15 to 20 percent by volume) and on decomposition it yields a relatively high level of nutrients, from 14–19 mg nitrogen, 8–10 mg phosphorus, 19–54 mg potash and 7–9 mg magnesium per 100 g of cinders. In fact, alpine plants even have been cultivated in pure lava cinders, to which only slow release fertilizer is added each spring. From a period of about April to July a slow release product such as Osmocote 16:10:13 is applied for optimal effect on healthy growth.

Calcium-loving plants thrive in standard soil mixtures, as long as one part of the coarse elements (sand or lava cinders) is replaced by crushed limestone (chat) or old wall mortar that has been crushed.

If one begins with a strongly alkaline soil, the pH level can be reduced by adding sulfur. (See page 15.) The pH level of acidic soils can be raised by applying lime. Lowering the pH level is generally more difficult than raising it, so it is wise to start with a growing medium as close to the plants' requirements as possible.

Lime-loving Alpine Plants (Calciphiles)

Acantholimon species
Acanthus species
Achillea ageratifolia ssp. *aizoon* and ssp. *serbica*
A. clavennae
Adenostyles species

Adonis species (except *A. brevistyla* and *A. pyrenaica*)
Aethionema species
Alopecurus lanatus
A. chamaejasme
Androsace lactea
Callianthemum anemonoides
C. kernerianum
Carlina species
Cyclamen species
Cypripedium calceolus
Dianthus species (almost all)
Dryas octopetala
Gentiana clusii
G. dinarica
Globularia species
Gypsophila species
Haberlea species
Leontopodium species
Potentilla nitida
Primula auricula
P. clusiana
P. marginata
Pulsatilla species (except *P. vernalis*)
Ramonda species
Saxifraga species, with a few exceptions, especially from the *Kabschia* and *Euaizoonia* sections

More or less Acid-loving Alpine Plants

Achillea herba-rotta ssp. *moschata*
A. nana
Androsace carnea
A. halleri
A. hedraeantha
A. imbricaria
A. obtusifolia
Astrantia minor
Campanula excisa
Chrysanthemum alpinum
Dianthus glacialis
D. microlepis
Dicentra cucullaria

D. eximia
D. formosa
Douglasia species
Erigeron aureus
Gentiana acaulis
G. frigida
G. sino-ornata
Helichrysum frigidum
Hieracium intybaceum
Houstonia species
Lewisia species
Lithodora diffusa
Lychnis alpina
Penstemon davidsonii
P. menziesii and other woody species
Potentilla aurea
Primula hirsuta
P. latifolia
Pulsatilla alpina ssp. *sulphurea*
P. vernalis
Saponaria pumila
Saxifraga cortusifolia
S. cotyledon
S. lilacina
S. pseudosancta
Sempervivum montanum
S. wulfenii
Senecio incanus
S. tiroliensis
Trifolium alpinum

Fertilizing Alpine Plants

Even plants which are extremely well suited to their location benefit from fertilization. Alpine plants growing at lower elevations (which permit extreme environments—long summers, decreased ultra-violet rays) typically exhibit higher metabolism and decreased frost-hardiness. Obviously, therefore, in the stressful environments of our gardens, alpines require fertilization. Potash-rich, complete fertilizer, 1 kg for each m³ (2 lbs/yd) should be added when first preparing rock garden beds. Soil for alpine plants should be admixed 1 to 2 kg/m³ (2–4 lbs/yd) of slow release (as Osmocote) or low solubility fertilizers, together with 100 g/m³ of a trace element concentrate (but only if trace elements are not in the general fertilizer) at the time of initial soil preparation. After the garden is planted, mulch the soil in late autumn with 1 cm of fertilized peat. Each m³ of peat (about 4 bales) should be enriched with about 3 kg (7 lbs) of an organic mineral fertilizer such as Hoof and Horn meal, seaweed concentrate, or other. Most fertilizers contain insufficient potash for alpines, so a few kilograms of wood ash, which contains up to 35% potash, should also be added.

Dwarf Plants For Rock Gardens

Almost all of the trees and shrubs mentioned in this book can be used in rock gardens, as long as their environmental requirements are met, and their size is suitable for the scale of the garden. The number of plants used is narrowed in an ecologically organized alpinum. The same holds true for smaller gardens which accommodate at best only a few, slow-growing trees and shrubs. Although all species and cultivars are theoretically usable, the species (and their cultivars) whose natural range of distribution is in the arctic, alpine or mountainous zones are most readily adapted to rock gardens.

The list on page 33 encompasses dwarf rhododendrons and other Ericaceae which are often found in alpine gardens. Because of their special environmental requirements, they will be dealt with in a separate section.

Plantings of dwarf forms of evergreen conifers should be emphasized in the design. A rock garden can hardly get by without them, especially in winter when

Dwarf Broadleaf Shrubs and Suffruticose Perennials (subshrubs) for Rock Gardens

Variety	Height		
	ankle-high	knee-high	up to 1 m
Aethionema grandiflorum	×		
Alyssum species	×		
Anthyllis hermanniae		×	
Aurinia species			
Berberis buxifolia 'Nana'	×		
B. candidula		×	
B. hookeri			×
B. × *stenophylla* 'Grawley Gem'			×
B. thunbergii dwarf forms	×		
B. verruculosa			×
Betula nana		×	
Bruckenthalia spiculifolia	×		
Cotoneaster adpressus		×	
C. dammeri cultivars	×		
C. horizontalis 'Saxatilis'		×	
C. microphyllus cultivars	×	×	
C. praecox		×	
Cytisus species	×	×	
Daphne altaica			×
D. alpina	×		
D. blagayana	×		
D. cneorum	×		
D. pontica			×
Dryas octopetala	×		
Empetrum nigrum	×		
Erica carnea species and cultivars	×		
Genista species	×	×	
Globularia cordifolia	×		
Hebe species	×	×	
Helianthemum species and cultivars	×		
Iberis species	×		
Leiophyllum buxifolium	×		
Moltkia petraea	×		
Muehlenbeckia axillaris	×		
Ononis fruticosa			×
Penstemon newberryi	×		
Prunus pumila var. *depressa*	×		
Rubus calycinoides	×		
Salix species	×	×	×
Sorbus reducta		×	
Spiraea decumbens	×		

most other plants are dormant. Choosing which specimens to use is largely a matter of personal taste, as long as the garden is not thematically organized, that is, an attempt to duplicate a specific geographical setting. Naturally, the environmental requirements of each species and cultivar, its habit (prostrate or upright), and its ultimate size, must be taken into account.

Besides the dwarf forms of conifers listed here, there are many taller-growing conifers which can be cultivated in larger rock gardens including the native alpine Mountain Pine, *Pinus cembra,* the southern European *P. leucodermis* and Balkan Pine, *P. peuce,* the Japanese White Pine, *P. parviflora* 'Glauca', the North American Bristlecone *P. aristata;* and *Cedrus brevifolia,* which is native to Cyprus.

Container Gardens

In recent years growing woody plants in containers (troughs and sinks) and planters has become increasingly popular. They are used not only as home gardens but also in public parks and malls, as well as along sidewalks. Traditionally, container gardening was restricted to window boxes, but today there are endless possibilities in use, size, shape. There are several advantages to planting containers with dwarf trees and shrubs. If they are chosen carefully, trees and shrubs last longer than the summer flowers usually planted in various sorts of containers, so the planting costs less, requires less care and is attractive the year-round—winter as well as summer.

Container gardens can be set up anywhere: inside courtyards, on terraces, balconies, roof gardens, on staircase landings, in sunken gardens, or any other place used for passage or leisure. They are irreplaceable wherever it is not possible to create a typical garden for want of space. This is particularly true of balconies on modern apartment buildings. Containers enhance the number of species plant-lovers can choose from, and give novice gardeners an opportunity to experiment with living plants.

A wide variety of containers, both in form and material, are available. They may be made of concrete, ceramic, wood or various plastic materials. Even deep planting containers are now produced in all shapes and sizes. Feed troughs, old fashioned hewn stone farm sinks, or smithy troughs, cut from various rock materials are especially useful. These are durable and fit easily into most garden spaces.

No matter what material is chosen, it should not be forgotten that the container is only a means to an end (except when growing Bonsai). Its shape and color should not be so dominant that the plants go unnoticed. Exotically-shaped or painted containers seldom harmonize with the plants in them, nor with the typical garden setting. The height of a container should be in a harmonious relation to container width and overall size of the planting. It is important that the container material be durable so it does not disintegrate quickly. Wall-thickness plays an important role in smaller containers. Soil organisms decay away thin wood containers quickly; purchase only wooden containers of thick walled design.

Many gardeners prefer natural stone containers. They are, consequently, quite scarce and highly priced. Marvelous substitutes are now available. They are unusual creations, not manufactured with hammer and chisel, but of sand, peat and concrete. Such manufactured containers can hardly be distinguished from those of natural stone. Both natural and manufactured stone troughs are much more attractive than any other containers available.

After many years of experimenting in the alpine garden at Pforzheim, Carl discovered that long-lasting containers can be made of coarse European peat, builders' sand and cement, in the ratio of 2:3:2. The higher the percentage of cement, the more the container resembles limestone. With a higher percentage of peat and added coloring agents, the container takes on the character of sandstone. After being taken out of the mold, the edges must be rounded and the surfaces roughened and sculpted to resemble stone before the material hardens.

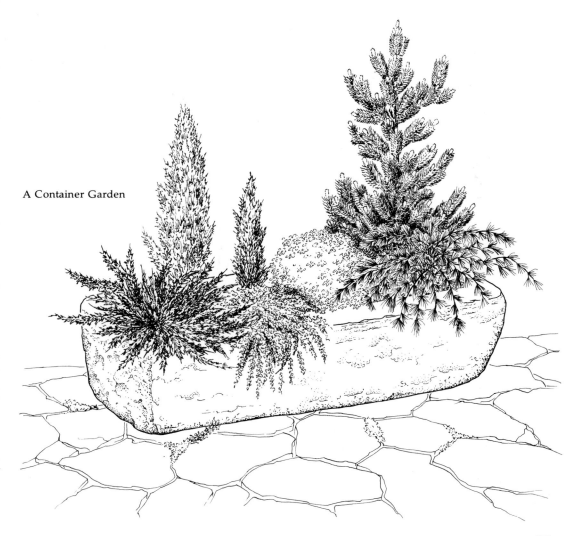

A Container Garden

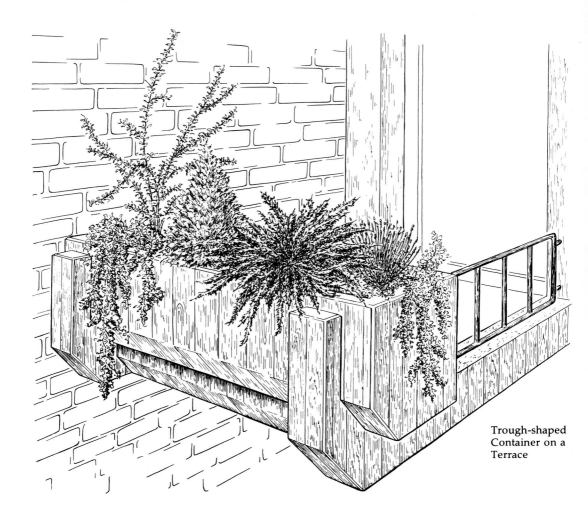

Trough-shaped
Container on a
Terrace

Preparation of Planting Media for Containers

Normally, trees and shrubs should last many years in containers. Therefore, preparations undertaken before planting are of great importance.

Before filling the container with soil, water drainage must be fully accounted for. Cover the drain holes at the bottom of the container with irregular rocks so that the soil will not be able to clog them. Then fill the container to 1/5 of its capacity (1/3 of the capacity of a deep container) with coarse gravel or rubble. If the drainage bed is covered with a permeable plastic filter or with a semiporous membrane, little of the mineral or humus content of the soil will wash down into the drainage layers. Place the container on flat stones to assist drainage.

The planting medium must be able to meet the requirements of the confined roots of the plants; however, the physical properties of the soil are more important in this case than are the chemical properties (pH & nutrient levels). The soil has to be structurally stable, as well as well-drained and aerated so that the plant roots obtain adequate fresh water and oxygen. A higher percentage of mineral materials (sand, silt and clay) minimizes planting medium shrinkage, compaction, and deterioration. Increased amounts of peat supply humus and accelerate aeration and water retentions. Clay colloids account for buffering and nutrient adsorption in the soil. According to Kurzmann, only 10 to 15 percent of the total volume of good container soil is made up of mineral components, and even when water-saturated, about 40 to 50% is air-filled, and the other 50 to 60% is filled with water.

Simon recommends using a 50% lava debris mixture or aggregate as the matrix for container soil. 10% should be bentonite which is the most useful clay mineral and vermiculite for nutrient, air and water storage. The remaining 40% of the medium should be made up of coarse sphagnum peat. The quality of peat is very important. Many commercial peats are too finely ground, therefore, it is important to select a coarse-grained peat. A commercial organic colloid can be added to increase the peat's capacity to retain water. Lastly, a concentrated, slow-release fertilizer should be added.

1 m³ (1 yd.) of container soil is made as follows: 2 bales of peat (compressed bales, each 0.17 m³),

0.5 m³ (½ yd.) of sand and
15 kg (35 lb.) bentonite or clay,
16.5 kg (40 lb.) vermiculite,
1 kg (2–2.5 lb.) of organic colloids such as kelp meal and
1 to 3 kg (2–7 lb.) Osmocote, or other slow-release fertilizer.

Substitutes for some of these components can be used. Lava cinders (aggregate) or gravel can be replaced by coarse sand and slow-release fertilizer can be replaced by fertilized peat. Carl recommends a simpler mixture as follows:

2 bales of fertilized peat (see page 9)

0.5 m³ (½ yd.) lava aggregate or gravel

25 kg (55 lbs.) bentonite.

Growing medium to be used in containers of ericaceous ornamentals such as rhododendrons, azaleas, heaths, heathers, *Pieris*, and others, as well as other humus-loving plants, should be admixed with 50 percent peat by volume, and lime and lime-releasing products omitted.

Hydroponic systems have proved effective in roof and container gardens. With the exception of fast-growing, deeply rooting shrubs, all coniferous and deciduous shrubs and bulbs tolerate hydroponic growing. Unlike house plants which die when soil remnants are inadvertently mixed into the hydroponic rooting medium, trees and shrubs can be grown hydroponically with their roots in loose balls of soil. For more detailed instructions on hydroponic systems, containers, media, management, and other aspects of soilless culture, consult a reference book dealing with hydroponics.

Culture

Watering, fertilizing and winter protection are central to managing container gardens. Container plants should be drought resistant, but they cannot get by without water during extended dry spells. The smaller the planting container, the more often it must be watered. Sensitive plants should be lightly watered every day in the late afternoon. Irrigation should be continued into late fall if dry weather hangs on; and it should continue into winter if clear, dry weather persists. Evergreen plants need a dampish soil the year around. If alpine plants are being cultivated, they should not be watered too often, and certainly, their soil should not be kept damp on a continuous basis.

After planting, additional fertilizing is not necessary immediately because the soil contains enough nutrients to sustain plants for approximately one year. In the second and subsequent years container gardens should be fertilized regularly each spring. Complete water-soluble fertilizers with trace elements should be added when watering. Trees and shrubs should be given applications of complete fertilizer such as Plant Marvel, Ra-pid-gro, or other soluble fertilizers following the manufacturer's directions. Potash, especially, is necessary to seasonal plant maturity and therefore, frost resistance.

Evergreen trees and shrubs should be completely protected with a light covering of brush in winter, to shelter them from drying frosts and intense sunlight. This covering will not keep the medium in the container from freezing but freezing does not hurt winter-hardy plants.

Plants for Container Gardens

The choice of tree and shrub species and cultivars is closely related to the size of the container. The smaller the container, the slower-growing the plants must be. When relating plant size to container size, mature plants, not young ones, should be kept in mind.

A planting exclusively of dwarf tree and shrub species and cultivars should include forms which have differing habits (columnar, globose, or prostrate) and they should be arranged in such a way that loose, harmonious groups result.

Preplanted containers can now be purchased which include a variety of trees and shrubs. Such preplanted containers are not very satisfactory. Frequently the plants die as they were planted at the wrong time, or plants too large at maturity have been used in order to present a full and pleasing appearance at the time of purchase. It does not help to prune back such trees and shrubs in order to restore them to an appropriate size. Pruning only results in increased growth or it destroys the natural growth habit of the plant. It is better to replace such trees and shrubs with suitable rock garden perennials or summer bedding annuals. Combining trees and shrubs with summer bedding plants is gaining popularity. Such groupings are more commonly called container gardens than are groupings of trees and shrubs alone.

Dwarf trees and shrubs are especially well suited to any kind of container garden. While drought resistant plants native to steppes, prairies, or arid moorlands may be used to landscape full-sized gardens, culturally demanding plants, which require a great deal of maintenance, especially water management, are often more easily grown in container gardens. All container plants should, moreover, be frost-hardy. Conifers and deciduous broadleafed plants are better in container gardens, therefore, than are broadleaf evergreen plants.

Broadleaf Trees and Shrubs

The species listed on page 39 are suitable for container gardens of all but the smallest sizes. The large-leafed evergreen species are not included. Most of them are best suited to containers in which the plants are frequently changed.

Broadleaf Dwarf Plants for Container Gardens

Species	Height		
	Ankle high	knee high	up to 1 m
Aethionema grandiflorum	X		
Alyssum species	X		
Aurinia species			
Berberis buxifolia 'Nana'	X		
B. candidula		X	
B. × *fricartii* 'Verrucandi'			X
B. gagnepainii 'Klugowski'			X
B. thunbergii, dwarf forms	X		
B. verruculosa			X
Caryopteris species and hybrids			X
Ceratostigma plumbaginoides		X	
Cotoneaster adpressus		X	
C. congestus			X
C. conspicuus 'Decorus'		X	
C. dammeri cultivars	X		
C. microphyllus 'Cochleatus'		X	
Cytisus × *beanii*		X	
C. decumbens	X		
C. purpureus		X	
Dryas octopetala	X		
Erica carnea species and cultivars	X		
Euonymus fortunei 'Minimus'	X		
Genista horrida		X	
G. lydia		X	
G. sagittalis	X		
G. tinctoria cultivars			X
Globularia cordifolia	X		
Hedera helix cultivars		X	
Helianthemum species and cultivars	X		
Iberis species and cultivars	X		
Ilex crenata cultivars		X	X
Lavandula angustifolia		X	
Lonicera albertii			X
Moltkia petraea	X		
Muehlenbeckia axillaris	X		
Perovskia species			X
Potentilla fruticosa cultivars			X
Prunus pumila var. *depressa*	X		
Salix species and cultivars	X	X	X
Sorbus reducta		X	
Spiraea japonica 'Alpina'	X		
S. japonica 'Little Princess'			X
Syringa meyeri 'Palibin'		X	

Dwarf Conifers For Container Gardens

Species	Prostrate forms which drape down in containers	Height		
		ankle high	knee high	up to 1 m
Abies balsamea 'Nana'		X		
A. cephalonica 'Meyer's Dwarf'		X		
A. concolor dwarf cultivars			X	X
A. lasiocarpa 'Compacta'				X
A. procera cultivars				X
Cedrus libani 'Sargentii'	X			
Chamaecyparis obtusa dwarf cultivars			X	
C. pisifera 'Filifera' forms				X
Ephedra distachia ssp. *helvetica*		X		
Juniperus chinensis 'Blaauw'				X
J. chinensis var. *sargentii* 'Glauca'	X			
J. connunis 'Compressa'			X	
J. communis 'Depressa Aurea'			X	
J. communis 'Echiniformis'		X		
J. communis 'Hornibrookii'	X			
J. communis 'Repanda'	X			
J. communis 'Suecica Nana'				X
J. communis 'Sibirica'		X		
J. conferta dwarf cultivars	X			
J. horizontalis 'wiltonii' (= "Blue Rug") and other dwarf cultivars	X			
J. procumbens 'Nana'	X			
J. squamata 'Blue Carpet'	X			
J. squamata 'Blue Star'		X		
Microbiota decussata	X			
Picea glauca 'Echiniformis'		X		
P. mariana 'Nana'			X	
P. omorika dwarf cultivars			X	X
P. pungens 'Glauca Globosa'				X
P. pungens 'Glauca Procumbens'			X	
P. pungens 'Glauca Prostrata'	X			
Pinus leucodermis 'Schmidtii'			X	
P. mugo dwarf cultivars			X	X
P. nigra cultivars				X
P. parviflora 'Adock's Dwarf'			X	
P. pumila and cultivars			X	X
P. sylverstris dwarf cultivars			X	X
Taxus baccata cultivars			X	X
T. cuspidata 'Nana'			X	
Thuja occidentalis 'Danica'			X	
T. occidentalis 'Tiny Tim'			X	
Tsuga canadensis 'Gracilis Oldenburg'			X	
T. canadensis 'Jeddeloh'			X	

Conifers and Ephedra

Slow-growing, prostrate specimens which may hang down over the container sides as well as slow-growing upright sorts are particularly well suited to container gardens. *Ephedra, Microbiota,* a few pines and junipers are reasonably drought resistant; all of the others have to be watered regularly. Dwarf spruces are suitable only in regions with exceptionally high humidity because droughty soil as well as dry air can easily result in devastating red-spider infestations, especially in some *Picea glauca* and *P. abies* forms. Forms of *Tsuga, Cryptomeria, Thuja* and *Abies* grow best in damp soil and high humidity.

Herbaceous Perennials, Grasses, Ferns and Bulbs

These plants are often more important in container gardens than the previously discussed trees and shrubs. They serve exceptionally well in highly ornamental plantings. Therefore, an extensive list is provided below. The list includes rarer, more demanding species, which can also be cultivated in rock gardens. Acid soil species which tolerate no lime are marked with an asterisk.*

Herbaceous Perennials, Grasses, Ferns and Bulbs for Container Gardens

Species and Cultivars	Container Size		Location	
	small	from 1 m	sunny	shady or partly shady
Herbaceous Perennials				
Achillea × *kellereri*		×	×	
A. × *kolbiana*	×		×	
A. umbellata	×		×	
Allium flavum 'Minus'	×		×	
Anacyclus depressus	×		×	
Androsace carnea ssp. *brigantiaca**	×		×	
A. hedraeantha*	×		×	
A. lactea*		×	×	
A. sempervivoides*	×		×	
A. villosa		×	×	
Andryala agardhii	×		×	
Anthyllis montana 'Rubra'		×	×	
Aquilegia flabellata	×		×	
A. discolor	×		×	
A. scopulorum	×	×		
Arabis ferdinandi-coburgi 'Variegata'			×	×
Armeria juniperifolia cultivars	×		×	
Asperula nitida		×	×	
A. lilaciflora var. *caespitosa*		×	×	
Aster alpinus cultivars		×	×	
Astilbe × *crispa* cultivars	×	×		×

41

Herbaceous Perennials, Grasses, Ferns and Bulbs for Container Gardens (cont.)

Species and Cultivars	Container Size		Location	
	small	from 1 m	sunny	shady or partly shady
Calceolaria polyrrhiza		×		×
C. tenella		×		×
Campanula aucheri		×	×	
C. carpatica		×	×	
C. cashmiriana	×		×	
C. cochleariifolia		×	×	
C. fenestrellata		×		×
C. raineri	×		×	
C. saxifraga		×	×	
C. tridentata		×	×	
C. waldsteiniana		×	×	
Centaurium chloodes	×		×	
Chiastophyllum oppositifolium		×		×
Chrysanthemum haradjanii		×	×	
Convolvulus boissieri		×	×	
Corydalis cheilanthifolia		×		×
Crassula milfordae	×		×	
Dianthus gratianopolitanus, slow-growing cultivars		×	×	
D. microlepis	×		×	
D. nitidus	×		×	
D. pavonius	×		×	
Diascia cordata		×	×	
Draba aizoides		×	×	
D. bruniifolia		×	×	
D. bryoides var. imbricata	×		×	
Epimedium diphyllum		×		×
Erysimum kotschyanum	×		×	
Gentiana farreri*		×	×	
G. sino-ornata* and hybrids		×	×	
Geranium argenteum		×	×	
G. dalmaticum		×	×	
G. farreri	×		×	
G. subcaulescens 'Splendens'	×		×	
Globularia repens	×		×	
Gypsophila aretioides	×		×	
G. repens cultivars		×	×	
Haberlea rhodopensis		×		×
Helichrysum milfordiae		×	×	
Heliosperma alpestre		×	×	
Iris pumila cultivars		×	×	
Leontopodium alpinum	×		×	
Lewisia species and cultivars	×			×
Linaria alpina		×	×	
Micromeria croatica	×		×	
Moehringia muscosa		×		×

Herbaceous Perennials, Grasses, Ferns and Bulbs for Container Gardens (cont.)

Species and Cultivars	Container Size		Location	
	small	from 1 m	sunny	shady or partly shady
Omphalodes luciliae		×		×
Onosma alboroseum		×	×	
O. stellulatum		×	×	
Orostachys spinosus	×		×	
Penstemon caespitosus		×	×	
P. pinifolius		×	×	
P. rupicola		×	×	
Petrocallis glaucifolia	×			×
P. pyrenaica	×			×
Phlox subulata slow-growing cultivars		×	×	
Phyteuma comosum	×			×
Plantago nivalis	×		×	
Polygonum tenuicaule		×		×
Potentilla aurea cultivars		×	×	
P. nitida	×		×	
Primula auricula		×		×
P. bauhini		×	×	
P. hirsuta		×		×
P. marginata	×			×
Pterocephalus parnassii		×	×	
Ramonda myconi		×		×
R. nathaliae		×		×
Saxifraga-arendsii hybrids		×		×
S. cochlearis		×	×	
S. cotyledon		×		×
S. hostii		×	×	
S. hypnoides 'Gemmifera'		×		×
S. longifolia		×	×	
S. oppositifolia 'Latina'	×			×
S. paniculata (*S. aizoon*)		×	×	
S. × urbium (*S. umbrosa*)	×			×
Sedum cauticolum		×	×	
S. pluricaule		×	×	
S. sieboldii		×	×	
S. spathulifolium 'Cape Blanco'		×	×	
S. 'Purpureum'	×			×
Sempervivum species and cultivars	×		×	
Silene alpestris		×	×	
S. schafta 'Splendens'		×	×	
Soldanella montana		×		×
S. villosa		×		×
Thalictrum kiusianum	×			×
Thlaspi stylosum	×		×	
Trachelium jacquinii ssp. *rumelianum*		×	×	
Veronica fruticans cultivars		×	×	

Herbaceous Perennials, Grasses, Ferns and Bulbs for Container Gardens (cont.)

Species and Cultivars	Container Size		Location	
	small	from 1 m	sunny	shady or partly shady
Viola biflora		✕		✕
V. × florariensis		✕	✕	
Vitaliana primuliflora	✕		✕	
Grasses & Sedges				
Alopecurus pratensis	✕		✕	
Carex buchananii		✕	✕	
C. firma 'Variegata'	✕		✕	
Festuca glacialis	✕		✕	
Poa alpina var. *vivipara*		✕	✕	
Ferns				
Adiantum pedatum	✕			✕
A. venustum		✕		✕
Asplenium platyneuron	✕			✕
*A. septentrionale**	✕		✕	
A. trichomanes	✕			✕
A. viride	✕			✕
Athyrium filix-femina		✕		✕
A. pycnocarpon		✕	✕	
Ceterach officinarum	✕		✕	
Cystopteris fragilis		✕		✕
Dryopteris cristata	™			™
D. goldiana		✕		✕
D. marginalis	✕			✕
D. noveboracensis	✕			✕
Onoclea sensibilia	✕		✕	
O. cinnamonea	✕			✕
Osmunda claytoniana		✕	✕	
Pellaea atropurpurea		✕	✕	
Phyllitis scolopendrium		✕		✕
Polypodium vulgare	✕			✕
Polystichum acrostichoides	✕			✕
Bulbs, Corms, & Tubers				
Crocus chrysanthus cultivars		✕	✕	
C. speciosus cultivars		✕	✕	
Cyclamen species		✕		✕
Eranthis × tubergenii		✕	✕	
Erythronium species and cultivars		✕		✕
Fritillaria pyrenaica		✕		✕
Galanthus species and cultivars		✕		✕

Species and Cultivars	Container Size		Location	
	small	from 1 m	sunny	shady or partly shady
Iris danfordiae		×	×	
Iris histrioides 'Major'		×	×	
Muscari azurea		×	×	
Narcissus asturiensis	×		×	
N. cyclamineus hybrids		×		×

* = lime intolerant
* = lime intolerant
* = lime intolerant

Roof Gardens

As cities become more and more crowded, there is less area available in which to plant gardens. Life would be more humane and attractive if the roofs of buildings (public and private), viaducts, bridges, and other structures, were adorned with greenery. Terraces and underground houses inspired the concept of roof gardens.

In order to create a successful roof garden, drainage, irrigation and isolating the roof surface are as important as choosing the right plants. The depth of the bed is not really very important and can be substantially shallower than is commonly assumed.

After many experiments, beds built up in a fixed sequence have been proved successful. On top of a layer of water-proof material to seal off the roof surface, a layer of coarse gravel or lightweight aggregate is placed, and is drained by plastic or other drainage pipes. Then a separating layer made of a porous fiber-glass mat is laid to prevent roots from penetrating the drainage bed. Next comes a layer of top soil, which must be as light as possible. It should be made of peat, or a soil mixture containing a high percentage of peat. The growing media described on page 42 can also be used for roof and terrace gardens.

The depth of the top soil is governed by the plants to be grown and the load-bearing capacity of the roof. Beds of 5 to 10 cm are deep enough for unassuming plants and greenery. 20 to 30 cm is necessary if trees, shrubs and exacting herbaceous perennials are to be planted.

Special cultural attention is important when gardening with a thin top soil. The garden has to be watered more regularly and fertilized more often.

There are several manufactured roof garden systems on the market today. These adapt to almost all home site situations.

Roof garden plants should be selected in keeping with their esthetic aspects. Plant arrangements, however, should be carefully thought out because they must adapt to the existing architectural and microclimatic limitations. The potential height of the plants must be taken into consideration. Atop high roofs and unsuitably proportioned locations, overly tall trees should be avoided. Evergreen trees and shrubs are ideal for roof gardens because they provide year-round effect. The exclusive use of drought resistant trees and shrubs which grow naturally on exposed prairies, steppes, and deserts is only necessary on high, open locations where it is either impossible, or too expensive, to irrigate during droughts. On private terrace, roof, or container gardens, where it is possible to provide more attentive care, plants of a more demanding nature can be used.

The environmental requirements of the roof garden, in particular soil requirements, are very similar to container gardens. Therefore, refer to the lists in the section on container gardens for plants which can be cultivated in a roof garden. Drought resistant species are listed in the section on steppe gardens.

A Roof Container
Garden

Entrance Gardens

The Romans used atriums as the central focus of their homes. Roman atriums, open to the sky and with a pool to catch rainwater, were enclosed within the walls of the house near the main entrance. When the Romans adopted the Greek pillared house (Peristyle) in the second century B.C., the atrium became a receiving room. Today, atriums frequently are used as open-air hallways which connect the ground floors of large apartment complexes and office buildings.

Architecturally, modern home atriums have evolved into small garden areas, more or less enclosed, at the front door. They are closely akin to the English dooryard garden. These small, entrance gardens sometimes suffer unfavorable environmental conditions.

Managing such a garden may be difficult, not least because of the cramped conditions. Far more difficult is the problem of light, especially where surrounding buildings are large. The gardening space in an entrance garden can be sunny and dry, or shady and damp, or it can be characterized by radical changes; sunny part of the day, shady the rest.

At any rate, the planting area in an entrance garden is very limited. Often an entrance garden offers amenities such as benches, and a fountain flowing into a decorative pool. Useful in the planting plan are the smaller sized flowering trees and modest-sized shrubs, especially broadleaf evergreens where they can be grown. Beds may be ground level, but some can be raised with good effect. Dwarf trees, shrubs and climbers (to cover bleak walls) are ideal for entrance gardens. They thrive in small areas, where plants of larger scale cannot. If mature plants are purchased, an atrium garden can be landscaped in a short period of time.

Plants for Entrance Gardens

The variety of plants to choose from is largely dependent upon the amount of light the atrium garden receives, but temperature extremes, soil reaction (pH) and other factors enter in. If the existing soil is not suitable for plants, it should be upgraded, or if need be, the top soil can be rebuilt much the same as for roof gardens. Drainage is a problem to be solved before any planting begins.

The plants listed for rock gardens, steppe and prairie gardens, and container gardens can be used for sunny, dry entrance gardens. The species listed below can tolerate the varying light conditions of entrance gardens or even enclosed courtyards, sunny as well as shady. Rhododendron and other Ericaceae which tolerate shade will be discussed in a separate section.

Wooded Areas

Taller-growing ornamental conifers and deciduous woody plants are ideal for shady or partly-shady locations in the entrance garden. Many of the recommended sorts (pages 49–51) will readily withstand overstory shade and root competition of standard trees.

Herbaceous Perennials Suitable for Shade

In an entrance garden, non-woody ornamentals which prefer shaded or partially shaded areas, or at least tolerate shade well, become important in the design due to building shadows. Select the most robust species which are well suited for any shaded situation. They can for example, be planted where immature trees and shrubs do not yet give shade, where

An Entry
Garden

48

the top soil has not yet been enriched with leaf mold, and where humidity and soil dampness fluctuate.

Especially desirable are low-growing species which can be used as ground covers, such as *Epimedium, Pulmonaria, Symphytum* and *Waldsteinia* species. Taller-growing, flowering perennials such as *Aconitum* and *Astilbe* species are also good, as well as all of the *Hosta* species. Grasses and sedges suitable for shade (*Carex morrowii, C. pendula, Deschampsia caespitosa* and *Luzula sylvatica*), together with numerous ferns, native and exotic woodland perennials and grasses and shade-thriving border perennials such as the Japanese Anemones and *Dicentra* species and cultivars should always be considered.

Herbaceous perennials suitable for sunny locations have already been dealt with in previous sections.

Trees and Shrubs for Entryway Gardens with Varying Amounts of Light

Species and Cultivars	Height (m)	Shady	Partly shady	Sunny	Under trees
Deciduous Trees & Shrubs					
Aesculus parviflora	3–4	×	×		×
Amelanchier species	6–13	×	×	×	
Aralia elata	2–3	×	×		×
Aucuba japonica	2–2.5	×	×		×
Berberis evergreen species	1–2.5	×	×	×	×
Buxus sempervirens cultivars	6–7	×	×	×	×
Cornus florida	4–5		×		×
C. kousa	5–7	×	×	×	×
Corylopsis species	2–4		×		×
Cotoneaster salicifolius	3–4	×	×	×	×
C. × watereri cultivars	3–7	×	×	×	×
Euonymus species	2–5	×	×	×	×
Fothergilla species	1–3		×		×
Hamamelis species	2–5		×	×	×
Hydrangea petiolaris	5–10	×	×		
Ilex evergreen species	2–6	×	×		×
Kolkwitzia amabilis	1.5–2		×	×	
Osmanthus heterophyllus	3–5	×	×		×
Parrotia persica	4–10	×	×		×
Parrotiopsis jacquemontiana	2–3	×	×	×	×
Prunus laurocerasus cultivars	1–2	×	×		×
Pyracantha cultivars	2–4		×	×	
Rubus odoratus	2	×	×	×	×
Sorbaria species	2–3	×	×	×	×
Staphylea species	3–4		×	×	×
Stranvaesia davidiana	3–4	×	×	×	×
Syringa species and cultivars	1–6		×	×	

Trees and Shrubs for Entryway Gardens with Varying Amounts of Light (cont.)

Species and Cultivars	Height (m)	Shady	Partly shady	Sunny	Under trees
Viburnum davidii	1–3	×	×		×
V. × burkwoodii	2	×	×		×
V. × carlcephalum	1.5–2	×	×		
V. × farreri	2–3	×	×	×	
V. × juddii	2–3	×	×		
V. plicatum	2–3	×	×	×	
V. × pragense	2–3	×	×		×
V. rhytidophyllum	2–4	×	×		×
V. utile	1–2	×	×		
Conifers					
Abies species and cultivars	to 30		×		
Cryptomeria japonica	10–20		×		
× Cupressocyparis cultivars	15–30	×	×	×	
Juniperus chinensis 'Pfitzeriana'	2–4	×	×	×	
Taxus species and cultivars	1–20	×	×	×	×
Thujopsis dolabrata	10–15		×	×	
Tsuga species and cultivars	1–30		×		

Trees and Shrubs for Shady Entryway Gardens

Species	Shady	Partly shady	Sunny	Under trees
Deciduous Trees and Shrubs				
Berberis species and cultivars	×	×	×	
B. × stenophylla cultivars	×	×		
Buxus sempervirens cultivars	×	×	×	×
Cotoneaster species and cultivars		×	×	
Daphne blagayana	×	×		×
D. laureola	×	×		
D. mezereum	×	×	×	×
D. pontica	×	×		×
Euonymus fortunei cultivars	×	×		×
Fuchsia magellanica		×		
Hebe species and cultivars		×	×	
Hedera helix cultivars	×	×		×
Hypericum species and cultivars	×	×		
H. calycinum	×	×	×	×
Ilex crenata cultivars	×	×		×
Ligustrum vulgare 'Lodense'	×	×	×	×

Species	Shady	Partly shady	Sunny	Under trees
Lonicera nitida	X	X		X
L. pileata	X	X		X
Mahonia species and cultivars	X	X		X
Pachysandra terminalis	X	X		X
Paxistima canbyi		X		
Prunus laurocerasus 'Otto Luyken'	X	X		X
Rubus irenaeus	X	X		
Sarcococca humilis	X	X		
Sasa pumila	X	X		X
Skimmia species and hybrids	X	X		X
Viburnum davidii	X	X		
Vinca minor	X	X		X
Coniferous Trees and Shrubs				
Abies species and cultivars		X	X	
Cedrus deodara cultivars		X		
Chamaeacyparis species and cultivars		X	X	
Cryptomeria japonica cultivars	X	X		
Juniperus chinensis cultivars		X	X	
J. horizontalis cultivars		X	X	
J. sabina cultivars		X	X	
Microbiota decussata		X	X	
Picea abies cultivars		X	X	
P. orientalis cultivars		X	X	
Podocarpus nivalis		X		
Pseudotsuga menziesii cultivars		X	X	
Taxus species and cultivars	X	X	X	X
Thujopsis dolabrata 'Nana'	X	X	X	
Tsuga species and cultivars		X	X	

Shady Garden Spots

Not only entrance gardens, but also in older "mature" gardens, larger trees and shrubs which can thrive in the shade are required. The fine old and dense trees of mature gardens should not be considered troublesome, just because they cast too much shade. They provide the opportunity to cultivate more delicate dwarf trees, shrubs and bushes. Density of shade is easily managed by expert pruning and thinning of larger trees.

In reviewing plants requiring shade, rhododendrons and other large-leafed ericaceous trees and shrubs or deciduous broadleaf woody plants such as *Acer palmatum* and *A. japonicum*, *Aesculus parviflora*, the yellow- or white-bordered forms of *Aralia elata*, the showy *Corylopsis* species, or *Cornus florida* and *C. kousa*, all thrive in partly-shaded locations where they readily attain full maturity and beauty. In addition, numerous broadleaf evergreen species of the following genera, *Aucuba, Berberis, Buxus, Cotoneaster, Hedera,*

Ilex, Lonicera, Osmanthus, Rhododendron, Skimmia and *Viburnum,* also possess this tolerance to partial shade.

The harsher the climatic conditions, the more shade these plants need. Low winter temperatures and strong, desiccating winds play as significant a role in plant survival as do summer conditions of drought and strong, searing winds. In humid, constant climates, trees and shrubs are more likely to get by without special protection than in more continental locations.

A simple shade planting

Dwarf trees and shrubs take on special significance in planting and enlivening shady garden spots sheltered by larger trees. Small-sized cultivars and dwarf trees and shrubs are seldom used singly; more often, they are used in larger or smaller groupings or even as a sort of ground cover planting. When using them, one must consider whether they are capable of surviving root competition and the water drip during storms from full-sized, over-story trees. Intolerant or noncompetitive species should be planted only in the shade beyond the dripline of a larger tree, as the dripline more or less defines the root zone of the tree.

The dwarf woody plants for shady areas, as well as taller growing coniferous and broadleaf trees and shrubs, listed for garden use in the previous section are all suitable for shady garden situations. Garden books dealing with perennials in detail supply additional information on shady beds and borders beyond the scope of this volume.

Terraces and Patios

People love to relax on terraces and patios. Such locations give plant-lovers the opportunity to sit and enjoy both the setting and the plant collection. Gardens close to terraces and patios ought to be especially colorful and contain a great variety of plants.

On terraces and patios, smaller forms of trees and shrubs, as well as herbaceous perennials, should be used whenever and wherever they do not block the view of the rest of the garden. Properly designed, the terrace planting ties the terrace or patio to the rest of the garden.

Not infrequently the terrace and the adjoining lawn are at different levels. This is ideal for a rock garden or raised rockery bed if the terrace is higher than the lawn, or for a sunken garden, if the terrace is lower. It makes no difference whether the area is sunny or shady. It can even vary; being sunny part of the day, and shady the rest.

If the terrace-bordering bed is higher than the pavement, and located in a sunny area, it can be laid out as a heath, steppe, or prairie garden. Specimen trees or shrubs or clumps of ornamental grass or rock garden herbaceous perennials can be planted in even the smallest areas. Where the lawn and terrace join such a planting will help break and soften the line separating the two. Planted containers are also useful in such cases.

It is not necessary to have a botanic or ecological theme when designing the garden. Personal taste and preference should dictate the choice of plants. The important thing to keep in mind is to use woody ornamentals and perennials which have similar environmental and cultural requirements. It is also important to make sure that the ratio of trees, shrubs and herbaceous perennials (or bedding annuals) is about equal. The garden should be as esthetically pleasing as possible, which means, the plants should be properly spaced and their shapes and colors complement each other.

Plants suitable for terraces and patios can be found in the preceding lists. The environment of your site need only be matched with the proper list. The trees, shrubs, and perennials may then be selected in keeping with personal preferences.

Front Yard Gardens

As lot sizes become smaller, the space available for gardens in the front of the house also shrinks. In fact, front yards are becoming so small, some gardeners no longer want to put time and energy into lawns. It seems much more attractive to convert the front yard into a garden filled with trees, shrubs, perennials, bulbs and

54

colorful summer annuals. The limited spaces remaining along walkways and driveways are better devoted to garden than maintaining them as a bothersome strip of grass.

Front yard gardens can be laid out and planted in much the same way as terraces and patios. Probably rock gardens should be designed and built only where the site is plagued with very steep slopes and height variations. In choosing plants, the amount of sunlight the garden receives must be taken into account. Oftentimes, plants suitable for shade are required. Front yard gardens usually have room enough for a few taller-growing woody plants; shade or flowering trees with nar-

rowish crowns, and ornamental shrubs. The list on page 60 includes some of the species which are especially suitable. The mature height and width of the plants must be taken into consideration before planting.

Conifers of a more or less columnar form are suitable in small or quite narrow front yard gardens. They do not, however, have to be the popular and common selections such as *Picea pungens* 'Glauca' or *Cedrus atlantica* 'Glauca', which will quickly grow far too large for small front gardens. Conifers should be planted so that they fit harmoniously with the proportions of overall landscape in the garden. The cultivars and species on page 61 will work well in small front yard gardens.

Ornamental Flowering Shrubs and Small-Crowned Trees Recommended for Front Yard Gardens

Species	Height (m)	Noteworthy Qualities
Acer ginnala	4–6	gorgeous bright red and yellow fall colors
Acer japonicum 'Aconitifolium'	2–4	decorative leaves with fiery-red fall color
Acer palmatum cultivars	1–3	cultivars have interesting leaf shapes and colors
Amelanchier species	6–13	adaptable flowering shrubs or trees with splendid fall colors
Aralia elata cultivars	2–3	ornamental, small-branched shrubs with very large, pinnate leaves, green or variegated white or yellow
Cornus controversa 'Variegata'	2–3	pagoda-like, erect shrub with vivid, white-bordered leaves, rare and choice
Corylopsis species	1–3	pretty, very early spring bloomer
Cotoneaster salicifolius var. *floccosus*	2–4	elegant, evergreen shrub
Cotoneaster × *watereri* cultivars	2–6	heavily berried, partially procumbent evergreen shrubs
Crataegus species	5–10	small-crowned, mostly white-blooming or rose-pink, heavily fruiting small trees
Hamamelis species	2–4	widely grown fall, winter or early spring flowers
Ilex aquifolium cultivars	2–8	mostly fairly narrow, upright evergreen shrubs suitable for shade
I. opaca cultivars	2–8	similar to above but fruits first year; hardier; leaves duller

Ornamental Flowering Shrubs and Small-Crowned Trees Recommended for Front Yard Gardens (cont.)

Species	Height (m)	Noteworthy Qualities
Kalopanax pictus	2–4	shrub with few branches, strong, decorative leaves
Kolkwitzia amabilis	1.5–2	especially beautiful in flower, but sometimes awkwardly growing shrub requiring regular pruning
Laburnum × watereri 'Vossii'	5–8	erect, vase-shaped small, deciduous tree, especially long, racemes of yellow flowers unfortunately poisonous
Magnolia species	2–10	decorative trees of various sizes with striking blossoms, some deciduous, some evergreen
Malus species and cultivars	3–10	heavily blooming, mostly small-crowned trees, some quite large at maturity
Parrotia persica	6–10	large, very upright shrub or small tree with beautiful fall colors and decorative bark patterns
Prunus kurilensis	2–3	especially slow-growing, heavily blooming ornamental cherry tree
Prunus laurocerasus and cultivars	1–3	evergreen shrub for shady locations
Prunus serrulata 'Amanogawa'	4–5	very slim, rigid columnar growth; all other Japanese ornamental cherry trees are just as desirable, but need much more room
Prunus subhirtella forms	2–6	more elegant form than *Prunus serrulata* species
Prunus triloba	2–3	commonly used in front yard gardens, but have somewhat stiff growth habit
Pyracantha forms	2–4	heavily fruiting, evergreen shrubs, very popular
Quercus pontica	4–6	bushy oak with peculiar, decorative leaves
Rhododendron species and cultivars	1–4	*Rhododendron* (and azaleas) should only be used in front yard gardens when suitable environmental conditions exist (humus, acid soil and lightly shaded sites)
Rhus typhina	3–5	large, ornamental shrub, very popular, too common in some areas
Robinia hispida	2–3	beautifully blooming shrub: easily broken, therefore, best cultivated on a trellis or staked
Rosa, shrub roses and wild types	1.5–3	beautiful flowering and fruiting shrubs for sunny locations
Salix matsudana 'Tortuosa'	8–10	popular specimen tree with corkscrew-like branches. *Salix × erythroflexuosa* is similar in structure but shrubby
Sorbus species	8–15	most species bear fruit and flowers abundantly and have beautiful autumn colors
Viburnum × farreri	2–3	interesting late winter and very early spring blossoms, *Viburnum × bodnantense* blooms at the same time
Viburnum plicatum	3–4	gorgeous blooming shrub with unusual fall colors
Viburnum × pragense	2–3	beautiful, evergreen shrub for partly shady to shady locations
Viburnum rhytidophyllum	3–4	large evergreen shrub for partly shady to shady locations

Conifers for Front Yard Gardens

Species	Height (m)	Noteworthy Qualities
Abies koreana	5–15	slow-growing, sets colorful cones even while quite young (knee-high)
Abies pinsapo	15–20	unmistakable with its rigid needles: very decorative and slow-growing
Araucaria araucana	5–10	huge tree of unusual form with dense branching habit and large, scaly leaves, winter hardy only in warm climates
Cedrus atlantica 'Fastigiata'	10–20	blue-needled, columnar form of Atlas Cedar
Cedrus brevifolia	6–8	slow-growing, short-needled and very beautiful
Cecrus libani var. *stenocoma*	10–20	thin, spruce-like, green needled form of Cedar of Lebanon
Juniperus chinensis 'Columnaris Glauca'	6–8	narrow columnar, silver-blue needled
Juniperus communis 'Horstmann'	3–4	loosely arranged perpendicularly pendulous branches, very decorative
Juniperus communis 'Oblonga Pendula'	3–4	wide growing, loosely erect, the upper branches are long and project elegantly
Juniperus rigida	5–6	branches spread widely, pendulous
Juniperus virginiana 'Glauca'	8–10	columnar, rapid and dense growth, steel-blue needles
Juniperus virginiana 'Skyrocket'	4–6	pencil-thin, blue-needled form of Virginia Juniper
Picea breweriana	10–20	the most elegant of all spruces, long-needled, vertically pendulous branches, grows rather slowly
Picea glehnii	15–20	thin, fine-needled and decorative
Picea likiangensis var. *purpurea*	10–20	especially elegant, very short needles
Picea omorika	20–30	generally well-known, with *P. abies* and *P. pungens* the most common spruces grown
Pinus aristata	5–10	especially decorative, small pine, oldest living conifer in the world
Pinus cembra	10–20	slow-growing, useful in small gardens
Pinus leucodermis	10–20	slow-growing, usually remains small-crowned
Pinus parviflora	5–12	the blue-needled form 'Glauca' is an especially important pine for small gardens
Pinus peuce	15–20	in habit it is similar to *Pinus cembra*, except it is a faster and taller grower, very important species
Pinus sylvestris 'Fastigiata'	10–15	especially narrow columnar form, blue-needled
Pinus wallichiana 'Densa'	10–15	narrow columnar form
Taxus baccata 'Dovastoniana'	3–5	erect form with projecting branches and pendulous twigs
Taxus baccata 'Overeynderi'	3–5	capable of developing large, wide columns
Tsuga canadensis	10–20	loose, elegant conifer with graceful habit
Taxus mertensiana	10–12	especially decorative with short, silver-white needles

A Front Garden

Dwarf Rhododendrons

In addition to dwarf rhododendrons, other representatives of the Ericaceae will be dealt with in this section because as a rule they have more or less similar cultural requirements and are botanically a tight-knit group. Examples of ericaceous genera are: *Andromeda, Cassiope, Chamaedaphne, Gaultheria,* × *Gaulnettya, Kalmia, Ledum, Leucothoe, Pernettya, Phyllodoce* and *Pieris.* Exceptions to this rule are: *Arctostaphylos, Bruckenthalia, Calluna, Daboecia, Erica* and *Vaccinium* species. These genera flourish under different ecological conditions than the other Ericaceae.

There is hardly another group of plants so well suited to beautify and brighten shady spots in mature gardens as rhododendrons and other Ericaceae. But no other group makes such specific demands of the environment, especially with regard to pH level, humus content, soil dampness, humidity and the amount of light received.

Planting Requirements

It is not absolutely necessary to prepare special beds for the widely grown cultivars of *Rhododendron repens, R. williamsianum* and *R. yakusimanum.* Like large blooming rhododendron hybrids or deciduous azaleas, they can be planted as a foreground for trees and shrubs, or beneath high-crowned trees. On the other hand, most of the small-leafed species and hybrids thrive best and are more conspicuous when planted in raised beds. Raised beds are commonly seen in rock gardens or terraces and in areas created expressly for the cultivation of dwarf rhododendrons. Lime-free rocks or wood (logs, ties, or close-set paths) are used to make retaining curbs. The space enclosed is then filled with a suitable acid humus soil to a depth of 30–45 cm (12–18 in.).

Natural Distributions and Climatic Demands

Most rhododendron species grow in damp to moist, acid, humus-rich soil, in mountain ranges. In the alpine regions, abundant precipitation and high humidity offset the high levels of solar irradiation in summer and plants are protected by snow cover during winter.

The evergreen leaves of rhododendrons transpire water during the winter. This moisture loss will not result in plant dessication if the plant can obtain moisture from the soil or if transpiration is greatly reduced by a protective layer of snow or ground level humidity. Because transpiration is increased considerably in wind-exposed locations, planting in a wind-protected site is one of the basic requirements for successfully cultivating rhododendrons. When the micro site is sufficiently humid, rhododendrons are decidedly light-loving plants; in less favorable locations, they do better in light shade under tall trees.

Sun and shade are environmental factors worthy of careful consideration. On a year-round basis, the higher the humidity, the more sunlight rhododendron can tolerate. When conditions are not ideal, or more sensitive species and hybrids are being dealt with (as *Rhododendron griffithianum, R. fortunei, R. williamsianum* and *R. repens* and hybrids of Japanese azaleas), light shade under deep-rooted trees is absolutely necessary. Oaks and pines are ideal deep-rooted shade trees. Suitable partners for small rhododendron species are, among others, slow-growing maple species *Acer rufinerve, A. japonicum, A. palmatum; Amelanchier* species, *Cornus controversa, C. florida,* and *C. kousa; Halesia carolina* and *H. monticola,* all magnolias, ornamental apple and cherry trees. The importance of wind

Dwarf Rhododendron
in a mixed planting

shelter and a humid atmosphere have already been mentioned. Rhododendrons are exceptionally sensitive to drying winds and therefore are unsuitable for roof gardens, exposed decks and balconies, and other drafty locations. Rhododendrons display their full beauty only with protection from wind near the sheltering wall of a house or on the lee side of a hedge, or when sheltered by large trees or shrubs. In newer gardens, rush-mats or interwoven slats of wood can be subsituted for hedges. Temperature is also a limiting environmental factor (see details in the encyclopedia section).

Soil Mixtures

All ericaceous ornamentals are decidedly shallow rooted. Their fine, fibrous roots, barely below the soil surface, require well aerated, loose, acid soil. Most sorts benefit from a permanent, porous mulch of oak leaf-mold, peat or similar humus source. With almost no exceptions ericaceous plants are highly sensitive to compacted or poorly drained soil. Luckily, however, many Rhododendrons are surprisingly adaptable where soil is concerned, otherwise they would not be able to grow in most gardens.

Before planting a garden, one should take a close look at the neighboring gardens. If these are marked by dark green, well leafed ericaceous plants, one can usually go ahead and plant similar ericaceous ornamentals without extensive soil preparations, as long as the soil is lime-free and not compacted, and a partly shady, wind-protected location is available.

In addition to suitable climatic conditions and soil structure, the pH level must be considered when cultivating rhododendron. The optimal pH range is between 4.5 and 5.0, that is, very acid. Planting in soil of a pH level under 3.0 and over 6.0 is very risky. High humus soils or forest floor soils covered with a layer of raw humus are natural habitats for rhododendrons. They also thrive well in sandy soil and sandy, loamy soil. If necessary, light soil can be made suitable for rhododendrons by adding organic material (peat, leaf mold, pine straw, bark compost and old, rotten cow manure) to increase water retention. Successful cultivation of rhododendrons in clay soil or heavy loamy soil is very unlikely. These soils are difficult to improve, even with large applications of humus. The fine, fibrous roots of ericaceous species have great difficulty in penetrating such soils. Neither overly compacted or non-acidic soils are suitable for rhododendrons. Such soils must be replaced with a special blended planting mix. It is usually not practical to prepare a planting site for only one plant; it is much better to prepare a bed for several rhododendrons and related ericaceous plants.

Cultivation in a Prepared Planting Media

Whenever the soil is not suitable for cultivating rhododendrons, it must be replaced. A 30 to 40 cm deep layer of top soil should be removed. A 5–10 cm layer of spruce trimmings, chopped brush shredded wood or wood chips should then be laid down. This layer promotes drainage and at the same time tends to prevent lime-bearing ground water from penetrating the planting media. When dealing with terraced or banked beds the original soil should be excavated to the same depth as the raised beds, to provide ample depth of suitable soil. There are numerous formulas for mixing suitable planting media. Good media contains a high percentage of humus, a pH level between 4.5 and 5.0 (see page 9 for treating the soil with sulfur to lower the pH level) and a structural stabilizer, which assures optimum drainage and aeration. 50% of the volume of all soil mixtures should be coarse-fibered peat. Different organic materials can be admixed with the peat; for example, leaf-mold, needle-mold, bark compost of fine granulation, hop residue (as is used in botanical gardens) or wood mulch, which has been composted for two years (chips, trimmings, hedge clippings). Suitable mixtures of trace elements and a slow-release fertilizer should be mixed in as primary fertilizers.

An artificial planting media lasts about

ten years, after which time the plants must be removed and the old medium replaced with new. This is due to soil micro-organisms which digest away all the humus as times passes. A permanent leaf-mold or peat mulch, renewed once or twice yearly, prolongs bed life. Even older rhododendrons tolerate being lifted and reset.

A good drainage system using lime-free rock or soil pipe should be installed if there is any question about drainage.

Watering

Soil moisture and water management play a decisive role in cultivating ericaceous plants. The soil has to be sufficiently damp for the plants needs, never soggy. Especially during the first year after planting and during the blooming season rhododendrons, like most ericaceous species, require an ample supply of water. Watering during these periods is absolutely necessary when rainfall is insufficient to keep the soil continuously damp. After a dry autumn they should also be watered so that moisture is available for metabolic processes during winter. The quality of water given to the plants is of great importance. Hard water containing a high percentage of calcium and magnesium is not suitable because these compounds raise the pH level of the soil. Hard water can be made tolerable by treating it with sulfuric, phosphoric or oxalic acids. The pH level of the water should be adjusted to 5.8 to 6.0. Berg and Heft (1979) recommend adding, for each degree of carbonate hardness in 1 cubic meter (265 gal.) of water, either 22.3 grams of oxalic acid crystals or 10 cc's of sulfuric acid. Moderately hard water can be softened by adding 500 g (20 oz.) of peat per m³ (cu. yd.). The peat is put into a muslin or gauze bag and hung in a 50 gal. water tank for at least 24 hours.

Planting and Maintenance

Planting sites for rhododendrons should be carefully chosen and prepared. It is advisable to improve all soils by adding organic materials, including even "good" garden soils. Normally, peat with fertilizer is used. About ¼ to ⅓ of a bale should be used for each plant. For each m³ (cu. yd.) of humus, 2 to 3 kg (2.5 to 6 lbs.) of a slow-release complete fertilizer should be added. The more unfavorable the soil conditions, the more organic matter ought to be worked in. If the soil is very limey and excessively heavy, then, by all means, replace it with an artificial planting medium as described above. A drainage system must underly the planting medium.

If the soil is prepared correctly, rhododendron plantings should be problem-free and easy to care for in the following years. About the only other care needed is maintenance of favorable soil conditions and winter protection for the touchier cultivars. It has already been mentioned that rhododendrons are shallow-rooted, but it should be stressed that every time the soil is disturbed, by cultivation or other digging, the roots can be injured. A better approach is to apply a deep leaf-mold or peat mulch, renewing it as necessary. It protects the roots, insures a cool root environment, reduces water runoff and evaporation, and through microbial action, supplies humus to the soil beneath.

It is well know that rhododendrons and other ericaceous plants tolerate mineral fertilizers rather well. When their leaves fade to a yellow-green or old leaves fall off earlier than usual, knowledgeable gardeners automatically realize they should add mineral fertilizers. They sometimes fail to considered other organic fertilizers (bonemeal, bloodmeal, and

In difficult soils, rhododendrons are planted in soilless planting medium made of peat, composted coniferous needles, bark compost and leafmold. This mixture overlays a drainage layer composed of coniferous prunings or mulched wood chips.

Normally, new branches develop below the blossom head. If there are only one or two new branches, they should be clipped short, thus encouraging the plant to branch more attractively.

similar acidic organic concentrates) which work just as well. It is recommended that 50 to 100 g/m² of one of these organic fertilizers mixed with 60g/m² each of superphosphate and ammoniated potash be applied.

A worthwhile aspect of rhododendron management is the removal of all withered rhododendron flowers, so-called dead-heading. This prevents seed formation, and the plants can direct photosynthates and nutrients toward the development of leaf and flower buds for the following year.

In the case of a few red flowered rhododendron cultivars pruning is especially important in the first few years after planting. Often shaping can be done simply by removing half the ends of leaf buds, just beyond the new spring shoots. Plants with too widely spread branches can be pruned well back even into the old wood, without adverse consequences.

Rhododendrons living in ideal soil and environmental conditions as outlined are much less prone to contracting disease as those not so situated. Calamitous plant diseases and deterioration almost always befall plants suffering from adverse growing conditions. Weak and disease-prone plants almost always can be brought to vigor by correcting the growing conditions.

Companion Plants for Dwarf Rhododendrons

In addition to the already listed ericaceous species with the same ecological requirements, a number of slow-growing trees and shrubs make excellent companion plants for rhododendrons. Some are the same size (*Ilex crenata* cultivars, *Skimmia* species and *Viburnum davidii*) while others are flat growing ground cover ornamentals which grow at a faster rate, but remain small (*Euonymus fortunei* 'Minimus' and 'Kewensis', *Linnaea borealis*, *Paxistima canbyi*, *Pachsysandra terminalis* 'Green Carpet', and *Rubus calycinoides*).

Herbaceous perennials, bulbs and ferns to be planted with dwarf rhododendron should include only slow-growing species. In addition to bulbs (*Eranthis, Galanthus, Muscari,* and *Scilla* species) and lilies (*Lilium martagon, L. speciosum,* Asiatic and Aurelia hybrid lilies), the following classic companion plants for rhododendrons are recommended (low and slow-growing species):

63

Astilbe chinensis 'Pumila'
Cardamine trifolia
Cortusa matthioli
Eomecon chionantha
Galax urceolata
Hacquetia epipactis
Hepatica nobilis 'Plena'
Hylomecon japonicum
Isopyrum thalictroides
Jeffersonia dubia
Liriope species
Meconopsis cambrica
Mitella diphylla
Primula alpicola
P. capitata
P. chionantha
P. secundiflora
P. sikkimensis
P. vialii
Sanguinaria canadensis
Saxifraga cortusifolia
Synthris stellata
Tolmiea menziesii
Trillium grandiflorum
Uvularia grandiflora
Vancouveria hexandra
Viola palmata

Dryopteris cristata
D. erythrosora
D. villarii
Phyllitis scolopendrium
Polystichum acrostichoides
P. aculeatum
P. braunii
P. lonchitis
P. scopulinum
P. setiferum-cultivars
Thelypteris decursive-pinnata
T. noveboracensis

Not only lilies, but especially ferns are traditional companion plants in rhododendron plantings, especially the slow-growing, lower growing species. Some choice ferns, growing 30 to 80 cm (10 to 30 in.) in height are:

Adiantum pedatum
A. pedatum 'Imbricatum'
A. venustum
Athyrium filix-femina
A. nipponicum
Blechnum penna-marina
B. spicant
Cyrtomium fortunei
Cystopteris fragilis
C. montana

Broadleaf Shrubs as Ground Covers

The use of ground covering shrubs is becoming increasingly widespread. Such plantings are practical as well as pleasingly decorative. They virtually eliminate the chores of weeding and cultivating the soil—which can only be viewed with relief by gardeners—provided the soil is deeply cultivated and treated with a herbicide before plants are set.

Ground covers are used wherever trees and shrubs are planted in loose groups which allow room for such a planting to thrive. They can also take the place of a lawn in locations where it is difficult for a lawn mower to operate, such as a narrow strip, under closely planted trees, or on steep slopes. In order for woody plants to be suitable as ground covers, they must have specific characteristics. They must be able to grow well in large drifts to be at their best when used in closely-planted, large areas. They should grow to a uniform, but low height, either by sending out prostrate, downward tending branches, or by sending up a dense stand of short, erect shoots which quickly cover the area with greenery. Dwarf plants

Broadleaf shrubs as a Ground Cover

spreading by underground runners are ideal. Prostrate and low growing shrubs normally grow in a dense, well-proportioned fashion and so meet the criteria of a good ground cover. The proper height of the ground cover planting in a given area is dependent upon the size of the planting area and the height of the trees and shrubs under which it is planted. The larger the planting site, the taller the ground cover plant can grow and still remain in character. Thus, *Cotoneaster dammeri* or similar absolutely prostrate species are, for example, the only plants which can be used under very small shrubs or dwarf conifers.

Ground covers must be as unassuming as possible, be able to tolerate shade, and be able to regenerate readily after pruning. If they are expected to suppress weeds, all weed roots and seeds must be carefully removed from the soil before the ground cover is planted. It is especially important to do basic soil preparations before planting ground covers because once the planting is in it is difficult to amend the soil short of removing the plants. Most ground covers will thrive for decades with very little care if the soil is properly prepared and maintained.

Though preparation of a ground cover site and the cost of plants and planting may be expensive, subsequent maintenance costs of the area are low, resulting in significant savings over the years. Therefore, they are a good choice for parking strips and similar sites. In two years, they can reach a height of 60 to 70 cm and at the same time, cover the ground thickly.

The plants in the following lists are eminently suitable for ground covers. Note that only rose cultivars not described in the encyclopedia section are listed. Other rose species and cultivars suitable as ground covers can be found in the encyclopedia section.

Broadleaf Shrubs as Ground Covers

Species	Height (cm)	Use	number of plants necessary for each m²
Arctostaphylos uva-ursi	20	only in acid, high humus soil	10–12
Berberis buxifolia 'Nana'	30	bushy, evergreen plant, suitable for containers	8–10
Calluna vulgaris	30	for light, acid soil, yearly pruning necessary	12–15
Ceratostigma plumbaginoides	25	prostrate, richly branched subshrub, builds a thick carpet, good for small areas, sunny or partly shady locations	8–10
Chaenomeles japonica	100	low, thick shrub with thorny branches and brick-red blossoms, for large areas and slopes	2–3
Cornus canadensis	20	for sandy or high humus soil; when well-grown provides a beautifully blooming carpet; North temperate zone only	15–20
Cotoneaster adpressus	25	compact shrub with prostrate branches, for sunny locations	2–3
Cotoneaster congestus	25	grows tight to the soil; evergreen leaves	3–4
Cotoneaster conspicuus 'Decorus'	100	elegant, fruits and blossoms abundantly	2–3
Cotoneaster dammeri	20	one of the most important low-growing ground cover used anywhere except very warm climates	8–10
Cotoneaster dammeri 'Coral Beauty'	50	selection from 'Skogholm' but with better fruits, does not lose as many leaves in winter	3–4

Broadleaf Shrubs as Ground Covers (cont.)

Species	Height (cm)	Use	number of plants necessary for each m²
Cotoneaster dammeri 'Eichholz	25	good, fast-growing ground cover for most locations, especially winter-hardy	4–6
Cotoneaster dammeri 'Juergl'	50	flat-growing, heavy bloomer and fruiter, gorgeous, winter-hardy	3–4
Cotoneaster dammeri 'Major'	20	grows stronger and is larger leafed than most *Cotoneaster* species and cultivars	8–10
Cotoneaster dammeri var. radicans	20	smaller-leafed than most *C. dammeri* types	8–10
Cotoneaster dammeri 'Skogholm'	100	popular, robust, chokes out weeds	2–3
Cotoneaster dammeri 'Streib's Findling'	10	very small leafed, slow-growing, ideal for small areas and graves	10–15
Cotoneaster microphyllus	100	thick branched, small-leafed evergreen, somewhat temperamental	3–4
Cotoneaster microphyllus 'Cochleatus'	50	prostrate, small, dark-green leaves	4–6
Cotoneaster praecox	50	similar to *C. adpressus*, grows somewhat faster	2–3
Cotoneaster salicifolius 'Parkteppich'	80	prostrate, evergreen shrub, covers quickly and thickly	3–4
Cotoneaster wateri 'Herbstfeuer'	50	heavily fruited and fast growing	3–4
Cytisus species		*Cytisus* species do not cover the ground well, not suited for large areas, all require sunny locations and light, nutrient-poor soil	
Cytisus × *beanii*	40	prostrate growth with upright flower clusters, deep-yellow blossoms	4–5
Cytisus decumbens	20	short, beautiful flowers growing along the length of the branches, for sunny locations and light soil	6–8
Cytisus × *kewensis*	30	short, creamy-white to sulphur-yellow blossoms	4–5
Cytisus procumbens	40	similar to *C. decumbens* but somewhat taller	4–5
Cytisus purpureus	60	low spreading, branches, dense	2–3
Diervilla lonicera	100	spreads by vigorous stolons, well suited for large areas, but coarse; deciduous	2–3
Empetrum nigrum	25	low-spreading, ascending branches, for light, sandy soil, good under trees, tolerates foot traffic; cool climates only	10–12
Erica carnea species	25	indispensable in heath gardens	12–15
Euonymus fortunei 'Emerald Gaiety'	80	white-bordered, large leaves, beautiful shrub for large areas in shade	3–4

Broadleaf Shrubs as Ground Covers (cont.)

Species	Height (cm)	Use	number of plants necessary for each m²
Euonymus fortunei 'Emerald'n Gold'	100	light-yellow bordered leaves, grows taller as it matures, somewhat like 'Variegatus'	5–6
Euonymus fortunei 'Minimus'	10	small-leafed cultivar, covers thickly, for large or small areas in shade	15–20
Euonymus fortunei var. radicans	30	prostrate or trailing shrub, covers well, tolerates very shady locations	6–8
Euonymus fortunei 'Variegatus'	30	better known as 'Gracilis' white to multi-colored leaves, for shady locations	6–8
Euonymus fortunei 'Vegetus'	100	wide, bushy, thick buds and large leaves, plant under larger trees and shrubs	2–3
Gaultheria procumbens	15	one of the prettiest of short ground covers for humus rich soil and partly shady locations	12–15
Gaultheria shallon	80	"Salal" as above	3–4
Genista sagittalis	15	prostrate shrub with upright flower shoots, for small areas in sunny, dry locations in nutrient-poor soil	10–15
Hedera helix	20	ivy; evergreen trailing plant, must be pruned to keep in bounds; several cultivars	6–8
Hydrangea petiolaris	40	trailing plant, covers ground thickly	3–4
Hypericum calycinum	30	short, evergreen shrub with stolons, occasionally tops freeze but always comes back, tolerates sunny and shady locations	6–8
Hypericum 'Hidcote'	80	evergreen ground cover for large areas in sunny locations	3–4
Hypericum kouytchense	80	deciduous, sometimes evergreen, similar to 'Hidcote', for large areas	3–4
Hypericum × moserianum	40	important partly-evergreen shrub for protected locations, yearly pruning required	4–6
Lavandula angustifolia	60	gray-leafed, erect-growing shrub for sunny locations, good in heath gardens, often used with roses	8–10
Ligustrum vulgare 'Lodense'	50	dense, mostly evergreen shrub, for large areas	2–3
Lithospermum purpureocaeruleum	30	trails with long, rooting sprouts, blossom clusters erect, thick, for sunny and partly shady locations, good under trees and shrubs but not too hardy	8–10
Lonicera japonica 'Halliana'	40	climbing plant with good ground covering qualities but over-vigorous and banned regionally in the United States	2–3

Broadleaf Shrubs as Ground Covers (cont.)

Species	Height (cm)	Use	number of plants necessary for each m²
Lonicera nitida 'Elegant'	80	fine-leafed more or less evergreen species, injured by winter temperatures in unsuitable sites	3–4
Lonicera pileata	40	extremely shade tolerant, especially useful for large areas	4–5
Lonicera xylosteum 'Clavey's Dwarf'	100–150	thickly branched, almost spherical growth for large areas	1–2
Mahonia aquifolium	100	important evergreen shrub, tolerates shade well, prune after blooming in April so it does not become leggy	3–4
Pachysandra terminalis	20	evergreen subshrub, best ground cover for shady locations in humus rich soil, "swallows up" fallen leaves under larger trees	12–15
Pachysandra 'Green Carpet'	10	slow-growing, suitable under small trees and shrubs, sunburns easily	15–20
Paxistima canbyi	25	fine-leafed evergreen dwarf shrub, weak stolons, for small areas in shade	10–12
Potentilla fruticosa cultivars	50–100	flat-growing, for sunny locations, gray-leafed 'Primrose Beauty' and var. *mandshurica* tolerate very dry locations	3–4
Prunus laurocerasus cultivars	100	evergreen shrub, grows well in light shade	1
Prunus pumila var. *depressa*	20	prostrate form of Sand Cherry, not a thick cover	4–5
Pyracantha cultivars	150–200	for large areas and sunny to partly shady locations; 'Soleil d'Or' cultivar especially good for parking strips	1
Rosa arvensis	60	shoots long and numerous, lay over each other, small white blossoms in June/July, for larger areas	2–3
Rosa nitida	60	elegant wild rose with strong stolons, blossoms single, pure pink, radiant brown-red fall colors, suited for small areas	4–6
Rosa × *paulii* (=*Rosa rugosa* 'Repens' × *Rosa* 'Alba')	40–60	trails, 5 to 6 m long shoots, thick, rooting at tips; pure white blossoms, short blooming period; one of the best available ground covers, needs only moderate amount of care; only for very large plantings	2–3
Rosa rugosa	80–100	robust wild rose, erect growing, forms many stolons, simple pink blossoms, in fall, many large hips	3–4
Rosa rugosa 'Alba'	100	white-blooming, wide, bushy growth, like *R. rugosa*, very good for larger areas	3–4

Broadleaf Shrubs as Ground Covers (cont.)

Species	Height (cm)	Use	number of plants necessary for each m²
Rosa rugosa 'Dagmar Hastrup'	60	cushion-like to flat, spherical growth, healthy, leaves, simple pink blossoms with strong fragrance, ever blooming, fruit sets better than R. rugosa, exceedingly salt tolerant, permits no weed growth; best in cool, mild climates	4–5
Rosa rugosa 'Max Graf'	30	especially flat growth, 2.5 m long shoots, many rose blossoms, glossy-green leaves, beautiful fall colors	3–4
Rosa rugosa 'Moje Hammarberg'	100–200	grows more quickly than 'Dagmar Hastrup' but not as compact, uneven height, dark violet blossoms, pleasingly fragrant	3–4
Rosa rugosa 'White Hedge'	110–130	erect and bushy, light green, healthy leaves large pure white moderately fragrant blossoms, densely covered with orange colored hips	3–4
Rosa × rugotida (Rosa rugosa × Rosa nitida)	80–120	erect, bushy, fine-branched, ground thickly covered by numerous stolons, leaves a bit larger than Rosa nitida, small, simple, light pink blossoms	3–4
Rosa rugosa 'Dart's Defender'	60–80	lower, bushier, larger violet-rose blossoms than R. × rugotida, rust-red fall colors, forms fruits moderately	4–5
Rubus calycinoides	10	trailing evergreen with rooting branches, deep green heart-shaped leaves, not completely frost hardy	6–8

With the exception of Salix repens and S. purpurea, dwarf willows are not suited for large areas but require exposed sites and full sun.

Species	Height (cm)	Use	number of plants necessary for each m²
Salix × ambigua	50	erect, with crowded, slender twigs, good ground cover	5–6
Salix arbuscula	50	also thick and erect, fine twigs, good ground cover	5–6
Salix caprea 'Pendula'	30	numerous, long shoots, flat growing, good coverer	2–3
Salix × grahamii	20	creeping habit, twigs form a dense cover	5–6
Salix purpurea 'Gracilis'	80	thick and bushy, numerous erect shoots, for large areas in sunny, dry locations	2–3
Salix repens ssp. argentea	100	flat growing, drought resistant, used on slopes and sand dunes	2–3
Salix repens ssp. rosmarinifolia (=Salix rosmarinifolia)	80	horizontal branches and erect catkins, drought resistant	2–3

Broadleaf Shrubs as Ground Covers (cont.)

Species	Height (cm)	Use	number of plants necessary for each m²
Salix retusa	20	strongly branched, mat-forming, completely covers soil	5–6
Salix waldsteiniana	30	flat laying, countless twigs, good cover	5–6
Skimmia species and cultivars	50–100	compact, evergreen plants for shady locations in humus rich soil	5–6
Spiraea albiflora	50	stiffly erect, dense growth	5–6
Spirea × *bu malda* cultivars	80	suited to low hedges on level ground	3–4
Spirea decumbens	20	almost forgotten small species, expands through stolons, completely covers soil	8–10
Spirea japonica 'Little Princess'	80	dense, compact growth	5–6
Stephanandra incisa 'Crispa'	50	arching, pendulous branches, tolerates shady locations	3–4
Symphoricarpos × *chenaultii* 'Hancock'	80	strongly branched, branches long and flat, tolerates shade; only suitable for large, rough plantings	2–3
Teucrium chamaedrys	25	broad, bushy, evergreen subshrub for small areas in sunny locations; elegant	10–15
Vaccinium vitis-idaea	20	evergreen ericaceous shrub, beautiful and satisfactory for light, acidy soil; many forms	12–15
Vinca minor	20	European forest plant, trailing stems which root down; tolerates very shady locations; substitute *V. major* in warm climates	10–12
Xanthorhiza simplicissima	80	quickly spreads by runners in light soil, good under trees	3–4

Coniferous Shrubs as a Ground Cover

Conifers as Ground Covers

Most prostrate and procumbent conifers are not ground covers in the truest sense. They cannot be used in the same manner as broadleaf trees and shrubs, which cover the ground quickly and can as a rule tolerate both root competition and shade under larger trees and shrubs. Almost all conifers require sunny, open sites with a minimum of competition. Only the *Taxus* species and cultivars can thrive in shady locations.

Microbiota decussata and the trailing junipers (*Juniperus communis* ssp. *alpina, J. conferta, J. horizontalis, J. procumbens*) only occasionally completely cover large areas in their natural habitat. They more often grow in loose groups on rocks and screes. Swiss Mountain Pine, *Pinus mugo,* and the East Asian, *Pinus pumila,* are the only gregarious species and cover larger areas with procumbent-ascending branches.

Therefore, only the above-mentioned pines, their varieties and cultivars, can be unconditionally recommended as somewhat "bushy" ground covers for large areas. However, *Juniperus conferta, J. horizontalis* and their cultivars, are widely used in the U.S. on sloping areas and in harsh climates where they will adapt and grow suitably in large-scale plantings. All other species and cultivars are better planted only in smaller areas; for example, small sloping areas and in rock and heath gardens. If used correctly, outstanding effects will result.

Conifers as Ground Covers

Species	Height (m)	Comments
Juniperus chinensis 'Rockery Gem'	0.8–1	short, flat growth, strongly branched, robust ground cover, blue-green needles
Juniperus chinensis var. *sargentii*	0.3–0.5	2–3 m wide cushion, creeping or flat-laying branches, suitable for poor soil
Juniperus communis ssp. *alpina*	0.5	flat-laying branches, with slightly ascending side-branchlets; to 2 m wide
Juniperus chinensis 'Hornibrookii'	0.2–0.3	mat-forming, densely branched, short, thick branchlets, silver-colored needles
Juniperus chinensis 'Repanda'	0.3–0.4	up to 1.5 m wide trailing form, branches grow uniformly slender branchlets
Juniperus conferta	0.4	long, low-laying branches, erect branchlets, makes thick cover
Juniperus horizontalis cultivars	0.2–0.3	almost all cultivars of *J. horizontalis* develop into a dense mat, generally 1.5–3 m wide, many forms have blue needles
Juniperus procumbens	0.6	low-laying, stiff branches, ends erect
Juniperus chinensis 'Nana'	0.3	short and dense, lower part of branches dense, cushion forming, well furnished with short, erect branchlets
Juniperus squamata 'Blue Carpet'	0.3	flat, widespread growth, blue-white needles, for partly shady locations

Conifers as Ground Covers

Species	Height (m)	Comments
Microbiota decussata	0.2	flat-laying branches, 2–3 m wide, creeping, carpet-forming; very branchy and densely covered with slender branchlets, for large areas
Pinus mugo ssp. *pumilio*	1–3	growth habit of horizontal branches in close whorls, heavily needled; shortest of its forms, takes years to reach mature height, can be kept shorter through pruning
Pinus pumila 'Dwarf Blue'	1–2	prostrate growth, used like other pines, decorative, blue needles
Taxus baccata 'Nissen's Corona'	1	strong, uniform growth; 1 m high, 5 m wide
Taxus baccata 'Nissen's Regent'	1	irregular growth; 1 m high, 5 m or more wide
Taxus baccata 'Repandens'	0.5	low-growing, 2 to 5 m wide, best selection if a low, uniform planting is needed

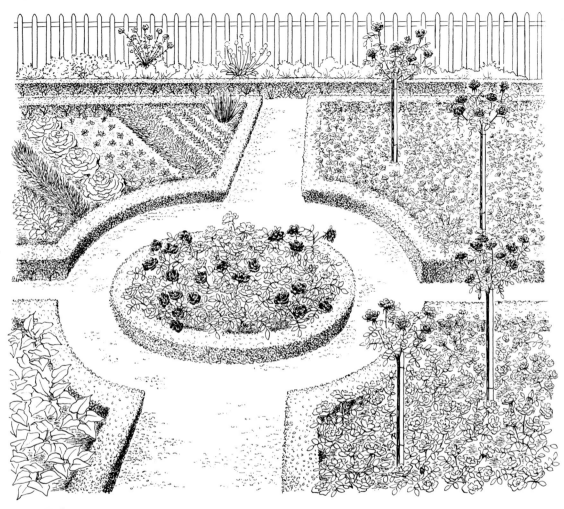

Low Hedges

Dwarf Shrubs as Low Hedges

Low hedges are not only essential in classic formal gardens where they define and enclose walks and beds, but are useful and sometimes even necessary in modern private gardens.

The following is a list of broadleaf and coniferous species which are well suited for sheared or unsheared hedges. Some species grow to a height of only 10 to 20 cm and so make ideal bed borders. Unsheared hedges of other species grow 1 m or more. Not all of the species listed here are suited for both pruned or free-growing hedges.

Dwarf Shrubs for Low Hedges

Species	Suitable for		
	low, sheared bed-borders	somewhat taller, sheared hedges	free-growing hedges
Broadleaf Shrubs			
Berberis buxifolia 'Nana'	✕		✕
B. gagnepainii 'Klugowski'		✕	✕
B. hookeri		✕	✕
B. thunbergii 'Atropurpurea Nana'	✕		
Buxus sempervirens 'Suffruticosa'	✕	✕	✕
Deutzia gracilis			✕
Forsythia ovata 'Tetragold'			✕
F. viridissima 'Bronxensis'			✕
Fuchsia magellanica cultivars			✕
Hypericum forrestii			✕
H. 'Hidecote'			✕
H. kouytchense			✕
Ilex crenata cultivars			✕
Lavandula angustifolia	✕		✕
Ligustrum vulgare 'Lodense'		✕	
Lonicera nitida		✕	✕
L. pileata		✕	✕
Mahonia aquifolium			✕
Potentilla fruticosa cultivars			✕
Prunus laurocersus 'Otto Luyken'		✕	✕
Ribes alpinum 'Pumilium'		✕	✕
Salix purpurea 'Gracilis'			✕
Spiraea albiflora			✕
S. ✕ *bumalda* cultivars			✕
S. japonica cultivars			✕
Teucrium chamaedrys	✕		
Coniferous Shrubs			
Picea abies 'Emsland'			✕
P. glauca 'Conica'			✕
P. omorika 'Nana'			✕
Pinus ✕ *hakkodensis*			✕
P. mugo var. *mugo*			✕
P. mugo var. *pumilio*			✕
P. pumila 'Glauca'			✕
P. sylvestris 'Hibernica' and other cultivars			✕

Planting, Cultivation and Winter Protection

Most nursery-grown dwarf trees and shrubs are sold in pots or containers. Container-grown plants offer great advantages to the gardener. They can be planted almost any time of year without the loss of parts of the root system (or possibly the plant itself) which occurs with field-grown plants which have to be dug.

We need not belabor the point that basic soil preparations must be undertaken before planting slow-growing dwarf trees and shrubs. However, it should be emphasized that slow-growing dwarf cultivars, grown beyond the limit of their natural range of distribution, make special demands on the physical and chemical qualitites of the soil. In the encyclopedia portion of this book, any special requirements of a particular species are noted. Species which do not demand special treatment will grow in any properly prepared garden soil (well drained soil which has been carefully spaded and worked up with fertilizers and enriched with organic materials, and above all, from which all weeds have been removed).

In choosing planting sites, the amount of sunlight received must be considered. Most dwarf plants grow best in sunny locations, but some thrive in shady spots, especially in warm, continental (inland) climates.

When planting, keep the following points in mind:
— Do not set plants any deeper than they grew in their containers or original soil.
— Cut the twine around the trunk of plants purchased balled and burlapped, but do not completely remove twine or burlap unless made of plastic materials. In short, neither strangle the trunk nor damage the roots by ignoring the method of packing. With the plant in its hole, fold down burlap so none projects above ground-level.
— Carefully loosen matted root balls of potted or container-grown plants.
— Do not apply mineral fertilizers directly to plant roots, except when using encapsulated, slow-release fertilizers, which should be placed below the root ball.
— After planting, the fill soil around the root ball should be pressed down firmly, but take care not to injure roots or compact the soil.
— Water newly set plants to soak the soil deeply—not with the full force of a hose nozzle, but rather with a slow-running stream from a watering can or hose, or water the bed with a sprinkler.
— Water plants regularly in dry weather; not too frequently however, because the plants can easily be drowned.
— Cover soil around plants with an organic mulch (peat, bark or compost). It keeps the soil damp, which is better than too frequent waterings.

Certain plant groups (heather relatives and rhododendrons) have special fertilizing requirements. This is true also of plants in various sorts of planters as well as roof gardens (see appropriate sections for specific information).

result of mold or mildew, so a better aerated cover of small evergreen branches or even very loose straw will serve better.

Winter protection is recommended for the species listed below (especially in harsh climates).

Dwarf trees and shrubs should be routinely fertilized, just as full-sized woody garden ornamentals are. The rule of thumb, with good soil, is to administer 100 g/m² (3.5 oz./sq. yd.) of a chloride-free fertilizer containing trace elements, in 2 to 3 applications from early spring to early summer. There are several organic base, complete fertilizers such as bone or bloodmeal blends, which are especially suitable for dwarf trees and shrubs. Maintain an organic mulch the year around. Nothing works as well in terms of maintaining soil texture as regularly adding to the humus level. Shredded bark compost or fertilized peat are especially well suited as mulch, as recommended in the section, "Fertilizing Alpine Plants."

Winter protection is important when growing some species or cultivars of dwarf woody plants. The climatic conditions of a display garden may be quite different from those of their native habitat. If they are to survive winters which are harsher than those of their natural habitat, some form of winter protection is necessary. Deep leaf mulching (dry, uncomposted leaves) is very effective. The leaves insulate and so reduce temperature fluctuations in the topsoil; limit frost penetration; and help keep the rooting area drier in very wet regions. Place not-too-large, bushy branches of needle evergreens (pine boughs carrying long needles are especially suitable) on top of the leaves so the leaf cover will not be blown away. Evergreen branches also protect evergreen plants from parching winds and intense, winter sunlight. In no case should the leaf dressing completely cover the foliage of evergreen plants, nor should the leaves be spread too deeply about the sides of evergreen plants or the leaves will yellow and abscise early. In wet climates, deep leaf coverings may harm plants as the

Broadleaf Shrubs
Aethionema grandiflorum
Amorpha canescens
Anthyllis hermanniae
Berberis buxifolia 'Nana'
B. × *stenophylla* cultivars
Caryopteris species and hybrids
Ceanothus species and hybrids
Cotoneaster conspicuus 'Decorus'
C. horizontalis 'Saxatilis'
C. microphyllus f. *thymifolius*
Daboecia cantabrica
Daphne laureola
D. pontica
Elsholtzia stauntonii
Erica cinerea
E. × *darleyensis*
E. vagans
E. × *williamsii*
Fuchsia magellanica cultivars
× *Gaulnettya* 'Wisley Pearl'
Genista species
Hebe species
Hypericum species
Ilex crenata forms
Lavandula angustifolia
Mahonia repens
Muehlenbeckia axillaris
Ononis fruticosa
Pernettya mucronata
Perovskia species
Rhododendron (see references as to frost-hardiness in encyclopedia section)
Rubus calycinoides
R. irenaeus
Santolina species and hybrids
Sarcococca humilis
Skimmia species and hybrids
Ulex europaeus
Conifers
Cedrus deodara cultivars
Chamaecyparis, yellow-leafed cultivars
Cryptomeria japonica cultivars
Podocarpus nivalis
Thuja orientalis cultivars

Pruning

Slow-growing dwarf plants should, in most cases, be pruned as little as possible. Most species and cultivars do not need to be pruned at all. Dense and compact habit is often destroyed by pruning.

Some summer-blooming shrubs are an exception to this rule and must be pruned severely. They include species and cultivars of *Caryopteris, Ceonothus Americanus* and *C. ovatus* (only), *Lagerstroemia, Rosa, Spirea* (not the spring-blooming nor tall-growing sorts) and *Stauntonia,* among others. In addition, shrubs grown for their colorful winter twigs, are renewed by pruning from the ground or low "stools", annually. Pruning them just above the soil in spring will stimulate the development of vigorous shoots and blossoms. In addition, with certain plants in the group, canes should be pruned in the fall to minimize freezing damage during the winter. Severe pruning is also recommended for this group after being planted. All of their canes should be pruned back from one-third to one-half of their length. This group is the exception as other dwarf trees and shrubs should be pruned minimally after planting.

Only a few dwarf trees and shrubs other than the deciduous, summer flowering shrubs need to be pruned regularly. *Deutzia gracilis* and dwarf *Forsythia* species fall into this limited category. In pruning these species, the oldest branches, recognized by dense branching on the upper part of the cane and its mature bark, should be pruned back to the crown. Only one-third to one-half of the older branches should be removed in any one year. If more than one-third to one-half of the canes are removed in a single year, the shrub will deteriorate or will develop too many new shoots.

Regular pruning is also necessary for the callunas and other ericaceous species and cultivars. Detailed information can be found in the section entitled "Heath Gardens."

All dwarf plants damaged by frost, snow or storm breakage or other similar injury must be pruned back to sound wood. Most broadleaf trees and shrubs tolerate being pruned back into older wood rather well. Of the conifers, only *Taxus* commonly sprouts again after being pruned back into older wood.

Occasionally, young shoots at the end of the branches of *Pinus mugo* cultivars and other pines are cut back. This is done in the spring to limit the height and spread of the plant. This form of control is discussed in more detail in the encyclopedia portion of this book.

Flat-growing or decumbent conifers propagated from lateral branch grafts (especially cultivars of *Abies procera* and *Picea pungens*) may suddenly develop an erect, leading shoot. It must be removed immediately if the dwarf habit of the plant is to be maintained.

Occasionally, regressive mutations occur in dwarf conifers. A standard shoot suddenly develops in the crown. It is very similar in habit and foliage to the original species, and so grows much faster than the dwarf conifer itself. Such shoots should

Summer-blooming shrub species from the first group, such as *Perovskia* or *Spiraea bumalda* hybrids, are cut back every spring.

Perovskia atriplicifolia

Spiraea bumalda hybrids

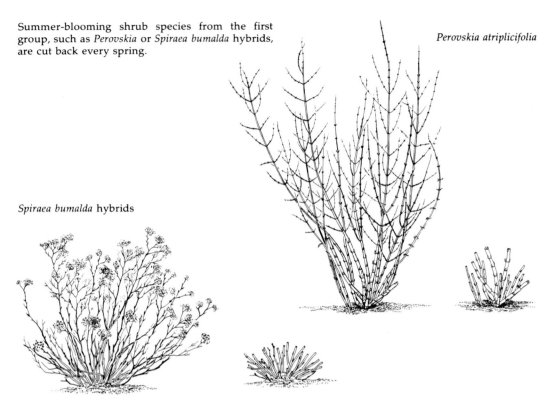

Deutzia gracilis and other shrub species from the second group should be thinned on a regular basis by complete removal of a few of the oldest canes after flowers have faded.

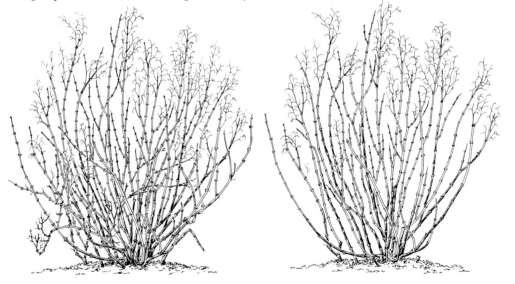

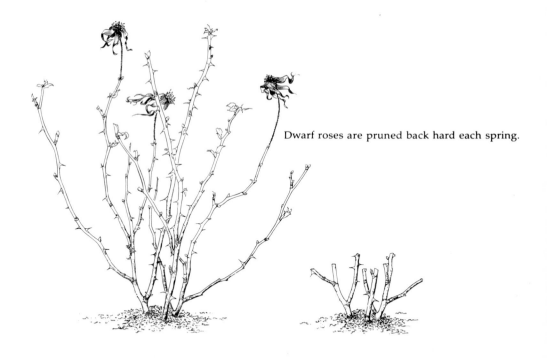

Dwarf roses are pruned back hard each spring.

also be removed as soon as noticed. In fact it should be noted that retrogression to normal form and growth habit is not an uncommon phenomenon with a few sorts of dwarf woody ornamentals; with other sorts it almost never occurs. Excepting some dwarf roses and the dwarf conifers, which are grown as grafts on rootstocks of normal-sized, compatible species, many dwarf woody plants grow on their own roots, having been propagated by seeds or cuttings.

The following is a list of species which need regular pruning. There are two different groups:

1. Summer-flowering shrubs which should be pruned back hard early each spring. Prune back the branches to just above the soil level.
2. Flowering and ornamental shrubs which should be thinned annually or semi-annually, cutting out a few of the oldest canes to the ground-line after flowering; they should also be pruned when young and only moderately branched.

The last column in the following charts describes recommended pruning practices.

Pruning Practices

Species	Group 1	Group 2	Remarks
Amorpha canescens	×		
Calluna vulgaris			Prune yearly to the previous year's branches
Caryopteris species	×		
Ceanothus species	×		
Daboecia cantabrica			Inflorescences and frost damaged shoots should be pruned back to undamaged wood.
Deutzia gracilis		×	
Elshotzia stauntonii	×		
Erica carnea, long shoot cultivars			Similar to *Calluna vulgaris.*
Erica vagans			Similar to *Calluna vulgaris.*
Forsythia species		×	
Fuchsia magellanica	×		
Genista tinctoria			Prune the previous year's growth in spring.
Hypericum calycinum	×		
Hypericum, other species			Prune only when plants have been damaged by frost; prune them back to the previous year's growth.
Lavandula angustifolia	×		
Lonicera albertii		×	
Mahonia species			If shoots loose their leaves, prune back into older wood.
Ononis fruticosa	×		
Perovskia species	×		
Potentilla fruticosa		×	Instead of thinning, prune yearly.
Prunus prostata		×	
Rhododendron			Most species and cultivars tolerate being pruned back into older wood.
Rosa nitida		×	
R. pimpinellifolia		×	
R. dwarf species			Prune yearly to just above the graft.
R. ground covers			No pruning necessary.
Santolina species			Prune the dry inflorescence, severe pruning needed if plant is damaged by frost.
Spiraea albiflora	×		
S. × *bumalda* cultivars	×		
S. bullata		×	
S. decumbens	×		
S. japonica	×		
Syringa meyeri		×	
Teucrium chamaedrys	×		

Some Fungicides, Insecticides, and Miticides Recommended for the Protection of Dwarf Woody Plants[1]

Chemical Name	Trade (Brand) Name	Comment
Aramite	Aramite	
Azinphos, methyl; guthion	Guthion	
Benomyl	Benlate	recently introduced fungicide; use in combinations.
Captan	Captan	
Chlorobenside	Mitox	
Diazinon	Spectracide	
Demeton	Systox	systemic insecticide
Dicofol	Kelthane	
Dimethoate	Cgon, Rogar	
Dimethylphosphonate	Dylox	
Dinocap	Karathane	
Endosulfan	Thiodan	
Ferbam	Fermate	
Folpet	Phaltan	
Malathion	Malathion	
Maneb	Manzate, Maneb, Dithane M-22	
metaldehyde	Slug-it, Snarol, Bugeta	for slugs and snails
Nicotine	Black Leaf 40	
Oxydemeton, methyl	Metasystox-R	systemic insecticide
PCWB	Terrachlor	
Parathion	Thiophos	systemic insecticide, extremely dangerous!
Tetradifon	Tedion	
Zineb	Dithane Z-78, Zineb, Parzate	

[1]Some of these chemicals may be found in garden shops; others are restricted for sale to professional applicators only. The agricultural departments of most governments make recommendations on disease and pest controls most suitable for local application and usually revised annually. Gardeners should utilize this information.

Insects and Diseases

The causes of insect damage disease to dwarf woody plants diagnostic symptoms, and the means of controlling them are presented in the following charts.

The use of control chemicals to combat diseases and insects should be undertaken only when it is evident that a disease is threatening, or when insects cannot be dealt with in any other way. Preventive measures should be employed routinely to minimize the likelihood of pest and disease outbreaks. Routine prevention measures include the early removal of spent flower heads, diseased leaves, removal of breeding sites (weeds, litter, etc.) for insects and disease-carrying organisms and in some cases routine spraying. Plant diseases, being internal, must be controlled by preventative spraying with appropriate fungicides or bacteriacides. Insect and arachnid infestations are external, so spraying can wait until a problem occurs.

With optimal cultural conditions (light, soil, moisture and free air movement), most garden trees and shrubs contract so few diseases that chemical measures are not necessary.

Roses must be watched carefully because they are regularly infected by pathogenic fungi. Red-spider, blue spruce gall aphids and woolly aphids are particular problems on conifers; weevils on numerous deciduous trees and shrubs, or fireblight on *Cotoneaster* species and other relatives of the rose.

Store chemical agents at cool room temperature, in darkness, and where they are accessible only to knowledgeable persons. Mix all insecticides, fungicides, and other toxic substances strictly according to the label instructions. If control chemicals are not measured and mixed in accordance with label instructions, plants could be harmed by the mixture. So, indeed, could the gardener.

If insecticides are used, they should be of a type which will not harm bees (see reference on package). Sevin (carbaryl) is a notorious poison for honeybees, while Spectracide (diazinon) and malathion are much less so. All are comparatively "safe" for the gardener.

In using the following table, note that the standard common name has been used for all pesticidal chemicals, rather than chemical or trade names.

Some Insects and Diseases of Deciduous Trees and Shrubs

Symptoms	Control
Betula	
Birch Leafrust (*Melampsoridium betulinum*) In summer, translucent spots from on the top of the leaves, orange-yellow pustules on the underside, the leaves discolor or turn yellow and fall off earlier than usual.	Apply a preventive (pre-infection) spray of a carbamate or thiocarbamate fungicide such as Zineb, Fermate, or Manzate
European birch Aphid (*Euceraphis betulae and other aphids*) Countless greenish-yellow aphids appear on the undersides of leaves and on the ends of new shoots. Honeydew usually appears as a shiny, sticky substance on lower leaves.	Apply an insecticide such as Malathion or Spectracide. A systemic insecticide such as Systox or Metasystox-R controls severe aphid infestations.
Buxus	
Box Leaf-miners (*Monarthropalpus buxi*) Tops of leaves pinpointed with yellow spots, blisters on the undersides are distended, inside whitish, or in later stages, yellow larva (⅛-inch long) are found. Cocoons form in the leaves in the spring. Adults emerge in May.	Spray Box repeatedly when weigelas bloom with Spectracide or Malathion to reduce egg-laying female midges. From mid-May to the end of June repeated treatments with Thiophes or other systemic insecticide (commercial applicator, only). Prune out diseased branches.
Buxus Canker, Twig Blight, Dieback. Infected branches begin spring growth late and foliage is off-color, usually pale or olive-hued. Leaves often lie closely adpressed to the twigs rather than spreading naturally. Later in the season leaves turn straw-colored, often with rosy or dark pustules. These diseases often follow winter injury.	In early spring prune to healthy wood (cankers on older wood may be whittled way and the wounds dressed with commercial tree paint *after* application of Bordeaux spray or lime-sulfur) clear away all fallen leaves. Spray Bordeaux mixture 3-3-50 or lime-sulfur 1-50, the first to dormant plants in early spring, the second when spring growth is half completed, third when spring growth is mature, fourth when fall growth is mature. Also, increase plant vigor with generous applications of cattle manure, and fertilizers and limestone as indicated by soil test.
Boxwood Psyllid (*Psylla buxi*) The terminal leaves cup upwards and new growth stunted. Leaves are sticky with honey dew secretions, later these are sooty-colored.	Repeated spraying with a systemic insecticide such as Metasystox-R or Spectracide from the initiation of growth in spring until the end of June, or spray weekly with Malathion from early spring through late summer.

Some Insects and Diseases of Deciduous Trees and Shrubs (cont.)

Symptoms	Control
Common Scale Insects Numerous oval, round, or sea mussel-shaped, gray, brown, or cream-colored scales, attached to twigs and leaves. Larva hatch from May to September and spread.	Spray at 5 to 10 day intervals with Spectracide or Malathion from May to September to control young insects, or spray at three to four week intervals with a systemic insecticide.
Calluna **Heather Beetles** (*Lochmaea suturalis*) Beginning in March, hibernating beetles emerge and feed off leaves and new shoots. From May to June the larva eat the leaves. Beetles appear again from mid- to late September.	Spray with Thiophes or other organic-phosphate insecticide.
Wilt Disease or Root Rot (*Phytophthora cinnamomi*) (see *Erica*)	
Japanese Beetle (*Popillia japonica*) Eggs in the soil hatch at various times through the year, producing white grubs that feed with ruinous effect on grass roots; after several molts grubs pupate, then adults emerge to feed on hundreds of species of plants, often clustered in large groups of beautiful, almost ½ inch long, metallic green beetle which are very active, feeding only in the daytime.	Deter increase of Japanese Beetles with milky spore disease applied to beds and leaves according to package instructions. Destroy at least some feeding adults by spraying at four week intervals with a systemic insecticide, or spray at five day intervals with Malathion, Guthion, Spectracide, or similar insecticide.
Clematis **Mildew** (*Erysiphe aquilegiae* or *E. polygoni*) White coating on leaves, sprouts and blossoms.	Repeated spraying with Karathane or Phaltan or summer-strength lime-sulfur.
Cotoneaster **Spider-mites** (*Brevipalpus obovatus*) Yellowish-white mottling on the underside of leaves caused by 0.3 mm long, bright-red mites.	Use a miticide such as Mitox, Kelthane or Tedion. Several garden insecticides reduce or control spider-mites, as Guthion, Malathion, Spectracide and dinitro compounds.
Scale Insects (*Eulecanium corni, Lepidosaphes ulmi*) Small, round or comma-shaped white "shells" adhering to branches.	When the young insects migrate (May to September) spray with control chemicals as listed under *Buxus*.
Woolly Apple Aphid (*Eriosoma lanigerum*) Overwinter in buds sometimes. White wax secretions, especially on bark injuries, the aphids go underneath the bark and when crushed exude blood-red juice.	Spray with Guthion, Malathion, or Spectracide every ten days to two weeks beginning when buds swell in spring until late summer (or when the infestation disappeared).

Some Insects and Diseases of Deciduous Trees and Shrubs (cont.)

Symptoms	Control
Fire blight (*Erwinia amylovora*) The leaves on new shoot-tips, then the shoot itself, wilt, turn brown or black and dry out. Leaves remain hanging on the ends of the dead shoots. Sufficiently serious in parts of the U.S. to limit successful cultivation of several cultivars (and other apple family species).	Consult a professional horticulturist to confirm diagnosis. If confirmed, dig out plant, including roots, and burn.
Cytisus **Mites** (*Tetranychus* species) Gray-green discoloration or mottling on leaves and shoots.	Spray with a miticide such as aramite or Kelthane at ten day intervals or with a mite-killing insecticide such as Guthion, Malathion, or Spectracide.
Thrips (*Thysinoptera* species) Silver-gray luster and tiny, black spots (droppings) on leaves.	Spray infested plants at five to ten day intervals with Malathion, Cygon, Diazinon or Metasystox-R. As control is very difficult, continue spraying with a systemic at four week intervals for several months.
Rust (*Uromyces laburni*) At first leaves have yellow spots, later they are completely yellow and are bordered with spores.	Spray with Ferbam, then prune out infected areas, and spray again, then repeat once or twice. Infection usually indicates a source of reinfection (second host, another species) in the neighborhood, which indicates a prophylactic spray application of Ferbam each spring.
Leaf Spot; Stem Spot (*Pleiochaeta setosa, Ceratophorium setosum*) Small, irregular dark brown spots appear first on leaves, later on petiole and branches, which increase in size.	Can kill out a planting as quickly as two weeks; prune out visibly infected branches, then spray with Bordeaux mixture at weekly intervals, or with a dithiocarbamate fungicide such as Fermate. The expense of Phaltan is justified for valuable plantings.
Daphne **Cucumber Mosaic Virus I** (*Marmor*) Chlorotic, irregular, or partial ring-shaped spots on leaves. Leaves wilt, turn yellow and fall earlier than usual.	Destroy diseased plants.
Cucumus and *M. medicaginis* **Daphne Leaf-spot** (*Marssonina daphnes*) 1 mm callus-like spots on leaves and petioles, in wet weather, white substance oozes out of them.	Repeated spraying with copper-based or dithiocarbamate fungicides. Pick and burn infected leaves.

Some Insects and Diseases of Deciduous Trees and Shrubs (cont.)

Symptoms	Control
Erica Mildew (*Oidium ericinum* and *Erysiphe polygoni*) Leaves and stems covered with mildew (white or gray felt-like mats).	Repeated spraying at 8-day intervals with wettable sulfur, Karathane, or Phaltan.
Gray Mold (*Botrytis cinerea*) Leaves and young shoots turn brown and die, later they are covered with gray-brown mold.	Control as above.
Heather Mildew (*Pucciniastrum ericae*) Leaves become chlorotic and then orange-yellow, yellowish powdery pustules appear on old lesions.	Spray with Zineb, Ferbam or Phaltan when the first signs of infection appear.
Heath Wilt (*Phytophthora cinnamomi*) Leaves on shoots tips grayish, tips of shoots wilt and droop, later they turn brown; ultimately, the entire plant dies as a result of the basal damage.	Remove plants and destroy them. Soil should be cleared of all plants, deeply loosened, and thoroughly fumigate with a product such as methyl-bromide or formaldehyde. (Plants are infected through organisms in the soil). Get details from your County Extension Agent.
Euonymus Mildew (*Oidium euonymi-japonici* and *Microsphaerea euonymi*) Thick, white mats of mold on both sides of the leaves.	As quickly as powdery mildew appears, spray with wettable sulphur (only with air temperature below 85°F.) or with Karathane; repeat twice at seven to ten day intervals.
Hedera Bacterial Leaf-spot and Stem Canker (*Xanthomonas hederae*) Small, well defined, glassy, translucent spots which quickly turn brown or black on leaves and stems. They spread quickly and run together.	Destroy infected parts. Spray frequently with a copper-based fungicide. High ground level humidity greatly contributes to this disease; avoid spraying ivy foliage, rather water from below with drip irrigation.
Fungus Leaf Spot (*Phyllosticta hedericola* and several other fungi) Round, brown, later gray spots on leaves with concentric rings and red marginal zones, leaf tissue often falls out, leaves eventually fall off. Stems sometimes are affected.	Preventive spraying with a copper-based fungicide every two to three weeks during the growing season.
Ivy Mite (*Tarsonemidae*) Leaf buds damaged, leaves remain small, do not develop and dry out; infected shoots are leafless and short.	Spray at seven to ten day intervals with a miticide such as Kelthane or with Malathion.
Two spotted Mites, Red-spiders (*Tetranychus urticae* and other species) Light mottling on leaves, later gray-brown discoloration, leaves dry out and fall off; fine, loose webs on dry leaves.	As with ivy mites.

Some Insects and Diseases of Deciduous Trees and Shrubs (cont.)

Symptoms	Control
Ivy Aphid (*Aphis hederae*) Crowded, scarcely moving aphids on crinkled leaves and shoot tips.	Spray when pests first appear with Guthion, Malathion, or Diazinon. Repeat once or twice at weekly intervals.
Ilex **Holly Leaf miner** (*Phytomyza ilicis* and *P. ilicicola*) Small, meandering mined tunnels in the leaves which appear as yellowish lines.	Spray repeatedly with Guthion or Malathion or Diazinon beginning with early expansion of new leaves in spring; spray weekly for one month, skip four weeks, then repeat four more applications.
Mahonia **Mildew** (*Microsphaera berberidis*) Whitish covering on leaves.	Spray with a neutral copper fungicide or with Manzate or Ferbam, covering both sides of the leaves and the canes.
Berberis Rust (*Puccinia graminis* and *Cumminsiella mirabilissima*) Tops of leaves have reddish-yellow spots, undersides have brown pustules with spores.	Prune in fall, spray with Ferbam in spring.
Potentilla **Mildew** (*Spaerotheca macularis* and *Coccomyces* species) White mildew covering on leaves and young shoots.	Spray with Cupricide or Karathane or Phaltan at onset of disease.
Prunus laurocerasus **Shot-hole Disease** (*Stigmina carpophila*) Small, round spots on leaves, tissue drops out later.	At onset, spray with Ferbam, Manzate or Captan preparations.
Burnt Spot Disease (*Gleosporium phacidiellum*) Red-brown, sharply defined necrosis on leaves, later they fade to gray-brown and have dark, concentric lines similar to small, black dots.	Spray with Ferbam or Phaltan.
Black Vine Weevil (*Otiorhynchus sulcatus* and *O. ovatus*) Leaf margins eaten in bow-shaped arcs, the bark of the root neck is gnawed near the soil line, the roots themselves are either gnawed or severed. These weevils attack numerous other trees and shrubs.	Slug and snail bait containing metaldehyde sometimes is effective for larval forms; spray adult beetles with Spectracide or Guthion.

Some Insects and Diseases of Deciduous Trees and Shrubs (cont.)

Symptoms	Control
Rhododendron Strawberry Weevil or Black Vine Weevil (see above)	
Leaf-spot (*Cercospora handeli, Phyllosticta maxima, Gleosporium rhododendri, Colletotrichum* species, *Pestalotia macotricha* and *Pestalotia rhododendri*) Mostly brown, irregularly shaped spots on leaves which lead to foliage loss.	From May to October at ten to fourteen day intervals spray with Ferbam; add a sticker-spreader. Avoid heavy applications on young shoots. Many leaf-infecting fungi of azalea and rhododendron enter through injured (sunscalded or winter-burned) leaves or attack foliage of plants weakened by poor cultural practices. Take steps to keep plants vigorous.
Azalea Leaf Gall (*Exobasidium rhododendri* and *E. vaccinii*) Leaves, especially on the ends of shoots are deformed, bladder-like; the tissue is condensed and fleshy, reddish colored and later has waxy whitish bloom.	Hand clip diseased leaves and shoots and destroy them, prevent by spraying captan or Zineb fungicide. As new growth emerges in spring, thin weekly until flowering is completed.
Botrytis Blotch (*Botrytis cinerea*) Appears on Rhododendrons grown in high humidity with poor air circulation; new shoots develop slowly, wither, and dry up before growth is complete. In high humidity, gray mold develops after the buds die. Infected rhododendron leaves die back from the tip, with various marbled markings and wilt.	Not generally as serious disease in the northern U.S.; generally occurs as a secondary infection, following winter injury. From mid-May to October spray every three to four weeks to prevent disease with Captan, Manzate, or Zineb.
Root Rot (*Phytophthora cinnamomi, Cylindrocarpon destructans* and *Cylindrocladium scoparium*) Leaves turn pale green and dull before they dry out and die. The cause is fungus-diseased stems; the fungus enters through the roots, injuring or killing them, then works its way up through the canes. Often mistakes in cultivation to blame, such as locations which are too wet or contain too much nitrogen.	Diseased branches should be cut out. If necessary remove the entire plant. In case of mild infection, saturate soil with Dexon or Terraclor mixed as per manufacturer's instructions for soil drench. Success of the treatment is limited.
Alpine-rose Rust (*Chrysomyxa ledi* var. *rhododendri*) Occurs usually on *Rhododendron ferrugineum* and *R. hirsutum,* Chlorotic or reddish to brown spots on leaves and stems. Beginning in August, yellowish-brown powdery pustules on the undersides, replaced by darker spots in late fall and early spring.	Control the same as in Botrytis Blotch. Not a general disease in the U.S.; first identified in 1954 in a commercial planting in Washington state, apparently introduced on infected European-grown plants.
Lace Bugs (*Stephanitis rhododendri* and *S. oberti*) Light yellow mottling on the tops of leaves, undersides have small, dark dots (droppings) and about 4 mm long, bugs with glassy wings and larva without wings. Leaf margins turn under, leaves dry up and fall off.	Mid-May to late June, repeated sprayings with Guthion, Malathion, or Spectracide. Or apply a systemic insecticide as flowers fade and new shoots are half-grown; repeat in four weeks with topical or systemic sprays, concentrate on undersides of all foliage.

Some Insects and Diseases of Deciduous Trees and Shrubs (cont.)

Symptoms	Control
White-flies (*Drialeurodes vaporariorum* or *D. chittenderi*) Yellowish mottling on leaf tissue, undersides of leaves have sticky droppings and 1 to 2 mm long winged, white insects, which fly when the plant is disturbed. Scale insect-like larva.	Control as for Lace Bugs, but continue spray applications through late summer.
Bud Mites (*Phyllocoptes azaleae*) Leaves at tips of shoots small and deformed, buds die, new shoots do not develop, often found on *Rhododendron japonicum*.	Prune diseased shoots, spray as new leaves unfurl with Guthion or Malathion at seven day intervals until growth hardens.
Gall Mites (*Eriophyes alpestris*) Tops of leaves rolled up on edge, blossoms are deformed.	Spray as above with Parathion or Thiodan.
Rosa **Mildew** (*Sphaerotheca pannosa*) Heavy mildew covering on tips and undersides of leaves, shoots and buds.	Repeated spraying with Karathane or Phaltan. All new growth must be completely coated with fungicide as it develops for effective control.
Rose Rust (*Phragmidium* species) Soon after the old canes leaf out and new shoots develop, a light orange-red callus appears on canes and leaves. In summer there are small yellowish or reddish spots on the tops of the leaves; on the undersides there are yellowish brown pinhead-sized pustules which turn black in the fall. Leaves fall off earlier than usual.	Before new growth appears, use copper-based agents. As soon as the plant starts growing, spray repeatedly with Foltan or with a Captan-Ferbam combined spray.
Black-spot (*Diplocarpon rosae*) In spring, and especially in warm weather, roundish, brown to violet-black spots appear which are as large as 1 cm. The leaves yellow, wither and fall off early.	Beginning as growth resumes in spring; Phaltan or Fermate or maneb combined with captan should be used every 10 days. Dead foliage should be burned.
Cane (Stem) Cankers (*Betryosphaeria, Coniothyrium, Cryptosporelle, Leptosphaeria* and other fungal species) On bark of previous year's shoots light-brown to brownish-red darker bordered spots. The bark dries up and cracks, the shoots wilt and die.	Prune out affected canes where possible. Spray with Cupricide before leaves come out. Do not mound with soil in the fall, rather cover deeply with pine needles, removing them early. Normal spraying at frequent intervals minimizes canilens.
Root Lesion Nematode (*Pratylenchus penetrans*) and **Rust Knot Nematode** (*Meloidogyne hapla*) The plant wilts, grows poorly; roots are more or less destroyed.	Before planting, treat the soil with EDB, Japam or VPM. Refer problems to County Extension Agent for diagnosis confirmation and for *in situ* control measures approved for your area.

Some Insects and Diseases of Deciduous Trees and Shrubs (cont.)

Symptoms	Control
Mites (*Tetranychus urticae* and *Panonychus ulmi*) Numerous chlorotic dots on the leaves; leaves discolor, dry up and fall off.	Before new growth appears, spray with dormant-strength lime-sulfur. Thereafter, spray repeatedly with Cygon, Mitor, Aramite or other miticide. Avoid use of Sevin in the garden as it destroys natural parasites of spider-mites which results in mite infestations.
Aphids (*Macrosiphon rosae* and others) Clustered green, rose-colored or black insects on leaves, shoots and buds 4 mm large. Leaves are deformed; honeydew glistens on leaves below the insect infestation.	Spray as needed with nicotine sulphate, Guthion, Malathion, or Spectracide—all of which also tend to repress other rose pests as rose slugs and spider-mites.
Rose Borers (*Blennocampa elongatula* and *Ardis brunniventris*) and Raspberry Cane Borer (*Oberia bimeculata*) Light brown caterpillars hollow out the canes, from the leaf axil upwards, or the tip downwards, signs include bored holes covered with white mold, or dead shoot tips. Cut stems reveal the "bored" pith.	Prune out and burn infested canes; treat rose root zone with granular systemic insecticide, or spray plants regularly with systemics. Often normal spray programs aimed at other common insects controls the borer population.
Scale Insects (various species) Small "shells" on branches in various sizes, forms and colors.	As new growth develops, spray at five day intervals with Guthion, or Malathion, or Diazinon. Dormant spray with lime-sulfur. Serious infestations respond to regular use of systemic insecticides.
Rose Leaf-hopper (*Typhlocyba rosae* = *Edwardsiana rosae*) Leaves are white-yellow spotted on top from May to September, leaves wilt and fall off; on the undersides of leaves, there are 3 mm long larva and winged leaf-hoppers; develop during droughts or extended dry periods.	At onset of infestation, spray with Guthion, Malathion, or Diazinon at eight-day intervals. As this insect overwinters in the egg stage under rose bush bark, dormant sprays reduce insect population.
Leaf-roller Sawflies (*Blennocampa pusilla*) From May to September the leaves are curled under from the edges to midribs by 8 to 9 mm long caterpillar-like larva.	Remove infested leaves, spray with Guthion, Malathion or Diazinon at eight-day intervals.

Some Insects and Diseases of Deciduous Trees and Shrubs (cont.)

Symptoms	Control
Salix	
Black Canker (*Glomerella miyabeana* = *Physalospora miyabeana*) Round or oval spots with concentric rings on shoots and leaves. Shoot tips wilt. A summer disease, will kill willows in two or three years.	Prune heavily as quickly as the disease is diagnosed. Spray with Cupricide or Bordeaux mixture from spring on.
Willow Scab (*Venturia saliciperda*) Irregular, sharply defined, dark brown spots on leaves, which after a rain are covered with smooth, olive-green fruiting bodies; on the under part of thin branches, blackish-brown necrosis, early leaf loss, tips of shoots die.	Beginning with first new growth, spray with Bordeaux mixture or Cupricide every two to three weeks.
Willow Rust (*Melampsora salicina* and other species) In summer, numerous yellow spots appear on undersides of leaves; later these darken with powdery spore-bearing pustules; disease begins on the older leaves, leads to early leaf loss, new shoots may die.	Beginning in early summer or late spring, repeated preventive spraying at two-week intervals with Fermate. Spray infected plants with Karathane or other dinitro compounds.
Willow Scale Insects (*Chionaspis salicis-nigras*) Numerous gray-white sea mussel-like "shells" up to 3 mm long on bark. In serious infestations, the bark may be completely covered with insects. Shoots may die.	Spray with Guthion, Malathion or Spectracide. With serious infestations apply dormant sprays, as oil with or without systemic insecticide.
Willow Twig Blight (*Venturia salicperda*) Soon after spring growth begins leaves and shoots blacken and shrivel. Ultimately the disease spreads to entire tree.	Prune out infected twigs and burn. At spring bud break spray at 7- to 10-day intervals with Bourdeaux Cupricide for three to five applications.

Some Insects and Diseases of Conifers

Symptoms	Control
Abies	
Balsam Wooly Aphid (*Dreyfusia nusslini* and *D. merkeri*) Wax-secreting insects on new shoots, branches and stem; needles curl, shoots dry out, stems encrusted with white casting.	Before new growth appears, spray with dormant oil, then in May-June, spray with Guthion or Malathion, or a systemic insecticide, any with sticker-spreader added.
Bagworm (*Thyridopteris euphemeraeformis*) Tiny caterpillars feed on needles enclosing itself in tough silken sac. Enlarges sac as it grows to two to three inches. Larva pupates in sac to emerge as moth in spring.	Pick off and burn sacs as soon as sacs noticed in spring. Spray with Guthion, Malathion, Spectracide or lead arsenate. Repeat twice at one week intervals.
Balsam Twig Aphid (*Mindarus abietinus*) The new shoots on *Abies alba*, *A. nordmanniana*, *A. sibirica* and *A. balsamea* infested with yellowish-green insects, needles and shoots are deformed and can die from infestation.	As above.

Some Insects and Diseases of Conifers (cont.)

Symptoms	Control
Juniperus	
Twig-blight (*Phomopsis juniperovora*) The tips of shoots of young plants turn yellow to dark brown; on blue-needled cultivars they turn gray-green to blackish and die; the disease progresses to larger branches; there is a marked difference between healthy and diseased shoots.	Preventive spraying in late summer with Ferbam, Maneb or Zineb. Prune out infected portions, destroy badly affected specimens. Good ventilation and full sunlight deter development of the disease.
Cedar-apple Rust (*Gymnosporangium juniperi-virginianae*) Whole plants or single shoots are stunted, wilt and eventually die. Woody galls and bark swellings appear on twigs and branches and in early spring orange jelly-like fruiting bodies appear during rainy weather.	Prune off diseased parts, spray with Acti-dione several times in spring. This disease transfers back and forth between certain junipers and members of the apple tribe. Avoid planting cultivars of *J.virginiana* which are exceptionally susceptible near ornamental crabapples, hawthorns, and other susceptible members of *Rosa*.
Spruce Spider Mite (*Oligonychus ununguis*) and other Spider Mites (*Tetranychus* species) Pale spots on needles and scales, later the branches discolor to gray and then reddish brown; webs of fine, white spider threads with mites, larvae and larvae cases on them.	Before new growth appears, spray with dormant oil; beginning in early spring use miticides as Dimite, Kelthane, Tedion, or with insecticides such as Guthion or Malathion, or with systemic insecticide such as Di-syston. Mites mutate quickly; change chemicals frequently.
Juniper Webworm (*Dichomeris marginella*) In spring ½ inch long light brown-striped caterpillars eat the plant from inside webbed mass of twigs and needles; in June, brown female moths with white stripes on their wing margins emerge; beginning in August, young caterpillars start eating the plant again.	At onset of infestation spray Guthion or Dylox or Spectracide under high pressure into the nests.
Scale Insects (*Diapsis visci, D. carueli, Carulapsis visci*) Tiny white or gray scales on branches, shoots and needles; sooty mold forms on the honeydew exuded by the scale. Needles turn yellow.	In April and again from July to September, repeated sprayings with insecticidal oils, or with Guthion or Malathion.
Picea	
Cytospora canker (*Cytospora kunzei*) Progressive browning of needles followed by death of the infected branch, usually beginning with lowest branches and progressing upward. Mechanical injury during cultivation or trimming seems to provide entry wounds for the fungus. Infected branches cannot be saved and should saved and should be removed immediately at the trunk. Paint the wound with pruning paint.	Spray lower branches and trunk as well as fallen needles beneath the spruce with Bordeaux mixture or with Cupracide, several applications at seven- to ten-day intervals beginning with first signs of bud growth in spring.

94

Some Insects and Diseases of Conifers (cont.)

Symptoms	Control
Needle Cast (*Lophodermium* species and *Rhizosphaera kalkhoffii*) Needles of lower branches show spots as they yellow and drop. Lower branches may be defoliated.	Spray as recommended for Cytospore Canker control.
Spruce Rusts (*Chrysomyxa ledi* var. *cassandrae* and other species) Needles yellow and drop prematurely; at early stages, white blisters on the lower surface of needles are symptomatic of rusts. Various alternate hosts (other species of plants) are required for the fungus to complete its life cycle. The government official can list those found in your area.	Remove alternate hosts if possible. Valuable specimens can be protected by applying protective fungicide such as Bordeaux mixture, Lime-sulfur (dormant strength in late winter, summer strength, 1:50, in warm weather), or Fermate, at seven to ten-day intervals through spring and early summer.
Spider-Mite (*Olygonychus ununguis*) Numerous light, later darker, pinpoint spots on the needles; later the needles turn completely yellow, then brown. Gray webbing on needles and twigs and inside are 0.2 to 0.4 mm long, greenish to brown mites and whitish larvae cases. Occurs on forms of *Picea mariana, P. pungens* and *P. abies*.	Preventive spraying with dormant oils in very early spring. In May to June, spray with any miticide (check local recommendations with government official). Spray alternately with Guthion, Malathion, or Black Leaf 40.
Spruce Aphid (*Liosomaphis abietinum = Elatobium abietinum*) In March to April, yellowish sections appear on older needles; later, needles discolor to red-brown and fall off. Caused by green aphids with red-brown eyes, which hatch in late winter. *Picea sitchensis, P. pungens, P. omorika, P. abies, P. engelmannii* and *P. smithiana* are all susceptible. Some spruce species do not lose needles, they just turn brown.	In late winter as temperature goes above 45°F. spray with dormant oil. As soon as symptoms appear spray with a systemic insecticide (even before new growth appears in some cases). In May-June, spray with a Guthion, Malathion or Spectracide.
Leaf-miner (*Epinotia tedella*) Yellowish to greenish-striped caterpillars bore into needles in June or July. Larva build a nest of pieces of needles and feces. The adult is a small gray moth.	Beginning in midsummer, repeated spraying with Guthion, Malathion, or a systemic insecticide such as Meta-systox-R.
Small Spruce Bud Worms (*Epinotia pygmaeana*) Green caterpillars bore into shoot tips, especially on *Picea pungens* and *P. omorika*.	Before new growth appears, spray with petroleum oil, from June on, spray with Thiodan.
Woolly Spruce Stem Aphids = Pine Leaf Chermid (*Pineus pineoides = Pineus pinifoliae*) Numerous white, woolly wax-covered aphids on stem and branches. Woolly nymphs overwinter on pine, move to spruce in spring (forming small galls), then return to pines in midsummer.	Before new growth develops, spray with dormant oil, later, spray with a systemic insecticide such as meta-systox-R. Also, spray nearby pines.

Some Insects and Diseases of Conifers (cont.)

Symptoms	Control
Spruce Gall Aphid and, especially, Cooley Spruce Gall Adelgid (*Sacchiphantes abietis, S. viridis, Adeleges laricis* and *Gilletteella cooleyi*) Pineapple-shaped galls of a few centimeters, green, later red or brown on young shoots.	From the end of March to the beginning of April, when the first adult aphids appear (in white, waxy blotches), spray once with dormant oil; at two-week intervals with Guthion, Spectracide or a systemic insecticide. Also spray Douglas firs as they are an alternate host.
Dried Needles on Serbian Spruces. Possibly a parasitic disease; it appears as a discoloration and drying out of leaves, which begins on the shoot tips and later spreads to the outer crown. Some plant pathologists applying fungicide as a prophylactic measure.	This disease is often treated with Zineb or Maneb. Do not plant *Picea omorika* in soil which is too heavy, acidy or damp.
Pinus White Pine Blister-rust (*Cronartium ribicola*) 10 to 20 cm long swellings or blisters develop on the stem and branches of *Pinus strobus* and other five-needled pines. In early summer blisters exude a sweetish secretion, later this forms membranous pustules which burst and release a yellowish powder. Alternate hosts are currants and gooseberries.	Diseased plants usually cannot be saved. They should be rooted out and burned.
Pine Bark Blister Rust, Bark Blister Rust (*Cronartium flaccidum, Endocronartium pini*) In summer, membranous, yellow, pustules develop on the bark of the shoots. They burst and release a yellow powder of yellow spores. Occurs on young shoots, as well as older ones. After repeated infection the shoots die.	Cut out diseased parts and burn them.
European Pine Leaf Aphid (*Pineus pini = Pineus pinifoliae*) During winter, white, waxy-woolly aphids live on the bark of one year old pine shoots. In spring, winged aphids move to the needles of spruces, form galls, and in summer return to the pines.	Spray with dormant oil before new growth appears, later, spray with Guthion or Malathion, Spectracide or apply a systemic insecticide.
Pine Bark Aphid, also called White Pine Bark Louse (*Pineus strobi*) White woolly masses in which aphids are embedded appear on twig undersides and on trunks. *Pinus strobus* and *P. cembra* are especially susceptible. Sometimes occurs on balsam fir, also.	As above.

Some Insects and Diseases of Conifers (cont.)

Symptoms	Control
Taxus	
Bud Gall Mite (*Eriophyes psilaspis*) Axillary buds are compressed and rounded, the new shoots are either deformed, or they simply do not develop.	Spray weekly with a miticide from early spring until midsummer.
Black Vine Weevil (*Brachyrhinus sulcatus*) This is the most destructive pest of yews in the U.S. Needles yellow and entire branches, then entire plants, die as root bark is gnawed away by beetle larvae. The larva is a white bodied, brown headed grub about ⅜ inch long. Just a few grubs will kill a large plant. The adult is a black snout beetle about ⅜ inch long which feeds on foliage at night	Control of the Black Vine Weevil and Strawberry Weevil is very difficult. Infested commerical plantings are quarantined until the infestation is destroyed entirely. Immediately notify your government official if you suspect an infestation. Spray foliage with Guthion, Malathion, or Spectracide, or have a commerical applicator spray with a parathion preparation. Apply granules of a systemic insecticide to the root zone. Also, scatter metaldehyde-containing pellets (Snarol; Bugeta) intended for slug and snail control near the stems of infested plants as larvae near the surface may by attracted to these.
Strawberry Root Weevil (*Brachyrhinus ovatus*) Grubs and larvae similar to the Black Vine Weevil but smaller, both being 1/5 to 1/4 inch long.	Control as for Black Vine Weevil. While destructive, this pest is not so devastating as the Black Vine Weevil.
Yew Lecanium Scale (*Eulecanium cornicrudum*) Large red-brown scale insects and their larva, which hatch mid-July to August on the bark of the branches.	Spray with a systemic insecticide before the plants resume growth in spring. Spray spring through midsummer at two week intervals with Guthion, Malathion, Spectracide or a systemic insecticide to combat new larva.
Thuja	
Tip blight (*Coryneum berckmanii*) Gradually, shoot tips or entire shoots discolor and die in early summer. There is a distinct difference between healthy and infected parts of the plant. Other *Arborvitae* blights are also controlled by spraying as for Tip blight.	If the disease developed the previous year, beginning in mid-May, spray 3 times at 14 day intervals with Cupricide or with Bordeaux mixture. With summer infections, spray when rain is forecast as spores are released by rainfall.
Arborvitae Leaf Blight (*Didymascella thujina*) Tiny leaves (scales) are yellow at first, then discolor to a brownish color and one or more pinpoint, round black or brown cushions of fungus appear on each. Young lateral branches fall off in autumn; often develops in nurseries.	From midsummer through fall, spray every 14 days with a neutral copper insecticide or Bordeaux mixture, or spray with Zineb or Maneb.

Encyclopedia of Deciduous Trees and Shrubs

Aethionema grandiflorum

Aethionema grandiflorum, Cruciferae

Natural habitat: the Caucasus mountains, the Transcaucasus, eastern Anatolia (Turkey), northern Iran and Iraq.

This subshrub (Zone 6) grows to a height of 20 to 25 cm. Shoots are unbranched, slender, relatively woody and leafy; Leaves are approximately 2 cm long, gray-green, straight-edged and linear-lanceolate. Fragrant pink blossoms appear from May to August in clusters 5 to 7 cm long and 2.5 cm wide.

A. grandiflorum is the most beautiful species in this genus. It is cushion-forming, suited to rock gardens, rock beds and dry walls in sunny, dry locations on poor, very well drained and porous soil.

Two superior cultivars with denser growth and brighter, larger flower heads are *A. g.* 'Warley Rose' and *A. g.* 'Warley Ruba'.

Alyssum montanum, Cruciferae

Natural habitat: central Europe, southern and central U.S.S.R. and Mediterranean locations. *A. montanum* (Zone 6) is found on plains as well as in alpine regions, on various sorts of stone, on dry, sunny cliffs, slopes, sandy wastelands, meadows and heaths.

A. montanum is a suffruticose to woody, heavily branched subshrub 10 to 20 cm tall; with prostrate-ascending stems, which sometime terminate in sterile rosettes of leaves which are covered thickly with stellate hairs; the other shoots have gray tomentose leaves and countless, clustered, yellow blossoms in April–May. Additional woody or suffruticose species suitable for rock gardens include: *A. alpestre,* 1 dm, yellow flowers; *A. murale,* 3.5 dm, yellow flowers; *A. serpyllifolium,* 3 dm, pale yellow; and *A. spinosum,* white, fragrant, with silver-white leaves, and *A. s.* 'Roseum' with violet-pink flowers.

All are ideal for rock gardens and dry walls and thrive in dry, porous, light, lime soil and a sunny location.

Alyssum montanum

Amorpha canescens, Leguminosae

Found on the dry prairies of central North America (Zone 2) it is reputed to be an indicator plant for lead, tin and silver.

This shrub reaches up to 70 cm tall and is finely branched. Elegant odd-pinnate leaves, gray-pilose on both sides, grow on slender, gray-pilose branches. In late summer, tiny purplish blue blossoms appear in 10 to 15 cm long terminal clusters.

The unusual, reduced, tubular flowers lack the flag petals of typical papilionaceous flowers (both wings and keel petals are absent); both pistil and stamens (with orange pollen) project beyond the corolla.

A. canescens thrives in sunny locations in dry, well drained, nutrient-poor soils on dry walls or in rock gardens, heath gardens, and prairie and steppe gardens. It is not completely winter hardy in wet climates. Shoots often freeze or are injured so badly in hard winters that spring pruning is required. Pruning does not interfere with blossom development. As is the case with many herbaceous perennials, blossoms develop on new shoots. Mulching completely around the plant in fall with evergreen boughs protects the shrub from frost damage.

101

Andromeda polifolia, Ericaceae

This is a characteristic plant of sphagnum moors in the northern zones of Europe (central Europe to the North Cape), Asia and North America (Zone 2). The cultivar *A. g.* 'Glauca' is most often used in garden designs with *Ledum palustre, Vaccinium oxycoccos, V. uliginosum, Betula nana, Calluna vulgaris, Rubus chamaemorus,* various *Carex* species and *Eriophorum vaginatum.* An elegant shrub, very bushy, *Andromeda polifolia* 'Glauca' will seldom exceed 20 cm. Its narrow, leathery, evergreen leaves are curled on the edges, dark green on top and light blue-green on the undersides. In May–June, small, light pink, urn-shaped flowers develop at the end of the shoots in umbels of 4 to 5.

A. polifolia thrives best in locations with high humidity or high precipitation, in moist to wet, infertile, raw humus, acid soil, in partly shady locations. If the soil is damp enough, it also does well in sunny locations. It is a fine companion plant with small-leafed trees and shrubs. In heath gardens, it thrives in wet soil with *Erica tetralix, Betula nana* and *Ledum palustre* as companion plants. Other cultivars, mostly described by their epithets, are *A. g.* 'Angustifolia'; *A. g.* 'Compacta'; *A. g.* 'Grandifolia compacta'; *A. g.* 'Major'; *A. g.* 'Minima'; *A. g.* 'Montana', more compact and with darker leaves; and *A. g.* 'Nana'.

A second *Andromeda* species, *A. glaucophylla,* is seldom cultivated. It comes from the cold peat moors of northern North America where, with *Ledum palustre* and *Chamaedaphne calyculata,* it forms low, dense carpets.

Anthyllis hermanniae, Leguminosae

Natural habitat: Corsica to Asia Minor, in Mediterranean rock heaths and subalpine locations in Zone 7.

This deciduous species develops thickly branched, thorny, nearly prostrate stems. It grows 40 to 50 cm tall. In its native habitat it grows into thorny, round cushions surrounded by stem-rooted offshoots. Its silky-haired leaves have apical leaflets 1 to 2.5 cm long. In June (April–May in its natural habitat) orange-yellow "butterfly" blossoms open. They

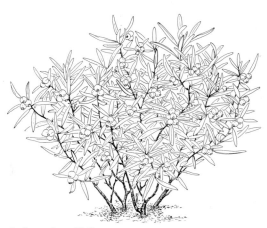

Andromeda polifolia

Andromeda glaucophylla var. *latifolia*

are approximately 8 mm long and are arranged in shortstalked heads.

This is a beautiful dwarf shrub for sunny, warm locations in rock gardens. The soil must be very well drained and porous, so that winter moisture drains away quickly. Winter protection with leaves or a covering of evergreen branches is recommended.

Arctostaphylos uva-ursi, Ericaceae

A. uva-ursi (Zone 2) can be found almost anywhere in Europe, in the Caucasus mountains, northern Siberia, and in northern North America. It forms extensive carpets on dry, sandy soil in conifer forests. In the Alps, it appears above the timber line in juniper thickets or in dwarf shrub heaths. It is found growing in almost all types of soil, but prefers a lime soil.

Its prostrate branches up to 100 cm long are thickly covered with small, dark green, leathery, alternate leaves. White, 5 to 6 mm, urn-shaped blossoms form in autumn and open in April–May in terminal, pendulous clusters. Glossy, bright red, pea-sized berries remain on the shrub through most of the winter and sometimes until the following spring.

It thrives best in sunny to partly shady (in areas with warm summers) locations on loose, not too moist, porous soil; it tolerates humus amendments, but not pure peat. Together with *Erica* and *Calluna,* it is an almost indispensable companion plant for bushy junipers and dwarf pines in a heath garden. Ideal locations are rock gardens and the upper edge of walls, from which its pendulous branches drape.

A relative, *A. nevadensis,* has its natural habitat in western North America (coastal mountain ranges and the Sierra Nevadas). It is less hardy than *A. uva-ursi.*

Arctostaphylos uva-ursi

At least 35 more species and a number of hybrids and cultivars are listed for this genus; many of them are grown locally as fine ornamentals and some are beginning to appear on the market. Watch for them!

Aurinia saxatilis, Cruciferae

Its natural habitat (Zone 6) stretches from the Jura mountains, through the area surrounding the Danube River and the northern Balkan Peninsula, to southern U.S.S.R. and Asia Minor. It is found mainly on sunny, dry rock and in the mountains on lime, basalt and mica schist.

A. saxatilis is a 15 to 30 cm tall subshrub with prostrate-ascending stems which end in sterile leafy rosettes and in flower heads; in April to May, countless yellow blossoms appear in thick clusters over the light gray, tomentose foliage.

Five common cultivars of *A. saxatilis* are well known: 'Citrina' flowers lemon-yellow; 'Lutea' flowers bright, clear yellow; 'Sulphurea' flowers sulphur-yellow, plants vigorous; 'Compacta', compact, thrifty eggyolk-colored flowers; 'Plenum' double flowers, rich gold-yellow.

All are used in the same manner as *Allysum montanum*.

Berberis buxifolia 'Nana', Berberidaceae

The true species comes from southern Chile (Zone 5) and is only cultivated in botanical gardens. *B. b.* 'Nana', however, is a very popular dwarf cultivar which is more tolerant in culture. It does not grow more than 30 cm tall as a round, dense bush, almost thornless, with small, oval, evergreen leaves. It seldom blooms.

B. b. 'Nana' thrives in all types of garden soil, tolerates sunny to partly shady locations and, thanks to its pruning tolerance, is well suited for low hedges. It makes a good undershrub, in single or group plantings in heath, rock or container gardens. Plants originating from the Southern Hemisphere, such as *Carex buchananii*, *Acaena* and *Hebe* species make good companion plantings with *B. buxifolia* 'Nana'.

Berberis buxifolia 'Nana'

Berberis candidula, Berberidaceae

B. candidula (Zone 5) comes from the mountains of Hubei Province in central China. It grows on cliffs and stony crags at altitudes of 2300 m. It was introduced into European culture in 1896.

It is one of the most beautiful of the evergreen barberries and grows hardly more than 50 cm tall. It grows very slowly and its upright-growing branches form dense bushes, oftentimes wider than they are tall. The narrow-elliptical, dark green leaves are 3.5 cm long, leathery, curled and lightly spined at the edges. Old leaves turn an intense yellow in autumn. Small, golden yellow blossoms appear in mid-spring amidst the foliage. Its egg-shaped dark blue fruits are white frosted and remain on the plant through the winter.

'Jytte' is a Danish cultivar. It is a round, compact grower. It is more frost hardy than the species and is, therefore, well suited for containers and hedges in colder areas.

B. candidula thrives in all humus soils. It grows best in sunny to partly shady, wind-protected locations. Growth habit is looser in shady locations. Above all, planting sites should be protected from winter sun. When there is insufficient snow or in exposed locations, a dome made of coniferous branches protects against winter sun. It is useful singly or in groups in front yard gardens, in sidewalk beds or on terraces. It is especially attractive when used with evergreen conifers, roses, ground covers or fall blooming plants such as chrysanthemums or asters. When planted among ground covering plants which reduce the penetration of frost, no other winter protection is necessary.

Berberis × frikartii 'Verrucandi', Berberidaceae

B. × frikartii (Zone 6) is a cross between B. candidula and B. verruculosa, having originated in Switzerland. This hybrid barberry grows to 1–1.5 m tall and is extremely frost hardy.

B. × f. 'Verrucandi' grows to 1.2 m tall with beautiful, compact, widespreading branches. It differs from B. candidula in that its leaves are a bit wider and flatter and the undersides are bluish white. It also grows taller and is more frost hardy.

Its cultural requirements and landscape uses are similar to B. candidula. Because it is more frost hardy and robust, it is very well suited for hedges and containers.

Berberis gagnepainii 'Klugowski', Berberidaceae

The species from western China, and the frequently cultivated var. lanceifolia, are not dwarf shrubs and, therefore, will not be dealt with in this book.

The slow growing cultivar B. g. 'Klugowski' remains, however, 1.2 m or under. It is a compact shrub wider than it is tall, with arching, pendulous branches. Its evergreen leaves are narrow, lance-shaped, 5 cm long, dark green on top, and blue-green underneath; sulfur-yellow blossoms appear in May either singly or in small clusters.

Its cultural requirements and garden uses are very similar to B. candidula. It is also well suited for hedges. It is especially frost hardy and rugged.

Berberis hookeri, Berberidaceae

B. hookeri (Zone 7) is native to climates supporting broadleaved evergreen forests. Its natural range includes the Himalayas, eastern Nepal, Bhutan, Sikkim and Assam, north India. The elevation at which it thrives ranges from 2400 to 3200 m. It was introduced into Europe in 1848 by Hooker.

This variable evergreen shrub grows to be 0.7 m tall. Its growth habit it looser and more robust and coarse than the other Berberis species. Its lance-shaped, spiny leaves are 6 cm long, glossy green on top and white bordered underneath. Leaves assume some beautiful red coloration in autumn. The greenish yellow blossoms do not fall off easily, nor do its blackish purple fruit.

It is a simple, almost frost-hardy shrub well suited for hedges. It can be used in a manner similar to the other evergreen barberrys.

Barberis gagnepainii 'Klugowski' (a young plant)

Berberis × stenophylla, Berberidaceae

B. darwinii and *B. empetrifolia,* which are the parent species of this hybrid (Zone 5) come from South America and are among the most elegant and striking evergreen barberrys. Both parent barberrys grow to 2 or 3 m tall, and are often substantially wider.

B. 'Crawley Gem', a × *stenophylla* cultivar, is much smaller, 50 to 60 cm tall, and can be identified by its wide habit and elegant, pendulous branches. Its matte green leaves are a bit wider than those of the hybrid, but are much more refined. Blossoms appear in late spring in clusters of 7 to 14. They are yellow and red on the outside, an unusual combination for barberrys.

Compared to the parent hybrid, this is a relatively frost-sensitive shrub, so should be planted in protected locations in heath, rock and container gardens. The soil should be mulched with, and a dome made of, needle-evergreen branches to protect the plant in winter.

'Irwinii', .05–1.2 m tall, is a wide, bushy shrub with broad, leathery leaves in clusters of three which resemble those of

Berberis × stenophylla 'Irwinii'

B. × *stenophylla* or *B. darwinii*. It flowers abundantly with relatively large, orange-colored blossoms. Its cultural requirements and use are identical to those of *B.* 'Crawley Gem'.

Berberis thunbergii, Berberidaceae

B. thunbergii (Zone 4) probably is the most popular of all the deciduous barberry. Its native habitat is the damp forests of Japan. It is densely branched and 1 to 1.5 m tall. It is notable for the countless coral-red fruits and intense, bright red fall foliage color.

Among the many cultivars of this species are some interesting dwarfs which are well suited for grave, rock, heath and container gardens. Whether they are planted singly or in small groups, they are not suited to be placed with fast growing, aggressive neighbors as they are non-competitive. They do well with slow growing, dwarf trees and shrubs.

All of the cultivars are robust and grow best in sunny locations in light, acid soil though they grow well in neutral, even slightly alkaline soils. They do not do well in nutrient-poor, acid, poorly drained soil. They are susceptible to *Verticillium albo-atrum*, a root-collar decay disease, in soil which is particularly soggy during long, cold, rainy periods (the leaves discolor to brown-red or reddish brown and fall off). The disease is very hard to control.

B. thunbergii 'Atropurpurea Nana' is most commonly used for low hedges. It is a thick, bushy, wide shrub reaching 40–60 cm tall. Its leaves are purple-brown. It has never been known to blossom. Recent comparisons in botanical gardens suggest tha *B. t.* Crimson Pygmy,' *B. t.* Little Gem', and *B. t.* 'Little Pygmy' are identical with *B. t.* 'Atroparea Nana'. Furthermore, the epithet *B. t.* 'Crimson Pygmy' takes precedence.

Especially slow growing is 'Bagatelle'. It is a flattened, ball-shaped dwarf cultivar which does not exceed 40 cm in height. Its smaller, more fragile shoots are very dense, but it is not generally suitable for hedges. Twigs are somewhat more slender than those found on *B. t.* 'Kobold'. The elliptic leaves are brownish-red when they first come out and turn to a blackish red later.

B. thunbergii 'Kobold' is similar to *B. t.* 'Bagatelle', except that its branches are more solid and knotty, and its leaves remain an unfading dark green until they fall off in autumn.

Berberis verruculosa, Berberidaceae

B. verruculosa (Zone 5) is native to western China, in climates which support both evergreen and deciduous broad-leaf forests. The altitudes in which it grows range from 1200 to 3200 m. It was discovered by E. H. Wilson and intro-duced in 1904.

This evergreen shrub grows slowly, to a height of 1–1.5 m and is wider than tall. Its yellowish brown branches are wide-spread, pendulous, and densely "warty" (verrucose). Leaves are 2.5 cm long, elliptic to egg-shaped, spine-toothed, glossy green above, glaucous beneath. In autumn, the older leaves turn fiery red. Large, gold-yellow blossoms are showy in late spring. Its black fruit is blue-frosted.

This is one of the most popular evergreen species due partially to its hardiness. It is very decorative, suited for almost any location, somewhat coarser in habit than *B. candidula,* but is more robust and frost hardy.

Betula nana, Betulaceae

As an arctic and alpine species, *B. nana* (Zone 2) has a circumpolar range of distribution. It appears in high moors in central Europe with species such as *Rhamnus frangula, Pinus mugo, Empetrum nigrum, Vaccinium* species, *Andromeda polifolia, Eriophorum vaginatum, Drosera* and various sedges. In the subalpine moors *Lonicera caerulea, L. nigrum* and *Rhododendron ferrugineum* are found with it.

   B. nana, with its low spreading habit, seldom grows to 50 cm tall. Its branches are either procumbent or slightly ascending. When old, the bark is blackish gray. Its young, hairy shoots bear round, serrate leaves which are 5–15 mm long. Young leaves are sticky and do not change color in autumn.

   B. nana is almost indispensable in heath gardens. It tolerates very damp locations in raw humus soil, but thrives just as well in dry, nutrient-poor, mineral soils of recent origin. It does especially well in sunny spots, but when necessary, does almost as well in partly shady locations. This is not a plant for areas with hot, dry summers.

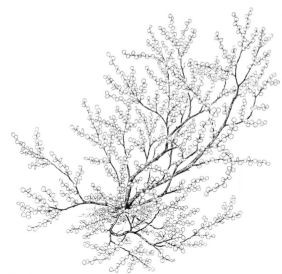

Betula nana

Bruckenthalia spiculifolia, Ericaceae

B. spiculifolia (Zone 5) is an important part of the understory flora of Austrian pine forests and the sub-alpine beech woods in the eastern Balkans, the Bithnean Olympic Mountains, and bordering mountains of Asia Minor. The altitude of its range of distribution is between 1200 and 1950 m. In these locations *Juniperus communis* and its var. *montana, Erica herbacea, Vaccinium vitis-idaea* and *V. myrtillus, Arctostaphylos uva-ursi* and *A. alpina, Daphne blagayana* and *Rhododendron kotschyi* also are found.

   B. spiculifolia is an evergreen dwarf shrub, 10 to 20 cm tall, with many similarities to heather. It has slender, erect branches densely covered with leaves. Its leaves are whorled and needle-shaped. Small, light pink, nodding, bell-shaped blossoms appear in late-midsummer on the shoot tips. The blossoms have a pleasing fragrance reminiscent of heliotrope.

   B. spiculifolia is used in the same manner as *Erica herbacea*. However, it is not as problem-free when grown in large groupings. It does best as a single plant or in small groups among large rocks. It requires lime-free, rather less moist, light soil. In cloudy climates it blooms better in sunny locations than in partly shady ones.

Buxus sempervirens, Buxaceae

The natural range of *B. sempervirens* (Zone 5) is central Europe, north Africa, the Caucasus Mountains and the western

Himalayas. It is usually found growing as an understory shrub in forests, but is also a relic plant of formerly forested areas destroyed by mankind, as is the case in the Balkan Peninsula. It appears along the Mosel River and in Baden in Germany. It colonizes there in warm, dry, sunny locations, often on gravelly hillsides. Only a few of the slow growing cultivars will be discussed:

B. s. 'Myrtifolia' is a short, loosely branched, slow growing evergreen shrub. It reaches 1 to 1.2 m tall and has beautiful, egg-shaped, gray-green leaves which are 6–18 mm long.

B. s. 'Suffruticosa' is well-known as an ideal shrub for low hedges. Unpruned, it hardly reaches 1 m. It is a very dense shrub with egg-shaped, emarginate leaves, 1 to 2 cm long.

The dwarf cultivars have the same cultural requirements as the species. They grow in sunny locations as well as in shade, thrive in any soil, even dry soil.

B. sempervirens 'Myrtifolia', which is looser growing and more beautiful, can grow in container gardens or in very shady locations.

Bruckenthalia spiculifolia

109

Calluna vulgaris, Ericaceae

With the exception of the southernmost regions, *C. vulgaris* (Zone 5) is found throughout Europe. To the east, it is found as far as western Siberia; in the Alps it grows up as far as the snow line; and in sunny, rocky, dry turf communities it grows in locations as high as 2700 m. It commonly appears in moors, sand dunes and in thin, dry forests. It is stopped in its universal advance only when it encounters meager, nutrient-poor, porous, lime soils. Its largest continuous distribution is in the Atlantic regions with constant, oceanic climates, from northern Spain to Scotland and Scandinavia. It is a decidedly gregarious plant and often occurs in large, extended colonies. It dominates nutrient-poor, loose sandy soil almost without competition.

Soil moisture dictates the species used for companion plants. In very dry, sandy soil, *C. vulgaris* is accompanied by some junipers, a few brooms and woadwaxens (*Cytisus scoparius, Genista pilosa, G. anglica*),

Calluna vulgaris 'Dart's Brilliant'

sedges (*Carex arenaria*), and grasses (*Festuca ovina, Koeleria glauca, Nardus stricta*). Typical shrubs in natural heaths are *Campanula rotundifolia, Hieracium pilosella, Dianthus deltoides, D. arenarius, Armeria maritima, Verbascum densiflorum* and *V. thapsus, Corynephorus canescens, Jasione montana* and *Antennaria dioica*. In damp transitional moors, *Vaccinium vitis-idaea, V. uliginosum, V. oxycoccos, Ledum palustre, Andromeda polifolia* and *Erica tetralix* appear together with pines and birches.

C. *vulgaris* is a densely branched, evergreen, low spreading shrub 20 to 100 cm tall which spreads by rooting stems to cover the ground. Its leaves are needle-shaped, 1 to 3 mm long. Lavender-pink blossoms appear from July–September; these have a straw-like texture and occur in 20 cm long shoot tip clusters. *C. vulgaris* is a monotypical genus of only one species with five natural varieties, but with numerous cultivars. The genera *Calluna* and *Erica* are closely related. *Calluna* is separated from *Erica* by its pigmented calyx, which is longer than the four-part corolla. Both calyx and corolla remain after the blossoms have faded. In *Erica*, the four, lance-shaped calyx leaves are only half as long as the corolla lobes; often they are green. Color display derives from the sepals in *Calluna*, and from the petals in *Erica*. The leaves are also arranged differently; *Calluna* leaves are crosswise opposite, often overlapping (shingle-wise), while *Erica* leaves are arranged in 3 to 4 leaf (also 5 to 6 leaf) whorls.

Calluna vulgaris is the most important plant in a heath garden, where it grows well. When laying out a heath garden, one need not confine the design to plants which associate with *C. vulgaris* in its native habitat. Numerous dwarf conifers and deciduous trees and shrubs, bushes, and grasses work exceptionally well in giving character to a heath garden, even if they are not phytosociological components of a natural heath.

See the Heath Garden section for a more detailed discussion of species to plant with *Calluna*.

The following list presents the most important cultivars of *C. vulgaris*.

Calluna Vulgaris **Varieties**

Cultivar	Flowers	Months*	Special Leaf Color	Height (cm)	Growth Character
'Alba Erecta'	Pure white	8–9		50	Erect
'Alba Plena'	Pure white, double	8–9		40	Erect, spherical
'Allegro'	Wine-red, currently the deepest red cultivar	8–9		40	Erect, improved form of 'C.W. Nix'
'Alportii'	Red to red-violet	8–9	Gray-green pilose	100	Strong, erect
'Alportii Praecox'	Red to red-violet	7–8	Same	50	Slow growing
'Annemarie'	Pink-red to purple-red	9–11		50	Erect, beautiful new growth
'Anthony Davis'	White	8–9	Silver pilose	40	Erect
'Aurea'	Light violet	8–9	Yellow, brownish red in winter		Slow growing

Calluna Vulgaris Varieties (cont.)

Cultivar	Flowers	Months	Special Leaf Color	Height (cm)	Growth Character
'Barbara Fleur'	Flesh-colored	8–9		50	Erect
'Barnett Anley'	Purple	8–9	Reddish on sun-exposed side	50	Bushy
'Battle of Arnheim'	Purple	9–11	Brownish green, esp. in winter	60	Erect, compact
'Beoley Crimson'	Purple-red	8–9		60	Erect
'Beoley Gold'	White	8–9	Robust yellow	40	Erect
'Blazeaway'	Delicate lilac-pink	8–9	Bronze-yellow, bronze-red in winter	40	Semi-erect
'Boskoop'	Light pink	8–9	Orange-red, brownish red in winter	40	Semi-erect
'Carl Roeders'	Violet-pink, double	8–9		40	Erect
'Carmen'	Violet-red	8–9		40	Erect
'Christiana'	White	9–10	Yellow-green, yellow in winter	50	Erect
'County Wicklow'	Light pink, double	8–9	Brownish green in winter	30	Compact
'Cramond'	Dark pink, double	9–11		60	Semi-erect
'Crimson Sunset'	Purple-red	8–9	Yellow, red in winter	30	Wide, compact
'Cuprea'	Purple	8–9	Yellow-green, red-brown in winter	40	Erect
'C. W. Nix'	Violet-red	8–9		60	Semi-erect
'Dainty Bess'	Light purple-pink	9–10	Bluish green, woolly pilose	10	Prostrate
'Darkness'	Purple-red	8–9		30	Thick, erect
'Dart's Brillant'	Lilac-pink	7–9		60	Erect
'Dart's Flamboyant'	Lavender	7–9	Yellow-orange, orange-red in winter	15	Prostrate
'David Eason'	Lilac	9–11		30	Procumbent
'Dirry'	Reddish violet	8–10	Dark green	15	Prostrate
'Elegantissima'	Pure white	8–9	Gray-green	50	Erect
'Elsie Purnell'	Pink-red, double	8–9	Gray-green	70	Ascending
'Fairy'	Purple-pink, sparse	8–9	Golden-yellow, orange in winter	40	Ascending
'Finale'	Purple	10–12	Brownish green	60	Erect
'Foxii Nana'	Violet-purple	7–9	Bronze in winter	20	Half-spherical, cushion
'Golden Carpet'	Pale purple-pink	8–9	Golden-yellow, bronze-yellow in winter	5	Prostrate, slow growing

Calluna Vulgaris Varieties (cont.)

Cultivar	Flowers	Months	Special Leaf Color	Height (cm)	Growth Character
'Golden Rivulet'	Light purple-violet	8–9	Gold-yellow, copper-red in winter	25	Wide and flat growing
'Gold Haze'	White	8–9	Remains gold-yellow	70	Erect
'Goldsworth Crimson'	Violet-red, sparse	10–11		60	Erect
'Hammondii'	White	8	Fresh green	70	Erect
'H. E. Beale'	Pink, double	9–10		60	Erect, loose
'Heidezwerg'	Lilac, sparse	8–9		15	Carpet-like
'J. H. Hamilton'	Salmon-pink, double	8–9	Bronze-green	25	Prostrate, compact
'Joan Sparkes'	Lilac, double	8–9		40	Wide, compact
'Kinlochruel'	White, double	8–9		30	Erect, slow growing
'Long White'	Pure white	9–10		45	Erect, loose
'Marleen'	Lilac-red	9–11		40	Erect
'Mrs. Ronald Gray'	Reddish	8–9		10	Prostrate, turf forming
'Mullion'	Dark mallow-lilac	8–9		30	Carpet-like, cushion-form
'Multicolor'	Light violet-purple	7–8	Yellowish green, twig tips red in winter	30	Wide and flat
'Orange Queen'	Mallow-pink	6–9	Yellow-green, yellow with orange in winter	50	Erect
'Peter Sparkes'	Deep pink, double	9–11		50	Semi-erect
'Radnor'	Light pink, double	8		25	Compact, semi-erect
'Ralph Purnell'	Purple-violet	9	Brownish green in winter		Prostrate, semi-erect
'Rica'	Pale lilac	7–8		10	Wide, compact
'Robert Chapman'	Pale lilac	8	Yellow; robust red in winter	40	Erect
'Roland Hagen'	Pale lavender	8–9	Bright gold-yellow; orange with bronze tops in winter	15	Prostrate
'Schurig's Sensation'	Purplish pink	9–10		60	Erect
'Serlei'	White	9–10	Emerald green	60	Erect
'Silver Cloud'	Pale lilac	8	Striking silver pilose	40	Wide and loose
'Silver Knight'	Pale lilac	8	Silver pilose	30	Erect
'Silver Queen'	Lilac	8–9	Silver-gray	30	Prostrate, semi-erect

Calluna Vulgaris Varieties (cont.)

Cultivar	Flowers	Months	Special Leaf Color	Height (cm)	Growth Character
'Sir John Charrington'	Purplish red	8–9	Yellow; reddish in winter	30	Erect; compact
'Spring Cream'	White	8–9	Fresh green cream-white branch tips	45	Erect
'Spring Torch'	Pink	8	Vermillion-red twig tips	30	Erect
'Sunset'	Pink, sparse	8–9	Bronze-yellow; redder in winter	20	Wide and flat
'Tenuis'	Scarlet-red	6–9		15	Loose and pendulous
'Tib'	Purple-violet, double	7–8		30	Erect; slow growing
'Tom Thumb'	Pink	8	Brownish green in winter	15	Moss-like
'Underwoodii'	Ivory- to silvery-pink	8–10		30	Erect
'Visser's Fany'	Pale lilac	8–10		50	Erect
'White Lawn'	White	8–9	Light green	10	Compact; prostrate
'Wickwar Flame'	Pale pink	8–9	Golden-orange, deep orange in winter	45	Erect

*In northwestern Europe; 1 = January, 12 = December

Caragana jubata, Leguminosae

Natural habitat: The deserts and steppes from eastern Siberia to western China and Turkey.

This species has short, thick branches which are densely armed with 3 cm long thorns emerging from the leaf axils. About 1 m high, it develops very irregularly and is sparsely branched. Its pinnate leaves, with 2 to 3 paired leaflets, are closely grouped, 1 cm long and oblong-lance shaped.

C. jubata (Zone 2) is a very striking, unusual dwarf shrub suited for dry, sunny locations in steppe gardens. It is extremely drought resistant and thrives well in lime soil.

Its relatives, *C. aurantiaca* and *C. pygmaea* are also quite drought resistant and lime-loving, but are usually only cultivated in botanical gardens.

Caryopteris × clandonensis, Verbenaceae

C. × *clandonensis* (Zone 5) belongs to a group of hybrids which originate from *C. incana* × *C. mongholica*. As a 0.5 to 1 m tall, aromatic shrub, it develops from a dense growth of canes.

Its leaves are lance-shaped, deep green on top and silver-gray tomentose underneath. Dark blue blossoms develop in the leaf axils in late summer or fall. It is notable as a drought resistant, summer-blooming shrub.

In addition to C. × c. 'Arthur Simmonds', developed in 1930 in England by A. Simmonds, the two following cultivars are also common in cultivatation:

C. × c. 'Heavenly Blue' is distinguished by its glowing, deep, dark blue blossoms and abundant inflorescences. This erect shrub grows to 1 m tall and is at least as wide. Its leaves are dull green on top and gray-tomentose underneath.

C. × c. 'Kew Blue' is an erect shrub. Leaves are green on top and silver pilose underneath. Dark blue blossoms are arranged in broad inflorescences with up to 20 blossoms.

Caragana jubata

Caryopteris incana is native to Japan and eastern China. It is an aromatic shrub, hardly more than 1 m tall. It has gray-tomentose branches and leaves; violet-blue blossoms open in September. It is used less often than the cultivars of C. × *clandonensis*, 'Heavenly Blue' and C. × c. 'Kew Blue'.

Caryopteris × *clandonensis*

These plants are particularly garden-worthy because they bloom late and their blossoms are blue, which is unusual among trees and shrubs. However, the canes are not very frost hardy. The soil around them should be mulched in winter. If injured by frost, cut out damaged stems in spring. These drought resistant plants grow best in sunny locations in well drained lime loam soil or other generally mineral rich soil.

They are used in rock, heath, prairie and steppe gardens, together with dwarf conifers, other gray-leafed trees and shrubs or silver-leafed shrubs (*Lavandula, Salvia, Achillea, Stachys* and *Veronica*) and grasses. They, like silver-leafed shrubs and grasses, are good companion plants for red and pink blossoming roses or *Potentilla fruticosa* cultivars.

115

Caryopteris 'Kew Blue'

Cassiope tetragona, Ericaceae

C. tetragona (Zone 3) is an attractive component of natural dwarf shrub heaths in subarctic and arctic Europe, Asia and North America.

An erect, evergreen, dwarf shrub, *Cassiope tetragona* grows to only 30 cm. It has tiny, thick, overlapping scale-like leaves, arranged in four rows. Its white, often pink-tinged, blossoms are bell-shaped and develop on the leaf axils or the shoot tips in spring.

Cassiope wardii (Zone 4) cultivar 'Edinburgh' originated in the Royal Botanical Garden in Edinburgh probably as a seedling of *C. fastigiata* × *C. tetragona*. This robust hybrid is distinguished by its vigorous, healthy growth, deep green leaves and large, cream-white, terminal blossoms. It is a good alternative to *C. tetragona*, which does not flower as well, but is more frost hardy and flowers better.

Other species in this genus are not as easily cultivated as *C. tetragona*. However,

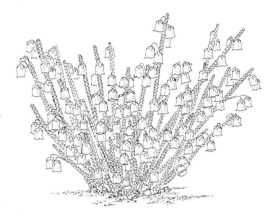

Cassiope 'Edinburgh'

Kummert (1977) claims that *C. lycopodioides* (Zone 3) from northeast Asia or *C. mertensiana* (Zone 5) from western North America (from Alaska and Canada southwards to the Cascade and Sierra Nevada Mountains) are easy to cultivate.

Cassiope species grow best in damp to moist, peat-rich, sandy-rocky, acid soils (pH levels of 4 to 4.5). Irrigation water should be as free of lime as possible. Cassiopes should be planted in a site having dappled light and partial shade, such as is cast by nearby trees, shrubs or even large rocks in rock gardens. *C. tetragona* is beautiful planted in groups and makes a good companion plant for rhododendrons. They cannot be grown in warm climates.

Ceanothus americanus, Rhamnaceae

C. americanus (Zone 4) is found on rocky or gravel hillsides in open, dry, deciduous forests and on the fringes of prairies in eastern and central North America. In central Oregon it grows in pure pumice soils in native pine forests.

This deciduous shrub is dense and widespreading to 1 m tall. It is one of the most frost hardy of the *Ceanothus* species. Its leaves are narrow egg-shaped, 3–10 cm long, sea-green on top and paler green underneath. From midsummer until autumn, myriads of small white blossoms, loosely aggregated into beautiful panicles, appear; these blossoms are intensely fragrant. Flower heads are located both in the leaf axils and at the end of new shoots. In late summer the plant is adorned with brownish red, flesh-colored or dried baccate fruits.

C. americanus will thrive in almost any well drained soil. It can be used in all kinds of locations, as long as they are sunny, warm, fairly dry and well protected. As is the case with many summer blooming dwarf shrubs, *C. americanus* may be pruned back to very short stubs (stools) in spring. In colder climates, the plant should be well mulched to protect from frost heaving and winter drought.

C. ovatus, from the Great Plains eastward, is very similar, almost as hardy, and far more showy as well as fragrant. This species is just coming on the market for the first time.

Ceanothus hybrids, Rhamnaceae

Included with the deciduous *Ceanothus* hybrids are all the cultivars of *C.* × *delilianus* (collective name for all blue flowered cultivars) and *C.* × *pallidus* (collective name for all pink and white flowered cultivars). Most of these hybrids were developed in France before 1900.

C. 'Gloire de Versailles' has dark blue, large panicles which bloom from midsummer to first frost. It grows vigorously, and is one of the most popular cultivars.

C. 'Henry Défossé' is a medium-sized plant with dark blue blossoms in large trusses.

C. 'Marie Simon' remains relatively short and is the most beautiful pink blooming cultivar. It blooms from midsummer to early fall.

C. 'Topaze' has delicate, indigo-blue blossoms. It blooms from midsummer to early fall and is more winter and summer fragile than most cultivars.

In locations where winter conditions do not stress the plants so they do not require heavy annual pruning, they may reach heights and widths of 1.5 to 2 m. Growing to that size, they can no longer be considered dwarf shrubs. Normally, however, these hybrids are pruned every spring, as is *C. americanus,* to prevent them from growing too large. As such, these are bushy, well branched shrubs about 1 m tall. Their landscape use and cultural requirements are similar to those of *C. americanus,* though these hybrids are, in general, intolerant of an inland climate. The following cultivars are winter hardy in U.S.D.A. Zone 6. (The soil should, however, still be mulched.)

Ceratostigma plumbaginoides, Plumbaginaceae

C. plumbaginoides (Zone 5) is found in the deciduous forests, steppes and arid regions of northern China.

This dense growing subshrub, 30 to 40 cm high, has a creeping habit with well branched, eight-sided upright twigs. Leaves are deep green on top, light green below, coloring bright red to reddish brown in fall. Deep blue, phlox-like flowers are borne in thick axillary or shoot-tip flower heads from September through October.

C. plumbaginoides is a very good deciduous ground cover for all sunny locations. It is also a beautiful solitary plant in rock and container gardens. It does well with other, warmth-loving plants such as *Ruta graveolens, Satureja montana, Artemisia abrotanoides, Helianthemum apenninum* and *Santolina chamaecyparissus.* It requires little care, quickly developing thick, uniform carpets. Its autumn blossoms and leaf color make it a very attractive addition to the fall garden.

Thriving in any loamy, well drained soil, *Ceratostigma* quickly spreads widely by way of vigorous underground runners. Soil should not be damp in fall. The plant also should not be fertilized too freely; too much moisture or fertilization encourage both overgrowth and a decrease in frost hardiness. Winter protection is recommended for harsher climates.

Chamaedaphne calyculata, Ericaceae

C. calyculata (Zone 2) is characteristic of dwarf plants in high and transitional moors in the northern part of the circumpolar temperate and arctic zones. It grows in the carpet of various *Sphagnum* species and in communities with *Betula nana, Andromeda polifolia, Ledum palustre, Vaccinium uliginosum* and *V. oxycoccos, Rubus chamaemorus* and various sedges.

C. calyculata is an evergreen shrub with wide spreading branches and firm, leathery leaves which are yellowish to rust-colored underneath. The terminal inflorescences bear drooping, bell-shaped blossoms and round, five-valved fruit capsules which open spontaneously.

C. calyculata 'Nana' is smaller than the species. Growing only 20 to 30 cm tall, its branches are short and spread horizontally. It is a beautiful, slow growing and long-lived moor plant. It prefers wet to damp locations in humusy, nutrient-poor

Chamaedaphne calyculata 'Nana'

soil. If humidity is high and air cool, it tolerates sunny locations, but in areas which have warm summers, it does better in partly shady locations. It can be used as a specimen plant, or in small groups in the garden on flat surfaces, in rock gardens, or damp sections of larger heath gardens. It looks well as a companion plant for rhododendrons.

Clematis alpina

Clematis alpina, Ranunculaceae

C. alpina (Zone 5) is native to the European Alps. Its distribution is limited largely to the limestone areas in the mountains where it vigorously sprawls over dwarf mountain pines and other shrubs, and is found growing with *Erica herbacea, Valeriana montana, Globularia nudicaulis, Veronica urticifolia, Homogyne alpine, Saxifraga rotundifolia* and *Sesleria varia.*

This trailing semi-woody creeper seldom grows as high as 2 m tall. It usually grows more horizontally over larger rocks or on small trees and shrubs. Its leaves are usually doubly ternate and the leaflets are evenly, finely serrate. In spring, dozens of solitary bell-shaped blossoms in various shades of blue are freely borne on the ends of the branches.

C. alpina prefers damp to moist, lime soil and cool, northern exposures. It tolerates shade well, and is an especially decorative rock garden plant, for niches of garden steps or partly shaded dry walls.

Clematis integrifolia, Ranunculaceae

C. integrifolia (Zone 2–3) is found along the Danube from southeastern Europe to southwestern Russia and western Asia. Natively it is exclusive to meadows, wet to dry slopes and bushy hillsides.

This herbaceous, non-climbing species grows 80 and 100 cm tall. Its leaves are undivided, sessile, oval and about 6–10 cm long. Its loose, bell-shaped blossoms droop gracefully. Flowers are 4 to 5 cm wide, and appear singly on the shoots in summer with wavy and often recurved sepals. Outside, they are lilac and inside, purple or dark blue. This species is especially attractive near the end of its

Clematis integrifolia

to the inside, and are lighter-colored inside. The blossoms appear as if they have been filled, and so distended.

This is one of the most beautiful of the hardy species for rock gardens. It has about the same requirements and is used in the same manner as *C. integrifolia*.

Cornus canadensis, Cornaceae

C. canadensis (Zone 2) is found in northern and arctic North America; east as far as the Allegheny mountain range, to the west along the Coast Range and south in the Cascades to northern California. On the western hillsides of the Cascades it appears as a ground cover in coniferous forests, together with *Mahonia nervosa*, *Rhododendron albiflorum*, *Menziesia ferruginea* and many other choice shrubs.

This species is not really a shrub, rather an evergreen perennial, but because it is raised in nurseries and sold as one, it is included here. This is also true of *C. suecica*,

blooming period, when feathery seed heads develop among the late blossoms.

C. integrifolia is an outstanding if large rock garden plant. It requires ample growing space and is attractive when allowed to spread over large rocks. It thrives in damp to moist, rich, lime soil. It is winter hardy and does well in shady locations.

Clematis macropetala, Ranunculaceae

C. macropetala (Zone 5) is native to the deciduous and coniferous forests of Manchuria and Siberia.

This slow growing herbaceous perennial seldom reaches 1m in height. Its leaves are usually doubly ternate and the 9 leaflets are egg-shaped to lance-shaped, coarsely serrate or lobed. Its drooping blossoms, borne singly, are 5 to 10 cm wide, the 4 sepals vary from blue to a more violet hue. Its numerous lance-shaped violet-blue stamminoides are arranged in concentric rings, shorter from the outside

Cornus canadensis

which is differentiated from *C. canadensis* by the terminal leaves which are opposite rather than whorled.

C. canadensis grows to be 10 to 20 cm tall. Its leaves are whorled, ovate, 2 to 4 cm long, with brownish red overtones in autumn. Its undistinguished, greenish red blossoms appear at the shoot tips in June. Flower clusters are surrounded by 4 large, white bracts in the manner of flowering dogwood. The berry-like clustered drupes are bright red in autumn; a beautiful sight.

C. canadensis thrives in partly shady to shady locations in damp, acid soils or acid humus of the woodland floor. If densely planted, they knit together and make a tight ground cover. They are a wonderfully decorative ground cover for moor beds and heath gardens, and are not at all competitive with dwarf trees and shrubs.

Cotoneaster adpressa, Rosaceae

C. adpressa (Zone 5) is found at higher elevations (about 3000 m) in the deciduous forests of western China.

It is a robust, low growing but densely branched, prostrate, deciduous shrub hardly reaching 25 cm tall. Its branches hug the ground. Its small, ovate, matte green leaves with wavy margins turn orange-red in fall. A June display of pinkish-white blossoms is followed by 0.7 cm long, nearly round, fruits. Bright red in fall and winter, the fruits are uncommonly showy.

C. a. 'Little Gem' is substantially smaller. This cultivar is a roundish bush, hardly more than 10 cm tall. Its prostrate branches root down, so the shrub spreads. Its leaves are 7 to 10 mm long, arranged in two rows, wavy, turn red in autumn and then fall off.

None of the *Cotoneaster* species require special consideration if planted in good garden sites. They grow in all soils, tolerate sunny to partly shady locations, and are very attractive to bees. They can be used many ways. The dwarf species can be used singly or in groups in all sorts of locations, together with roses, barberrys, brooms and coniferous trees and shrubs. Cotoneasters often show stress where summers are hot.

C. adpressa thrive in rock gardens, and *C. a.* 'Little Gem' is very well suited for container gardens.

Cotoneaster congesta, Rosaceae

The evergreen laurel forest regions in the Himalayas, in which the climate is characterized by high summer temperatures and heavy precipitation, are the natural habitat for this species.

C. congesta (Zone 6) is a beautiful dwarf shrub with prostrate branches which nestle against the contours of the earth. Together with close-set ovate, 6–12 mm long, evergreen leaves, they form a thick, compact mat. The plant rarely exceeds 70 cm tall. Its leaves are a neutral green on top and white below and take on a reddish tinge in fall. Blossoms are light pink and are large for cotoneaster. Flowers appear in spring and are followed by a sometimes sparse set of berries. Both the fruit and blossoms are often hidden beneath the foliage.

This plant is especially good for rock and container gardens. See *C. adpressa* for cultural requirements.

Cotoneaster conspicua 'Decora', Rosaceae

In its alpine sites and the damp summer forest of southeastern Tibet, the native species, C. conspicua (Zone 6), can grow to be taller than a person, given time.

The growth habit of C. i. 'Decorus', on the other hand, is mat-like with short, spreading branches. The branches are covered with handsome, thick, dark, evergreen leaves which are pilose beneath. Innumerable small white blossoms appear in spring, followed in autumn by an abundant crop of roundish, 9 mm long, bright orange-red fruit.

This is an elegant dwarf shrub for rock and heath gardens. It may be damaged in severe, sunny winters when no snow is present to protect it.

Cotoneaster dammeri, Rosaceae

Its natural habitat is the alpine deciduous forest of central China.

C. dammeri (Zone 5) is a creeping, evergreen shrub which covers the ground with rooting branches. The branches are covered with 2–3(5) cm long, oval, leathery leaves arranged formally in two rows. In contrast to the garden cultivar C. d. 'Major', its leaves do not turn color in fall. In spring, large, white to light pink blossoms appear. Round, scarlet-red fruit clings to the shrub well into the winter.

C. dammeri and its garden cultivars are very hardy and require little special maintenance. They grow in any good garden soil in sunny to partly shady locations. All of them make ideal ground covers. In using them, however, the individual habit of the various cultivars must be kept in mind. Fast growing cultivars 'Coral Beauty', 'Eichholz', 'Hachmanns Winterjuwel' and 'Skogholm' can only be planted in larger areas.

With the exception of the slow growing C. d. 'Streib's Findling', all the cultivars are vigorous growers. When used as ground covers or to face down shrub borders, they cover the area between trees and shrubs very quickly and develop a dense mat. They can be troublesome for slow growing dwarf plants, but are not so overwhelming as to deter most bulbs from flowering. These cotoneasters are very well suited for container gardens or atop garden retaining walls; in fact, walls are quickly covered by their thick-leaved, pendant branches.

C. dammeri 'Major' is a very popular cultivar. It differs from the species only by more vigorous growth and longer leaves, which turn a showy shade of yellow-orange in fall.

C. dammeri var. radicans is found in western Sichuan Province. It differs from the species in that its leaves are smaller (1–1.5 cm long) and it is more frost hardy.

Vigorous growing, large leaved selections such as 'Mooncreeper', 'Rapid' and 'Typ Sürth' or the slow growing, small leafed 'Schweizer Typ' can also be cultivated in some areas.

C. d. 'Streib's Findling' varies markedly in habit from the other cultivars. Its growth is slow and compact and its leaves are small (8–15 mm long) and elliptic. It is especially well suited for small containers.

Cotoneaster horizontalis 'Saxatilis', Rosaceae

This plant's natural range is, as is the case of many East Asian species, in the higher elevations of deciduous hardwood forests in western China (Zones 4–5).

This is the most commonly planted *Cotoneaster* cultivar. It seldom exceeds 40 cm tall, but is often many times wider. When used as a trailing shrub against a wall however, the normally prostrate branches grow as much as 2 m up the wall.

C. h. 'Saxatilis' is really more of a slow growing selection than a truly dwarf shrub. Its fish-bone-like, almost horizontal branching is even more uniform than the species. It even looks a little stiff. Its thick, almost round leaves are only 8 to 10 mm across. They are not as intensely colored as the leaves on the species, and its ability to produce fruit leaves something to be desired.

This plant makes a good summer half-evergreen, rock garden plant. Because of its slow growth, it can be used in small areas. It needs a protected site as it can be damaged in severe winters.

Cotoneaster microphylla 'Cochleatus', Rosaceae

The evergreen species is found at higher elevations in the evergreen forests of western and southwestern China and the Himalayas (Zone 5–6). Plant this delicate cotoneaster clone only in quite sheltered sites because it is barely frost tolerant.

C. m. 'Cochleatus', which is sometimes labeled *C. m. melanotrichus* in nurseries, is much frost hardier than the species. At 30 to 40 cm tall it is also shorter than the species' height of 1 m. It has thick, pendulous branches and small, oval, glossy dark green leaves. Fruits begin to redden as early as September. It is a gorgeous *Cotoneaster* with an impressive habit.

C. m. 'Cochleatus' is best planted singly in rock or container gardens; it is also well suited for enlivening small display gardens. It thrives in sunny to partly shady locations and tolerates rather dry sites.

C. m. f. *thymifolia,* which originated in Kashmir and Sikkim, is undoubtedly the smallest and most beautiful of all *Cotoneaster* cultivars. Its growth is very compact with flat prostrate branches. Leaves are thick, spirally arranged, glossy dark green and 4 to 15 mm long. It is not fully frost hardy and requires a partly shady, protected location.

Cotoneaster praecox, Rosaceae

The native range of *C. praecox* (Zone 5) is the rocky steppes in the Nan Shan

Cotoneaster horizontalis 'Saxatile'

mountain range in the western Chinese province of Sichuan. Some taxonomists consider this plant to be a variety of *Cotoneaster adpressa.*

This deciduous shrub grows to only 50 cm tall. Its branches are gracefully pendulous and may spread to a width of 1 m. Its leaves are waxy, glossy dark green, turn brilliant red in autumn and fall off soon thereafter. Numerous large pink blossoms develop in spring; 8–12 mm red fruits mature in autumn, and fall soon after turning red. This is an exceptionally good garden ornamental.

Plant *C. praecox* as a specimen shrub in larger rock gardens or plant singly in containers. It can be kept fairly dry in sunny to partly shady spots. It does not do well planted on flat surfaces.

Cytisus, Leguminosae

This genus includes a great number of dwarf species. Almost all of them originated on the rocky steppes in Mediterranean or sub-Mediterranean

Cotoneaster praecox

chaparral, rough meadows, rocky slopes or scree slopes. Their natural habitat gives a good clue to their preferences for planting sites in gardens: all thrive best in sunny, warm locations in well drained, lime or sandy-humus, nutrient-poor soils. They can easily lose their typical habit if soil is too fertile. They do well in heath, rock and container gardens, on retaining walls and in niches of garden steps. They can be accompanied by other dwarf plants, shrubs and grasses, for example: *Ruta graveolens, Santolina chamaecyparissus, Lavandula angustifolia, Dianthus deltoides, Thymus serpyllum, Centranthus ruber, Euphorbia myrsinites,* the smaller lilies, *Festuca glauca* and *F. scoparia.* They also make companion plants for dwarf pines and spruces.

Cytisus × beanii, Leguminosae

This hybrid of *C. ardoinii* (Zone 7) (which comes from the western Mediterranean area) and *C. purgans,* was bred in 1900 in Kew Gardens, London, England.

C. × beanii grows to 40 cm tall and 80 cm wide. Its habit is nearly prostrate and wide-spread. Its leaves are simple, linear and about 12 mm long. Its deep yellow pea-like blossoms are arranged in clusters of 1 to 3 at the leaf axils. This is a beautiful, low growing broom, which flowers heavily in spring.

Refer to *Cytisus* for cultural requirements and garden uses.

Cytisus decumbens, Leguminosae

C. decumbens (Zone 5) is found in Albania, through Dalmatia, Yugoslavia and central Italy to southern and central France; in rough meadows as well as in sparse pine and oak forests on lime soil.

C. decumbens grows 15 to 20 cm tall. Its branches are prostrate, wide-spreading or creeping. Despite its low height this shrub can cover several square meters within ten years. Its simple, elliptic leaves are 8–20 mm long and thickly pilose beneath. In midspring the entire shrub is densely covered with gold-yellow blossoms.

With its numerous blossoms, this is one of the most beautiful of all dwarf Brooms. It is also frost hardy and drought resistant. It should be planted singly or in small groups alongside rock plants. If it is planted in heavy soil, or too close together, it soon loses its leaves and deteriorates.

Cytisus × kewensis, Leguminosae

Cytissus × kewensis (Zone 6) was developed in 1891 in Kew Gardens, London, England, as a hybrid of *C. ardoinii* and *C. multiflorus*.

C. × kewensis is only 30 cm tall, but up to 2 m wide. It is a creeping, prostrate shrub with slender, projecting branches. Its leaves are usually trifoliate, rarely simple. Large, cream-white to sulfur-yellow blossoms appear in May on the previous year's shoots.

Cytisus purpureus, Leguminosae

C. purpureus (Zone 5) is found in central and southeastern Europe in scrub forests and on rocky slopes. It thrives especially well on lime rock debris in sub-Mediterranean climates.

C. purpureus is a procumbent shrub 60 cm tall with green spreading-ascending branches. The leaflets of its trifoliate leaves are elliptic, up to 2.5 cm long and glabrous or ciliate. In late spring its branches are covered their entire length with large, lilac or purple-pink blossoms.

C. purpureus 'Atropurpureus' is considered to be more valuable in the garden than its species because of its numerous, dark purple-pink blossoms and flat, more prostrate habit. The species was considered passé in Holland, whereas this cultivar was distinguished with 2 stars when judged along with hundreds of others at Boskoop.

Other cultivars of *C. purpureus* include: *C. p.* 'Alba'; *C. p. albo-carneus*, flowers pale pink; *C. p.* 'Erectus', upright-growing; and *C. p.* 'Elongatus', with slender branchlets and violet-purple flowers.

Cytisus scoparius 'Dukaat', Leguminosae

This F_2 selection originated from a cross between *C. praecox* × *C. scoparius* 'Burkwoodii' at the Boskoop Experiment Station in The Netherlands.

C. × 'Dukaat' grows densely and stiffly erect to a height of 50 cm. Individual branches may grow more vigorously than others, so it is important to prune them out in order to maintain the plant's dwarf habit. Its large blossoms are two tones of yellow (its flag and keel are light yellow, the wings are darker). *C. ×* 'Dukaat' blooms longer than other *Cytisus* species and cultivars.

This is the only cultivar available among brooms which has the potential to grow as tall as a man, yet it remains dwarfed and is valuable in a garden. It is also called 'Golddukaat' in nurseries.

Cytisus scoparius 'Prostratus'

Daboecia cantabrica, Ericaceae

D. cantabrica (Zone 5) occurs on acid peat in heaths along the oceanic coastlines from northern Ireland to northern Portugal and in the Cantabrica Mountain Range in Spain.

This well branched evergreen dwarf shrub reaches to 25–30 cm. It has small, leathery, elliptic leaves; wavy on the edges, glossy green on top, and white-tomentose underneath. Convex, cylindrical blossoms are borne from summer through fall. Flowers are purple, and arranged in 10 to 12 cm long, terminal clusters.

As is the case with many other species, popular cultivars of *Daboecia* have been vegetatively reproduced for sale in nurseries. The following are examples:

D. 'Alba Globosa' has white, more or less globe-shaped blossoms which are 10 mm long. Leaves are light green and its habit is tall and stiffly erect.

D. 'Cinderella' has globe-shaped, white blossoms with delicate pink tinges. Leaves are dark green. Habit is wide spreading and erect. It is a beautiful cultivar and received a Gold Medal at the Herfstweelde 1978 in Boskoop, The Netherlands.

D. 'Praegerae' has interesting, salmon-colored blossoms. It is more frost tender than other cultivars, but was nevertheless awarded 3 stars in South Holland.

D. 'Wijnie' has a broad, erect habit and grows to a height of 35 cm. Blossoms are pinkish red, with 12 mm long, wide elliptic leaves. This cultivar also won a Gold Medal at the Herfstweelde 1978 in Boskoop, The Netherlands.

D. 'William Buchanan' is a very important cultivar despite its small, 8 mm long blossoms. It grows to be 20 to 25 cm tall, has violet-red blossoms which bloom from July to October, and glossy, dark green leaves.

D. cantabrica and its cultivars are ideal in small heath gardens. If used in larger heath gardens, Calluna or Erica species and cultivars should be interplanted in drifts. It requires damp, light, peaty, lime-free soil and open, sunny locations. Outside its natural habitat it is only moderately hardy and should be covered with evergreen branches for winter protection. It is intolerant of hot weather, either humid or dry.

Daboecia cantabrica

Daphne alpina, Thymelaeaceae

D. alpina (Zone 5) is found in the Pyrenees, in southern France, in the Alps, the Juras and in the hills and alpine levels from the Tyrol to Dalmatia, Yugoslavia. It grows in moist, calcium-rich, rocky subalpine soils and scree-covered slopes. In such locations it is accompanied by Juniperus communis, Globularia cordifolia, Stipa pennata, Polygonatum officinale, Helianthemum nummularium, Teucrium alpinum and Thymus serpyllum.

D. alpina is a 15 to 30 cm tall, dense, deciduous shrub with short, twisting, ascending, tangled branches. Its leaves are gray-green and are compactly arranged on the branch tips.

White, strongly vanilla-scented blossoms in clusters of 4 to 10 develop in late spring in the axils of the upper leaves .Red fruit is oblong-ovate.

D. alpina is a robust, long-lived Daphne, often planted in alpine gardens, in sunny locations in loose, lime-humus soil to which crushed rock or sharp gravel has been added. It sometimes reseeds itself in gardens, even in sandy-acid soil where it is short-lived.

Daphne altaica, Thymelaeaceae

D. altaica's (Zone 5) natural habitat is in the mountain ranges of Altai and Sungari.

This usually deciduous shrub may be evergreen in favorable climates. When mature, it reaches a maximum height of 75 cm, and has about the same circumference. Its dull green leaves are narrow, oblong and 3 to 6 cm long. Its white, lightly fragrant blossoms appear in late summer in terminal clusters of 6–10. Normally it develops a second, comparatively rich flower display in autumn.

Daboecia cantabrica 'Alba'

D. altaica is one of the most robust and long-lived of the *Daphne* species. It thrives in a humus-rich, well drained, alkaline soil in sunny to partly shady locations.

Daphne blagayana

Daphne blagayana, Thymelaeaceae

The midpoint of *D. blagayana*'s (Zone 6) natural habitat is Bosnia-Herzegovina and Serbia in Yugoslavia. From there, it radiates out to Albania, Bulgaria and Romania. It is found in the inner Balkan Austrian pine forests, the *Pinus leucodermis* forests and Bosnian mountain ranges under *Picea omorika* in lime, dolomite and serpentine soils. It is usually found growing with *Juniperus communis* var. *montana, Rhamnus fallax, Erica carnea, Daphne oleoides, Genista sylvestris* var. *pungens, Thymus hirsutus, Globularia nana, Helleborus odorus, Anemone nemorosa, Potentilla carniolica, Primula elatior* ssp. *elatior* and *Scilla bifolia*.

    D. blagayana is a 15 to 30 cm tall, low spreading, twiggy, evergreen dwarf shrub. In its natural habitat, creeping branches sprawl, but in gardens they form a dense, tight cushion. Its 3 to 4 cm long, obovate leaves are clustered on the ends of the branches. Yellowish white, strongly fragrant blossoms are borne in terminal clusters of 10 to 20 in early spring.

D. blagayana thrives in a partly shady to shady site in porous, stony, lime enriched woodland soil. The soil should be well drained, but should not be allowed to completely dry out.

Daphne × burkwoodii 'Somerset', Thymelaeaceae

This is one of the most commonly cultivated Daphnes. It is a hybrid between the deciduous *D. caucasica* and the evergreen *D. cneorum*.

D. 'Somerset' (Zone 5–6) grows 1.5–1.8 m tall and in most areas is deciduous. In warm climates it grows much taller and is usually evergreen. It is bushy when young but as it matures becomes more open; leaves are narrow, dark green. In May, its branches almost disappear beneath masses of fragrant light pink blossoms. The blooming period is comparatively long. *D.* 'Somerset' begins to bloom in late summer as a very young shrub, and continues to do so regularly as it matures.

This beautiful shrub fits well in heath gardens with pines and junipers. It thrives in sunny locations in any well drained, pH neutral garden soil. Unfortunately, it is very susceptible to several fungus diseases.

Daphne cneorum, Thymelaeaceae

D. cneorum (Zone 5) is found in northern Spain, southern and central France, Switzerland, northern Italy, Austria and from the northern Balkans into Russia. It is native to the mountainous areas of the northern Alps and central European mountains. In the southern Alps, it grows into the alpine zone. It is a typical member of a group of plants which require a warm, sun-drenched habitat and which are often found growing in meadow communities, on sunny slopes and meager hillsides with *Cytisus nigricans, Genista sagittalis, Aster amellus, Prunella grandiflora, Geranium sanguineum, Pulsatilla vulgaris, Adonis vernalis, Helianthemum canum* and *Bupleurum longifolium.*

D. cneorum is an evergreen, cushion-like shrub 20 to 30 cm tall with brown branches. Leaves, which are dark green above and blue-green on the undersides, are crowded toward the shoot tips and resemble rosemary foliage. Blossoms appear in early spring with a scent very much like carnations; they are arranged in terminal clusters of 6 to 8. The shrub is so heavily laden with them that its foliage may be almost obscured.

Many beautiful dwarf *Daphne* cultivars have been developed. England has many such cultivars. *D. cneorum* var. *verlotii* is an example. It originated in southeastern France; and is distinguished from the species by looser inflorescence and even heavier flowering, longer calyx tubes and narrower calyx segments.

D. 'Eximia' also blooms heavily. It is taller than the species and its blossoms are deep pink. Similar attributes are true of *D.* 'Major', which is found in Holland.

D. cneorum thrives in the alpine garden, in dry walls, or rock gardens, preferably in sunny or lightly shaded areas. It requires limy, well-drained soil to which humus, gravel, pumice or lava cinders have been added to ensure good drainage and aeration. *D. cneorum* is a good companion

Daphne cneorum 'Eximia'

plant for *Cytisus decumbens*, *Genista pilosa*, *Dryas octopetala*, *Globularia cordifolia*, *Gentiana angulosa* and *Sedum sexangulare*.

Daphne laureola, Thymelaeaceae

As a typical forest plant, *D. laureola* (Zone 6–7) is found in sub-Mediterranean-Atlantic beech wood regions in the western Mediterranean. Elsewhere, it is found in North Africa, the Azores, southern Germany, Scotland and from the southern Alps to the Balkans. In mature forests of oaks and beech in central Europe, *D. laureola* is accompanied by *Helleborus foetidus*, *Euphorbia amygdaloides*, *Hepatica nobilis*, *Primula acaulis*, *Luzula nivea*, *Sanicula europaea*, *Asperula odorata* and *Teucrium scorodonia*. In warmer loca-

tions, such as the stoney meadows near Lake Garda in northern Italy, it is accompanied by *Helleborus niger*, *Dictamnus albus*, *Ruta graveolens*, *Inula hirta* and *Carex baldensis*.

D. laureola is an erect, evergreen shrub with laurel-like foliage. Under favorable conditions it grows to 1 m. The glossy, oblanceolate, dark green, leaves are up to 8 cm long. Yellowish green blossoms, sessile or with short pedicels, appear in spring in clusters of 5 to 10. Fruit is bluish black, ovate.

D. laureola ssp. *philippi* is found in the Pyrenees. It is shorter than the species, reaching a height of 20 to 40 cm, and is also more frost hardy.

D. laureola is a decorative, evergreen dwarf shrub suitable for all partly shady locations. It does well under dappled shade from trees, as long as the soil is kept damp. It thrives in moist, porous, lime-humus rich woodland soil. Where winters may be harsh, protect the plants with a mulch of humus and mound a loose covering of evergreen boughs over the plants.

Daphne mezereum, Thymelaeaceae

D. mezereum (Zone 4) has the largest natural range of any daphne species. It extends from the Pyrenees throughout western Europe, southern England, Scandinavia and Finland to central Siberia.

D. mezereum grows naturally through a range of ecosystems on lime substrate. It is found in forested highlands as well as in lower mountainous locations; in pure or mixed beech woods rich in herbaceous species where the soil is porous, loose, humusy, and continuously moist.

When mature, *D. mezereum* is an almost ball-shaped, moderately branched, deciduous shrub 1 m tall. Its branches are flexible, glabrous and thick. Leaves are thin, bright green on top and bluish-green underneath. Long before leaves appear, the branches are covered with clusters of fragrant, carmine blossoms. During the summer, bright red berries develop, replacing the flower clusters. Berries are beautiful but very poisonous; if eaten, can lead to serious stomach and intestinal problems.

In addition to the species, there are a few varieties worth mentioning:

D. mesereum f. *alba* appears in the wild and can be reproduced by seed, often coming true. Growth is narrowly upright; blossoms are pure white and the fruit is pale yellow.

D. m 'Ruby Select' or 'Ruby Glow' cultivars are not true vegetatively reproduced clones; rather, they are a population of plants, out of which dark blooming cultivars are chosen and used for futher propagation.

D. mezereum is one of the best known late winter flowering shrubs. Plant it in locations where children cannot get hold of its poisonous berries. It takes partly shady to shady locations, but can thrive in open locations where the climate is not too harsh winter or summer, and the soil is not too dry. It grows in forests in fertile, damp, lime soil. The cultural requirements of *D. mezereum* are not especially demanding as it will grow in loamy soil, but does better in sand. It does well when planted with other late winter and early spring flowering ornamentals such as *Erica carnea*, *Galanthus nivalis*, *Eranthis hyemalis*, *Helleborus niger*, *Leucojum vernum*, *Hepatica nobilis* and *H. transylvanica*.

Daphne pontica, Thymelaeaceae

D. pontica (Zone 6) is found in humid, damp mountainous forests of the eastern Balkan Peninsula and the Caucasus Mountains, with *Fagus orientalis*, *Abies bornmülleriana*, *Rhododendron ponticum*, *R. flavum*, *Hypericum calycinum*, *Prunus laurocerasus*, *Hedera colchica*, *Ilex colchica* and *Buxus sempervirens*.

D. pontica is distinguished from *D. blagayana* by its more upright, 80 cm tall habit, leathery, glossy dark green leaves and greenish yellow blossoms. Its abundantly produced, strongly fragrant blossoms develop in mid-spring, mostly 2 to a short penduncle, which develop in the leaf axes of the upper leaves.

D. pontica is not as difficult to grow as *D. blagayana*. It thrives on damp, lime-humus soil as well as fertile, loam soil. It is tolerant of shady locations as well as the drip of rainwater from larger trees and shrubs.

Daphne tangutica, Thymelaeaceae

D. tangutica (Zone 5–6) is native to the northern Chinese provinces of Gansu and northern Yunnan, where the winters are cold and the summers dry.

    D. tangutica is an evergreen shrub about 1 m tall. Year-old shoots are stout, gray bristly-pilose, and bear elliptic-oblong leaves which are 3 to 8 cm long and glossy on top. In early spring fragrant blossoms appear in terminal, 5 cm wide clusters. The flowers are purplish pink outside and lighter pink inside. Especially attractive are the clustered red fruits, which are about 1 cm diameter.

Deutzia gracilis

Deutzia gracilis, Saxifragaceae

D. gracilis (Zone 4) is an example of the very rich flora found in the warm, damp deciduous forests of Japan. It was introduced into Europe in 1840.

    D. gracilis is one of the most beautiful deutzias. It grows stiffly erect, to a height of hardly more than 70 cm. Its leaves are 3 to 6 cm long, light green and oblong-lanceolate. In late spring, pure white, 1.5–2 cm wide blossoms appear, grouped in 4 to 9 cm long erect clusters.

    D. gracilis is lovely when planted in groups in front gardens and narrow beds. Thanks to its rigid habit, it is also well suited for low hedges. It prefers damp, loam soil that also contains some lime; the plant is stressed by poor, sandy soil. It must be watered regularly in all soils. Annual recurrence of a full-blossoming cycle can only be expected when the plant is grown in sunny locations.

Dryas octopetala, Rosaceae

D. octopetala (Zone 2) is circumpolar in the high mountain ranges of the Northern Hemisphere. It is usually found in dry to damp, coarse or fine rock debris (screes or moraines), on calcium and dolomite limestones at altitudes up to 3000 m. In Scandinavian, carpathian and alpine areas, *D. octopetala* is often accompanied by *Salix reticulata, Arctostaphylos alpina, Polygonum viviparum, Parnassia palustris, Silena acaulis, Veronica saxatilis, Astragalus* and *Saxifraga* species. In dwarf shrub heaths on alpine humus, it is also accompanied by *Rhododendron hirsutum, Erica carnea* and *Rhodothamnus chamaecistus*.

    D. octopetala grows a thick, turf-like cushion, which conforms to the contours of the earth. Its evergreen leaves, which are glossy green on top and white-tomentose below, are deeply notched, curled at the edges, and with a heart-shaped base. Throughout the summer months, white, 4 cm wide, long-stalked flowers appear. The flowers fade leaving feathery, silvery-white fruits, which remain on the plant until winter.

D. × *suendermannii* (*D. drummondii* × *D. octopetala*) differs from *D. octopetala* in its drooping, yellow blossoms, an especially heavy set of flowers and fruit, and in its faster growth.

Both Dryas' are well suited for alpine gardens, heath gardens or any other sunny to partially shady location which is not excessively dry. *D.* × *suendermannii* grows so vigorously that it has to be kept in check or it will overgrow slow growing dwarf trees and shrubs.

Elsholtzia stauntonii, Labiatae

Natural range of distribution: northern China.

Only a few winter hardy trees and shrubs are found in the *Labiatae* family. *E. stauntonii* (Zone 5) is a 1–1.5 m tall, deciduous, twiggy, aromatic subshrub

Elsholtzia stauntonii

with opposite, somewhat pendant, lanceo-late leaves. In the fall, light purple to nearly carmine-red labiate flowers develop on the shoot tips in thick, long, spike-like clusters.

The extremely late blossoms, which occasionally get caught by the first frost of the season, make this charming shrub a valuable ornamental. It thrives in sunny sites in heath and rock gardens and requires a deep winter mulch where climates are humid. Low growing native wildflowers and, especially, late blooming grasses, make excellent companion plants for this little shrub. It grows in all soils, including lime soil. As is the case with most summer blooming subshrubs, severe yearly pruning in spring is recommended.

Dryas octopetala

133

Empetrum nigrum

Empetrum nigrum, Empetraceae

E. nigrum (Zone 2) is a habitat-vague dwarf shrub. It grows as well in high moors as it does in dry sand dunes, on sunny rocks, or in arctic-alpine dwarf shrub heaths. In all these locations, however, the soil must be nutrient-poor and acid, moist during the growing season and there must be a snow covering in winter months (the exception being along the coastline). It can be accompanied in moors by *Calluna vulgaris, Ledum palustre, Andromeda polifolia, Rubus chamaemorus, Eriophorum vaginatum* and *Vaccinium* species. In dwarf shrub heaths, *Loiseleurea procumbens* and *Arctostaphylos alpina* are found, but *E. nigrum* often forms a pure stand in such heaths. It is found circumpolar over the entire Northern Hemisphere.

This ericaceous, evergreen dwarf shrub makes a turf-like cushion with its prostrate, densely branched shoots. The branches curve upwards at the ends, and are thickly covered with alternate, needle-like, 5 mm long leaves. Blossoms are rather insignificant, and are located singly in the leaf axil. Its large, round, glossy black fruits are much more noticeable.

E.n. 'Smaragd' is a cloned cultivar. It was found in the dunes of northern Germany and is particularly attractive for its especially thick habit and its lasting, fresh green foliage.

E. nigrum, a typical heath garden plant for sunny locations, can be used in fresh,

134

raw humus soils as well as in nutrient-poor, sandy soils. It is often used as a design element to tie together groups of *Erica, Calluna* and taller trees and shrubs in heath gardens. Unlike *Erica* and *Calluna, E. nigrum* tolerates some foot traffic as well as competition from standard trees and shrubs, including birches, which have surface root systems. The cultivar *E. n.* 'Smaragd' is especially well suited to such situations. The Empetrums will not grow where summers are hot.

Erica carnea, Ericaceae

Natural habitat: eastern and central parts of the Alps, the maritime Alps, the Apennines, and the northern Iberian Peninsula. It is the most common ground cover in slightly alkaline to neutral soils in thin, mountain to sub-mountain pine forests. It is often found among *Pinus mugo, P. sylvestris* and *P. nigra.* It appears as a pioneer on rocky lime soil and slopes covered with rock debris. It is often accompanied by *Rhododendron hirsutum, Arctostaphylos uva-ursi, Vaccinium vitis-idaea, Daphne stricta, Helianthemum alpestre, Polygala chamaebuxus, Carex humilis, C. ornithopoda, Globularia cordifolia, Sesleria caerulea, Pirola minor* and *Gentiana clusii.*

As a prostrate dwarf shrub, *E. carnea* (Zone 6) hardly reaches 30 cm tall. Many branches break from the main stem. They are covered with needlelike, whorled, evergreen leaves. Flesh-colored flowers form in the fall. They are clustered in 3 to 10 cm long, terminal, one-sided spikes. This heath blooms during or shortly after the winter snows have melted.

One would be hard pressed to find *E. carnea* cultivars not listed on pages 134–135. This author only knows of a few specialty nurseries which grow others.

Next to *Calluna vulgaris, E. carnea* is the most important plant in a heath garden. It should be planted in masses in a sunny, sloping to flat site where it serves as a good companion plant for all dwarf trees and shrubs, not limiting itself to heath gardens.

E. carnea tolerates somewhat limey, loamy soil, as long as it has been generously ammended with humus. It also does well in neutral to acid, humus-sandy soil.

E. carnea's companion plants were mentioned in the section entitled "Heath Gardens".

Erica cinerea, Ericaceae

E. cinerea (Zone 5) occurs natively in humid, constant climates from England and coastal areas along Scandinavia to northwest of the Iberian Peninsula. It thrives in dry *Ulex* and *Calluna* moors and heaths, or in sparse forests in acid, nutrient-poor silicate soils. Often, it is accompanied by *Ulex europaeus, Calluna vulgaris, Genista pilosa, Arenaria montana, Jasione montana* and *Molinia caerulea.*

E. cinerea grows 30 to 40 cm tall, with a prostrate-ascending habit. Its branches are gray-pilose; densely covered with leaves in whorls of three, dark green on top and gray-green beneath. Through summer, violet-pink blossoms with ovate corollas in 10 cm long, whirled clusters appear on the shoot tips and sides, completely covering the plant with flowers.

Of the 70 or so cultivars, the first begin blooming in late spring; the last, as late as October. The cultivars listed on page 134 are considered to be some of the best at present. Each of them was awarded at least 2 stars at the competition in The Netherlands in 1978.

E. cinerea, as is the case with other ericaceous species, makes the best show when planted in more or less large drifts in sunny locations. It requires an acid, moist to dry, sandy to raw humus-rich soil. Outside its natural range of distribution it is only moderately hardy. A brushwood covering is recommended during winter if no snow is present.

Erica × darleyensis, Ericaceae

This plant was developed about 1890 in England as a hybrid of *E. carnea* and the non-winter hardy, Mediterranean species, *E. erigena.*

E. × darleyensis (Zone 6) is in habit, foliage and blossom, hardly distinguishable from *E. carnea.* It grows somewhat more vigorously, reaching 40 cm tall, blossoms through the late fall, winter, and early spring months, and is not quite as frost-hardy.

The following cultivars are, at present, important:

E.d 'Darley Dale' is considered to be typical of the hybrids. It grows slightly loose and widely erect, its blossoms are light lilac-pink and it tolerates alkaline soil.

E. × d. 'Silberschmelze' is more frost hardy than other cultivars of this cross. It has rich green, rough foliage, which often russets in winter. Its silver-white blossoms open in long spikes from December to April.

'White Perfection' is considered an improvement over *E.* 'Silverschmelze.' It has rich green foliage, which holds without discoloring the year-round, and a more pure flower color.

Cultural requirements and landscape uses are similar to those of *E. carnea;* though these cultivars are more frost

hardy, they should be protected from cold winds in winter.

Erica tetralix, Ericaceae

E. tetralix (Zone 3) is found in Spain, Portugal, England, Ireland, central Sweden and the Baltics. It thrives in peat moors, transitional moors, moor forests and damp, low lying heaths. Its most common associates are *Calluna vulgaris, Myrica gale, Salix repens,* and *Erica ciliaris, E. scoparia* and *Ulex minor* in southern France.

When cultivated, *E. tetralix* reaches a height of 30 to 40 cm. Wild, it reaches up to 60 cm. Its gray-green, glandular-hairy, needle-like leaves are borne three to four in each whorl. Barrel-shaped, delicate pink blossoms appear in summer and early fall, usually 5 to 12 in each terminal one-sided spike.

The cultivars listed below are considered very valuable in gardens.

E. tetralix grows best in sunny locations with moist to damp, acid sandy loam with plenty of raw humus. It can be planted either singly or in small groups on damp sites in *Calluna* gardens. Small woody species with similar ecological requirements are *Ledum palustre, Arctostaphylos uva-ursi, Chamaedaphne calyculata, Vaccinium* and *Andromeda* species.

Erica vagans, Ericaceae

E. vagans (Zone 7–9) is native to the Atlantic coastal areas of Europe, from central Spain to southwestern England and northwestern Ireland; in heaths and sparse forests on acid soil.

Cultivated, it grows to scarcely 30 cm, but can be 90 cm tall under suitable condi-

Ericea cinera Cultivars

Cultivar	Flowers	Months of bloom	Height (cm)	Observations
'Alba'	white, in long clusters	8–9	25	wide habit, pendulous branches, apple-green leaves
'Atrosanguinea'	glowing reddish pink	9–10	15	light green foliage, especially beautiful and heavily blooming
'C. D. Eason'	pink-red	6–9	20	bushy, dark green foliage, one of the most often cultivated
'Cevennes'	lavender-pink in stiffly erect clusters	8–10	25	a beautiful, heavily blooming cultivar
'C. G. Best'	salmon-pink, in long clusters	8–9	30	erect, greenish-red to gray-green foliage, best cultivar in salmon-pink
'Coccinea'	striking, intense red	6–8	10	prostrate habit
'Golden Drop'	lilac-pink, few blossoms	6–9	25	yellow-orange foliage, bronze-red in winter, mat-like, wide, dense growth, frost tender
'Pallas'	pure lilac, blooms abundantly	6–9	35	erect, winter hardy and heavy blooming.
'P. S. Patrick'	violet-red	8–9	40	slender, erect clusters of blossoms
'Rosea'	pale carmine-rose	6–9	25	dense, bushy growth

Erica carnea Cultivars

Cultivar	Flowers	Months of bloom	Special foliage color	Height (cm)	Observations
f. *alba*	white	3–4			very dense
'Alan Coats'	pale pink to purple	2–5		15	dense and wide
'Ann Sparkes'	pink	3–4	gold-orange to golden, red-bronze edges	15	
'Atrorubra'	carmine	4–5	deep green to bluish	20	somewhat lower habit than most
'Aurea'	pink	2–5	copper to yellow	15	bushy and wide
'Cecilia M. Beale'	pure white	2–5	pale green, slender shoots	15	dense and compact
'December Red'	pink to pale pink	1–2	deep green	15	good cultivar, blossoms in strong spikes

Erica carnea Cultivars (cont.)

Cultivar	Flowers	Months of bloom	Special foliage color	Height (cm)	Observations
'Foxhollow'	soft pink	2–3	yellow to yellow-brown, bronze-yellow in winter	20	certainly the most beautiul yellow-foliaged cultivar
'Heathwood'	dark lilac-pink	3–4	bronzish green tips in winter	25	short and compact
'James Backhouse'	pale pink, large	3–4	glossy green	25	vigorous, coarse branches, dense growth
'Lohse's Rubin'	ruby-pink	3–4		15	broadly erect, somewhat weak to modestly vigorous growth, compact
'Loughrigg'	intense purple	2–3	blue-green; branch tips bronze in winter	15	
'March Seedling'	dark pink	3–4		25	spreading-erect, fast growing, especially well suited for large areas
'Myretoun Ruby'	intense wine-red, large	3–4	dark green	20	prostrate and outward spreading growth; one of the best of the newly introduced cultivars
'Pink Sprangles'	very dark pink, large and numerous	2–4		30	vigorous, wide and loose
'Pirbright Rose'	bright pink	2–3		15	
'Praecox Rubra'	light purple-red	11–3	dark green	15	wide and flat, good ground cover, very valuable
'Ruby Glow'	ruby-red	2–5	dark green, bronze in autumn	15	vigorous and wide
'Snow Queen'	pure white, numerous	2–3		15	compact, very valuable
'Springwood Pink'	light pink, numerous	2–3		20	as 'Springwood White'

Erica carnea **Cultivars (cont.)**

Cultivar	Flowers	Months of bloom	Special foliage color	Height (cm)	Observations
'Springwood White'	pure white, large	2–4		25	broad, flat growing branches, slow growing
'Vivellii'	violet-red	2–4	dark bronze in winter	15	beautiful; somewhat slow growing, an important, popular cultivar
'Winter Beauty'	deep pink, numerous	12–3	dark green	15	very compact, widely cultivated in Europe

Erica tetralix **Cultivars**

Cultivar	Flowers	Months of bloom	Special foliage color	Height (cm)	Observations
v. *alba*	white	6–9	silver-gray	30	often found growing wild
'Alba Mollis'	pure white	6–9	silver-gray, pilose	20	compact, erect when mature
'Con Underwood'	dark reddish brown	6–9	gray-green	35	open and erect when mature
'Hookstone Pink'	light pink	6–8	silvery	30	loose, denser when mature, heavy bloomer
'Ken Underwood'	carmine-pink	6–9	dark gray-green	30	erect, heavy bloomer, highly recommended

Erica vagans Varieties

Cultivar	Flowers	Months of bloom	Special foliage color	Height (cm)	Observations
'Diana Hornibrook'	reddish-pink	6–9	deep green, paler when young	30	dense and compact
'Lyonesse'	white, flowers densely crowded	8–9	deep green; shoots bright yellowish gray	30	vigorous and compact growth
'Mrs. D. F. Maxwell'	dark pink	8–9	deep green; shoots yellowish brown	35	beautiful; bushy
'St. Keverne'	pure salmon-pink, heavy bloomer	8–9	bright green	35	compact and bushy

Erica cinerea 'Cevennes'

tions. This is a half-hardy species and develops into a wide and luxuriant heath. Its needlelike, dark green leaves, borne 4 to 5 per whorl, are larger than those of *E. carnea*.

Pink blossoms with an almost globe-shaped corolla appear from midsummer to early fall in terminal, uniformly rounded spikes. The species is usually only cultivated in botanical gardens, but the four cultivars listed in the table are indispensable in a garden.

Cultivars of *E. vagans* are more frost hardy than the species; therefore, in protected locations winter coverings are not necessary. The cultivars thrive in sunny to lightly shaded gardens and can be planted in loam soil. For best effect plant these in small to larger drifts accompanying *Calluna* or *Erica;* or in front of groups of pines or junipers, in order to protect them from severe winter winds.

Erica × williamsii, Ericaceae

A natural hybrid, *E. × williamsii* (*E. tetralix × E. vagans*) was discovered about 1910 by P. D. Williams in St. Keverne, Cornwall, Wales, growing as a natural hybrid.

Erica vagans 'St. Keverne' and 'Lyonesse'

This vigorous hybrid grows to be a compact, 20 cm high shrub. Its branches are lightly pilose, with pale green leaves, 4 to each whorl. In winter, leaves on the shoot tips turn golden-yellow. Its best attribute is its rather long blooming period. It begins blossoming in late spring and continues through late fall, even after light frosts. Its closed-bell-shaped, pink blossoms are borne 5 to 6 per cluster, with 10 or so clusters united on shoot tips, in exquisite spikes.

E. × *williamsii* is an especially alluring member for the heather-heath community, with the same cultural requirements and winter hardiness of *E. vagans*. In addition, it tolerates heavier soil, so long as it is lime-free.

Euonymus fortunei, Celastraceae

E. fortunei (Zone 5) is found in central China. It grows in the damp, hardwood forests as well as in humid, broad-leaved evergreen, forests. It was discovered and introduced into Europe in 1907.

With anchoring rootlets, *E. fortunei* climbs to 5 m or more; or it can also be prostrate. The species is ordinarily not cultivated. Its cultivars, however, are often used as ground covers or as dwarf shrubs. They are very shade tolerant. Many of the cultivars derive from the variable variety *radicans*. It, too, can either grow prostrate or erect, in which case, it can reach up to 2 m.

In this book only slow growing, dwarf cultivars are dealt with. Cultivars which placed high in the judging in The Netherlands (Experimental Station for nursery stock in Boskoop), and which are commonly cultivated, are given special attention. Cultivars selected at the Dar-

thuizer Boomkwekerij in the last few years have not yet been grown long enough to fully assess their qualities in cultivation.

E. 'Emerald Charm' is erect, up to 1 m tall with broad, elliptic, glossy, light green leaves. Its abundant, yellowish white fruit have orange arils. It is considered one of the best green-leaved 'Emerald' cultivars. It originated in the U.S. and is a good group shrub for shady locations and a good ground cover for larger open areas.

E. 'Emerald Gaiety' is a variegated cultivar, broad and up to 1.25 m tall. It has large, gray-green leaves which are irregularly white-edged. It is taller than *E.* 'Variegatus' and, with its distinctive leaves, is much more decorative. It makes a good group shrub for sunny to shady sites.

E. 'Emerald'n Gold' at first appears to be similar to 'Variegatus', but as it matures, its distinct qualities appear. It grows very slowly, to about 1 m tall. Its small, light gray-green leaves, with a wide golden-

Euonymus fortunei 'Vegetus'

yellow margin, turn purple-pink in winter. This is a good group plant for partly shady to shady locations.

E. 'Goldtip' is a 70 cm tall, erect shrub. Its medium-sized leaves are golden-yellow edged at first, but later becoming creamy-white edged, discoloring very little in winter. This plant is used in the same manner as is E. 'Emerald'n Gold'.

E. 'Minimus' is an especially lovely small-leafed cultivar, well suited for limited spaces. Its leaves are only 15 mm long, round and glossy green. With E. 'Kewensis', it is one of the smallest cultivars of the genus. It hardly reaches 10 cm tall and grows well even in very shady locations.

E. 'Silver Queen' is an erect, 80 cm tall shrub, which will grow even taller when planted against walls. Its elliptic to ovate leaves are 4 to 6 cm long. When leaves first unfold, they are edged or spotted creamy-yellow, but later the variegation turns creamy-white. It is an especially beautiful

Euonymus fortunei 'Gracilis'

mutation of the older 'Carrierei'. Unfortunately, it is not as frost hardy as many other cultivars.

E. 'Sunshine' originated as a mutation of E. 'Emerald'n Gold' and was awarded a Gold Medal in the Boskooper Herfstweelde in 1978.

E. 'Variegatus' is usually prostrate, but can also grow to a height of 1.5 m. Its relatively small, elliptic to ovate leaves have a narrow, white edge. Its leaves are often tinged or spotted purple-red in winter. It is a well proven, winter hardy cultivar. It is best used as a ground cover, but also works well against low walls.

All *E. fortunei* cultivars thrive in partly shady to shady locations. With sufficient humidity, they can also be used in sunny areas. They grow well in heavy soil. The taller cultivars can be used in groups, the shorter are valuable ground covers.

Forsythia ovata 'Tetragold', Oleaceae

The species (Zone 5) is found growing wild in the damp deciduous forests of Korea. It is not much used in gardens, as its flowers may be uncommonly unattractive.

'Tetragold' is a cholchicine-derived tetraploid clone, developed in 1963 at the Experimental Station for nursery stock in Boskoop, The Netherlands. This deciduous shrub is bushy and grows to 1 m tall. Its fine display of gold-yellow blossoms are 3 cm in diàmeter, substantially larger than is typical. Flowering begins in late winter or very early spring, much earlier than those of *F.* × *intermedia,* which is more frequently culivated.

Dwarf forsythias are beautiful shrubs for front gardens and narrow beds, as low, unpruned hedges and in containers. They thrive in sunny to lightly shaded sites in nutrient-rich soil which is not too dry. They wilt quickly in light sandy soil during droughty periods so must be watered accordingly.

Forsythia viridissima 'Bronxensis', Oleaceae

The wild type of this species from China, as with *F. ovata,* is not often cultivated. The cultivar *F.v.* 'Bronxensis' originated from Japanese seed in the Bronx Botanical Garden, New York, U.S.A., in 1939. This 50 cm tall dwarf cultivar has very short internodes and very small leaves. It produces only a few flowers. Since 1939, choice selections have been propagated and now, as is the case with 'Selektion Weber', many blossom regularly and heavily.

Its cultural requirements and landscape uses are much the same as *F. ovata* 'Tetragold'.

Forsythia viridissima 'Bronxensis'

Fuchsia magellanica, Onagraceae

F. *magellanica* (Zone 7) is one of the few native woody ornamentals of the Southern Hemisphere which beautify northern gardens. This deciduous shrub comes from the Patagonian laurel forests of southern Chile and Argentina. These forests are composed principally of *Nothofagus* ssp. *F. magellanica* was introduced into England sometime before 1820.

In its natural habitat, it grows to be 3 m tall. In our gardens, it seldom exceeds 1 m due to winter injury which necessitate pruning to the crown most springs. In the axils of the opposite, lanceolate-ovate leaves, slender pendant blossoms appear from midsummer to first frost. The exquisite blossoms have blood-red stems and sepals, and purple petals.

Because they are hardier than the species, the following two cultivars are most commonly recommended:

If *F.m.* 'Gracilis' is allowed to grow freely, it can reach a height of 2m. Normally, however, it is pruned back yearly, and grows less tall. Its branches are a lovely shade of red. The leaf petioles are also red. From midsummer until frost it produces elegant blossoms with carmine-red stems, sepals and purple petals in the leaf axils.

F.m. 'Riccartonii' is differentiated by its more vigorous growth, shorter, slightly pendulous branches, and longer petioles. The blossoms have bright red peduncles and purple-violet petals.

Fuchsias are among the most valuable group of late summer blooming shrubs, as long as their environmental requirements are met. In mild climates fuchsias thrive in any well prepared, nutrient-rich garden soil. They should be kept moist in summer,

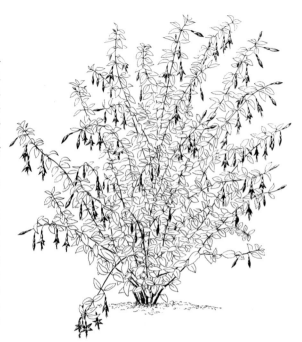

Fuchsia magellanica 'Gracilis'

and as dry as possible in winter. It is important that the plant's site is partly shaded and sheltered from wind. In winter, the plant must be protected from excess cold and moisture. A deep mulch of dry leaves is satisfactory, with coniferous branches placed on top to hold the leaves. In the U.S., gardeners in cold areas often mound a bushel measure of soil or Cornell-type potting mix over the fuchsia's crown in late fall. *F. magellanica* cultivars can be used as house plants in containers. Over the years, such house plants reach a splendid size and, with their finely segmented blossoms, are very decorative.

145

✕ Gaulnettya; G. wisleyensis 'Wisley Pearl', Ericaceae

The bi-generic hybrid cultivar 'Wisley Pearl' is a typical example of—✕ *G. wisleyensis* (Zone 6). It originated in 1930 in the garden of the Royal Horticultural Society at Wisley as a cross between *Gaultheria shallon* and *Pernettya mucronata.*

This evergreen ericaceous plant develops into a very dense, 1 m tall shrub with 4 to 6 cm long, oblong-elliptic leaves. In late spring it blossoms heavily; the flowers, 6 to 15, develop in glandularly pilose clusters on the shoot tip axils. A fine

Fuchsia magellanica 'Riccartonii'

✕ *Gaulnettya wisleyensis 'Pink Pixie'*

display of a reddish brown to wine-red 8 mm fruit provide a fall and winter display.

This is a striking, evergreen dwarf shrub. Its cultural requirements and landscape uses are similar to *Gaultheria shallon*, which is not as frost-hardy as *G.w.* 'Wisley Pearl'.

Gaultheria itoana, Ericaceae

G. itoana (Zone 6) is found growing wild in high, open locations in China and Taiwan. It thrives at altitudes between 2200 and 3600 m.

This handsome, evergreen dwarf shrub rarely reaches 20 cm tall. Its thin, firm leaves are oblong, 1 to 1.5 cm long, serrate, the edges curled downward. Not very ovate, tubular, 4 to 5 mm long, white blossoms appear in late summer in sub-terminal clusters. Its round white fruits are 6 mm in diameter.

G. itoana makes a beautiful specimen or group shrub in an alpine garden or as a companion for rhododendrons; in sandy-humus, moist soil in sunny to partly shady locations.

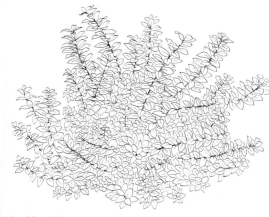

Gaultheria itoana

Gaultheria miqueliana, Ericaceae

Natural habitat: Japan.

This dwarf evergreen shrub grows only to 30 cm tall. Leaves are 2 to 4 cm long, ovate to obovate, glandular and serrate on the edges. In mid-spring white, urn-shaped blossoms appear in the leaf axils near the shoot tips. Later, rather large round white fruits develop.

In spite of its height, *G. miqueliana* (Zone 5) is not used as a ground cover, rather, as a specimen or grouped shrub in a rock garden, or as a companion plant for rhododendrons. As is the case with all gaultherias, it thrives in acid, sandy-humus, constantly moist soil, in partly shady locations.

Gaultheria procumbens, Ericaceae

In eastern North America, from Canada to the Carolinas, *G. procumbens* (Zone 3) grows in sparse deciduous forests and forest glades, often in acid, sandy sterile soil.

This dwarf shrub, which ony reaches 15 cm tall, makes a dense ground cover in only a few years, spreading by under-ground stolons. Its leaves are evergreen, glossy, dark green, 1 to 5 cm long, clustered at the shoot tips. New leaves are copper-colored as they unfold in spring, and the foliage turns reddish in autumn. The species blooms with single, white to pink, nodding, tapering, urn-shaped blossoms throughout summer. Its round fruits are glowing red. They contain salicylic acid, which is a principle ingredient of "wintergreen oil". The chemical today, mostly of synthetic sources, is used in the U.S. as a flavoring for candy, gum and toothpaste. It is also widely used in fruit preservation.

G. procumbens is one of our most important ground covers. It is without peer for plantings between rhododendrons. It thrives in acid, moist, sandy-humus soil in partly shady locations. It grows moderately, and does not interfere with the growth of dwarf trees and shrubs and tolerates early blooming bulbs, corms, and tubers such as *Eranthis hyemalis. E. hyemalis,* with its yellow blossoms, is a beautiful contrast to *G. procumbens'* red fruit.

Gaultheria shallon, Ericaceae

G. shallon (Zone 5–6) is a native to the North American coastline, from southern Alaska to northern California, in the Pacific Northwest coniferous forests. In some areas, it makes dense, waist-high ground covering thickets.

This evergreen species develops into a 60 cm–1 m tall, vigorous shrub with many, erect shoots and ground-level stolons, and hard, leathery, ovate, 5–10 cm long, and sharply serrated leaves. Red-tinged, white, urn-shaped blossoms appear in spring and early summer in pendulous, terminal and axillary clusters. The fruit, which appear in fall, are black-red.

G. shallon is a decorative massing shrub in gardens. As an understory shrub in damp to moist, sandy-humus, acid soil, it is invaluable.

Genista, Leguminosae

It is often possible, and sometimes necessary, to have drought resistant dwarf shrubs in the garden. This is especially true in rock gardens, heath gardens, in dry walls as well as on top of them, under eave-edges, in containers and raised beds. Some *Genista* species are well suited for such use. In their natural habitat (heaths in Atlantic Europe and maquis and garigues in the Mediterranean region) they grow in sun-drenched southern exposures with little water and sharp drainage.

All genistas are small, often very dense and compact-growing shrubs or sub-shrubs. Foliage is absent or simple, sometimes trifoliate. With the exception of the white blooming *G. monosperma*, all species have yellow blossoms. Their pale to golden-yellow blossoms appear from spring to midsummer in terminal clusters or on single-flowered spurs in the leaf axils.

All thrive in sunny, warm locations in well drained, dry, light, nutrient-poor soil. A drainage system made of rock and gravel should be constructed under the soil before planting. The various species have differing requirements with regard to the lime content of the soil. Decidedly lime-intolerant are *G. germanica* and *G. anglica, G. radiata, G. sericea, G. silvestris; G. lydia* and *G. hispanica* are lime-loving, whereas *G. pilosa* and *G. tinctoria* are indifferent.

Although in their natural habitats *Genista* species are gregarious, they are valuable in a garden as specimen plants. They can be used with all other dwarf trees and shrubs in rock and container gardens and also in heath gardens, as long as their cultural requirements are similar. Their charm is brought out in steppe-like, well articulated rock gardens, together with *Ephedra* species, *Salvia officinalis, S. × superba, Acantholimon androsaemum, Asphodelus albus, Asphodeline lutea, Geranium sanguineum, Hypericum olympicum, Stipa capillata* and *Achnaterum calamagrostis.*

Most species grow best in oceanic climates with mild winters, and tolerate

Genista hispanica

Genista hispanica

Genista saggitalis

long periods of drought in summer. In continental climates, winter protection is absolutely necessary. The soil surrounding the plant should be deeply mulched with dry, hardwood (oak) leaves. Place coniferous branches on the leafy mulch to deter their being wind-blown. Additional boughs may be domed over genistas to prevent winter sun scald. Frost damaged shoots should be pruned out in spring; all *Genista* species quickly regenerate new growth.

Of about 100 species in the genus, only a few are considered generally useful in gardens, such as *G. lydia*, *G. pilosa* 'Goldilocks' and *G. tinctoria* 'Plena'. The other species listed here are used only in special situations, but when used correctly they are very charming.

Genista Species

Species	Natural Habitat	Habit	Bloom
Genista anglica	the Atlantic coast from central and western Europe to the Iberian Peninsula in peaty soil and damp heath sands	low spreading, strongly branched, thorny, 40 to 80 cm tall	mid-spring; golden-yellow in short, terminal clusters
Genista germanica	central and western Europe to the southern Alps, in dry, nutrient-poor sand; calcium-loving plant	prostrate limbs with ascending branches; twigs matted pilose, mature plants become thorny; 30 to 50 cm	midsummer; golden-yellow, in 2 to 5 cm long, terminal clusters
Genista hispanica	Spain to northern Italy in warm, dry, limestone soils	dense, almost ball-shaped shrub with crowded, thorny, thickly pilose, dark green branches; 30 to 70 cm tall	early summer; golden-yellow flowers, up to 12 in terminal clusters; heavy blooming and beautiful
Genista horrida	dry, rocky hillsides in the Spanish Pyrenees	cushion-like, dense, rigid and pungent, 30 to 60 cm tall	summer through early July; yellow flowers, 1 to 3 in terminal clusters, delicate; blooms only in dry, sunny locations
Genista lydia	in lime soils in the Balkan mountain ranges, and the Lydia region of Asia Minor; thrives in well drained soil	30 to 60 cm tall, cushion-like, dense prostrate branches; when mature it is many times wider than it is tall, branch tips are thorny	spring; golden-yellow, borne on the sides of branches, one of the heaviest flowering species
Genista pilosa	Atlantic Europe, from southern Sweden to Portugal, most often in dry, sandy heaths, seldom found in calcium soil; unpretentious in the garden	prostrate, limbs root down; short, erect, fine-pilose branches; 10 to 30 cm tall	spring; golden yellow, on small blossoms, 1 to 3 axillary spurs.
Genista pilosa 'Goldilocks'	a selected cultivar from Boskoop, The Netherlands	vigorous and bushy growth, 40 to 60 cm tall, when mature, much wider than tall	spring; golden-yellow; many more blossoms than the species
Genista radiata	central Italy to southeastern Europe in dry, shallow alkaline soil; sometimes found in cracks of solid rock	erect with radiating branches, 70 to 80 cm tall; wider than tall; lives longer than other species	spring; lemon-yellow, up to 20 in terminal clusters

Species	Natural Habitat	Habit	Bloom
Genista tinctoria 'Royal Gold'		50 to 80 cm tall, shorter and denser than the species, plants in fertile soils grow too fast and break apart in heavy rain	midsummer, abundant golden-yellow blossoms
Genista tinctoria 'Plena'		with prostrate limbs bearing ascending branches; 30 cm tall; good ground cover for small areas	late summer to early fall; orange-yellow blossoms in compact clusters borne on branch tips

Genista horrida

Globularia cordifolia,
Globulariaceae

Only a few *Globularia* species are sub-shrubs; most are truly woody. *G. cordifolia* (Zone 5) is native to slopes, dry hillsides, and gravelly, grazing meadows in the Alps, at altitudes up to 2800 m.

In its natural habitat, the rosettes are evergreen, spatula-like, 2 to 2.5 cm long, deep green; leathery leaves form thick carpets which spread like turf.

This 2 to 5 cm tall dwarf shrub bears quantities of ball-shaped blossom heads in late spring. Small blue labiate flowers cluster tightly in the globular inflorescences which name the genus.

G. cordifolia thrives best in sunny locations in well drained, well-weathered, mineral soils.

Hebe, Scrophulariaceae

Almost all of the 100–140 species of this genus are native to New Zealand, only growing there as evergreen trees and shrubs. Their closely crowded leaves are opposite, scale-like, lanceolate, round or ovate. Some species are decidely xerophytic, which, due to the dryness of their environment, and are seen as plants with greatly reduced branches and twigs of small, leathery, closely appressed leaves.

In continental climates, the shrubs remain much smaller than in their natural habitat. Even in protected, warm and dry locations, they require winter protection. They will thrive in any good garden soil, but do especially well in rich, loamy soil.

They are often used in rock and heath gardens, where their unusual, often distinctly odd, character is very noticeable. They can also be used in containers and in trough gardens. For the most effective landscape value they should be planted with other New Zealand dwarf shrubs such as *Muehlenbeckia axillaris* or *Coprosma petrii*, with the sedge *Carex buchananii*, or creeping or low growing herbaceous perennials such as *Cotula dioica, C. squalida, Epilobium inornatum, Mazus pumilio, Acaena* and *Raoulia* species.

Of the many species, the following are most often cultivated:

Hebe armstrongii; Zone 7. This densely branched shrub, the best known and hardiest species, grows to 60 cm with curving, ascending branches. Its leaves are scale-like, 2 mm long, and olive-brown. They are pressed tightly to the twigs, and are reduced to a keeled, stubby point. This shrub seldom blooms out fully. Its small, white blossoms have purple anthers and are borne in terminal tufts of 4 to 8.

Hebe buchananii; Zone 7–8. Grows very compactly and reaches a height of 15 to 25 cm. Its erect branches are covered with thick, leathery, concave, 3 to 6 mm long, blue-green, oblong to round leaves. White blossoms appear in midsummer, often in 2 to 4 tufted spikes near the shoot tips.

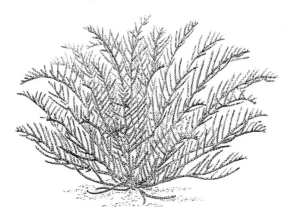

Hebe armstrongii

Hebe buxifolia; Zone 7–8. This shrub reaches a maximum height of 50 to 100 cm. It attracts attention because of its foliage. The leaves are 8 to 12 mm long, glossy green on top and lightly spotted beneath. They are arranged in 4 rows, opposite each other on the branches which, when young, are light green. This shrub blooms in midsummer with dense, white, 2.5 cm long spikes located in the axils of the upper leaves.

Hebe cupressoides; Zone 7. *H. cupressoides* develops into an erect, almost globe-shaped dwarf shrub with crowded, slender branches; cypress-like in appearance; to about 50 cm tall. The scale-like linear leaves are 6 mm long on young plants, but when the plant matures, leaves are only 1.5 mm long. They are crowded and closely adpressed to the twigs. In midsummer pale blue-lilac blossoms appear, borne 3 to 8 in small clusters on the shoot tips. This is an especially beautiful and hardy species.

Hebe pinguifolia

Hebe pinguifolia; Zone 6. This is a thick twigged, 0.3 to 0.7 m tall, prostrate or slightly erect shrub. Its round, thick, leathery leaves are blue-green, generally reddish on the edges. They leave noticeable scars on the branches when they fall off in autumn. The white blossoms have blue anthers. Blossoms appear in mid- to late summer in small spikes on the branch tips.

Hedera helix, Araliaceae

This is the only evergreen climber native to central Europe. Many of its cultivars are well known. As a result, the climbing and/or trailing cultivars will not be discussed; rather, the emphasis will be concentrated on a few of the shrubby cultivars. Zone 5.

All are slow growing, evergreen dwarf shrubs. They grow best in shady or partly shady locations in the garden. They grow well in most garden soils, but an alkaline pH gives the best results. If the location is too sunny, the soil must be kept moist and

Hebe buxifolia

rich in humus. If the soil is not sufficiently friable and rich, lime marl, compost and leaf mold should be added.

The cultivars discussed here are valuable companion or bedding plants for all shady and partly shady locations. Because they are very winter hardy, they can also be planted in containers in all but the coldest climates.

H. h. f. Arborescens is an older form, maintained in shrub-form through vegetative reproduction. It grows as a round shrub to 1 m tall and flowers and produces fruit regularly. The leaves are relatively large, unlobed, and in late summer, greenish yellow blossoms appear which are very attractive to bees. Its black fruit ripens during the second season. This form may be propagated from any form of climbing *H. helix* that has develoed flowering branches. Select 3 year or older flowering shoots and root in damp soil or perlite.

H. h. 'Congesta' differs from the following cultivar in that its leaves are not

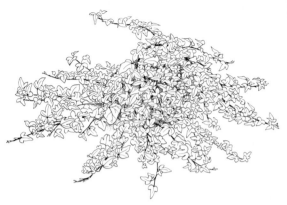

Hedera helix 'Minima'

wavy on the edges. This slow growing cultivar is densely bushy with stiffly erect branches. Its leaves are very small, triangular-three-lobed, and heart-shaped at the base.

H. h. 'Conglomerata'. At first, the branches of this dwarf cultivar are stiffly erect. They soon twist, lay over and lie prostrate on the soil. The plant has small, 1.2 to 3.5 cm long, three- to five-lobed, matte-green leaves. They are very wavy on the edges, heart-shaped at the base, and often are arranged in two rows.

H. h. 'Conglomerata Erecta' differs from *H.* 'Conglomerata' in that its branches do not turn downwards but remain erect. It is 30–50 cm tall, 120 cm wide. Its distinctive, two-ranked leaves are sharply three-cornered and deeply grooved. The lateral lobes are small and sharp, the base is flattened heart-shaped.

H. h. 'Spetchley' is named after Spetchley Park in England where it was discovered. In nurseries, it is called *H.* 'Minima'. It is a very slow growing, creeping cultivar with prostrate, rooting shoots. Its oblong, unevenly three-lobed, irregularly wavy leaves are 0.5 to 2 cm long. They are dark green except for a paler green zone along the main veins. The

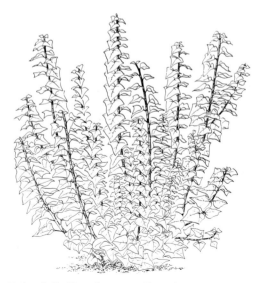

Hedera helix 'Conglomerata Erecta'

young stems are dark purple. The plant's early branching habit results in a dense little shrub. This is a very decorative cultivar and very winter hardy.

Helianthemum apenninum,
Cistaceae

As a western Mediterranean-Atlantic area plant, *H. apenninum* (Zone 6) colonizes dry, sunny, rocky slopes, and hillsides covered with rock debris and dwarf shrub heaths. It is found with species such as *Pulsatilla vulgaris, Anemone sylvestris, Geranium sanguineum, Helianthemum canum, Thalictrum minus, Alyssum montanum, Dictamnus albus* and *Salvia pratensis*. They grow as well in limey soil as they do in lime-free soil.

This species is considered a "Plant Lover's Choice": *H. a.* var. *roseum*, which is native to the Alps, is a very important and widely used plant.

Related species and cultivars are also very popular among gardeners. They include *H. alpestre* 'Serpyllifolium', *H. canum* and *H. lunulatum*.

H. apenninum is a free-branching, broadleaf evergreen subshrub with 10 to 30 cm long branches. The leaves on *H. a.* var. *roseum* are simple, opposite, lanceolate and 3 to 5 cm long. They are green on top and gray-pilose beneath. In late spring, 3 cm wide, pink blossoms appear (the species has white blossoms), 3 to 10 in clusters, on top of the foliage.

Like many Sunroses, *H. apenninum* is used as a specimen plant or in small groups in rock gardens, dry walls, containers and terraces. Although plants grow together and make a thick cushion when planted in groups, it is not well suited as a ground cover as it cannot restrain weed growth.

Open, sunny locations are best suited for its cultivation. Avoid planting helianthemums near large trees and shrubs because they cannot tolerate shade or root competition, and are easily crowded, shaded, or starved out.

Soil should be well drained, easily warmed, nutrient-poor and alkaline. It should not be too damp in winter. Heavy, damp, fertile soils are not satisfactory for *H. apenninum*.

All helianthemums bloom again in summer following the main spring flower production. *H. apenninum* should be pruned immediately following the second bloom period in late summer. If they are not pruned annually, they lose their foliage and take on the appearance of a "wornout broom". Because helianthemums can be damaged by frost, a light covering should be used in winter.

Helianthemum hybrids, Cistaceae

Helianthemum hybrids are readily distinguished from their parent species. It goes without saying that these hybrids are much more valuable in a garden than are their parents. They have large, simple to double, richly colored blossoms, which can completely cover the plant during peak bloom!

The choicest selections for hybridizing have been *H. nummularium, H. nummularium* ssp. *grandiflorum* and *H. apenninum*, which originate in central and southern Europe, as well as Asia Minor. All are found growing in dry, alkaline grasslands or in rocky grass meadows or in limey, well-drained sandy-rocky, loamy soil that is dry in summer. This furnishes a good indication as to the plant's cultural requirements.

155

Helianthemum selections have been rated critically by Hansen (1970). Of the numerous cultivars assessed, the ones listed in the table were given the highest ratings. These hybrids have the same cultural requirements and landscape uses as *H. appenninum*.

Helianthemum hybrid

Helianthemum 'Wisley Primrose'

Helianthemum Cultivars

Cultivar	Rating	Blossom color	Blossom type	Evergreen
'Braungold'	*	dark carmine	double	yes
'Cerise Queen'	**	dark carmine	double	yes
'Frau M. Bachtaler'	*	carmine-red	single	—
'Gelbe Perle' (= 'Double Yellow'; 'Luteum Plenum', 'Sulphureum Plenum')	**	lemon-yellow	double	yes
'Golden Queen'	***	yellow	single	no
'Lawrenson's Pink'	**	carmine-pink	single	yes
'Pink Double'	*	carmine-pink	half-double	yes
'Praecox'	*	lemon-yellow	single	—
'Rubin' (= 'Rubro Pleno', 'Amabile Plenum', 'Mutabile Coccineum')	**	dark carmine	double	—
'Sterntaler'	**	yellow	single	—
'Wisley Primrose'	**	lemon-yellow	single	—

Helianthemum Choicest Cultivars in North America

Cultivar	Blossom color	Blossom type	Notes
'Boule de Feur'	crimson red	double	
'Dazzler'	bright crimson red	single	
'Double Apricot'	plant pink	double	
'Double Orange'	copper orange	double	
'Flame'	flame pink	single	
'Golden Nugget'	yellow very large	single	plant dwarf, prostrate
'Goldilocks'	yellow	single	silver green leaves
'Mrs. Mold'	bronze salmon	single	
'Peace'	apricot peach	single	evergreen
'Pumpkin'	pumpkin orange	single	
'Rose Glory'	rose pink	single	
'Seattle'	bright copper	single	
'Snowball'	pure white	double	
'St. Marys'	pure white	single	
'Sun Fleck'	golden yellow	double	

This list is characteristic but not totally inclusive—there are *dozens* of others, and all quite good.

Hypericum androsaemum, Hypericaceae

H. androsaemum (Zone 6) is widely distributed from the Caucasus Mountains and the western Mediterranean regions, to the Canarys and Azores. This species prefers maritime locations where fogs are commonplace. It is common in the North Atlantic regions of Spain in shady thickets and in the age-old mixed forests of the Caucasus as a forest ground cover.

This partially evergreen, upright-spreading shrub grows to 1 m. Oval-oblong leaves are 5 to 10 cm long, and nearly clasp round the stem; in spring they emerge violet or brown, and turn red in late autumn. The yellow flowers are relatively small with only a 2–2.5 cm diameter. The individual blossoms are short-lived, but the plant blooms continuously from late spring to the beginning of early fall. Fruits develop near the end of its blooming period. They are red-brown, and as they mature turn glossy black. The fruits remain on the plant into late winter.

Whereas *H. androsaemum* requires a moist and shady to partly shady location, the other species grow best in light, warm, more-dry-than-damp soil, in sunny to partly shady locations. They are especially suitable for tightly knit foreground plantings, with the exception of *H. calycinum,* which is suitable only for larger areas due to its vigorous stolons. The taller species (not including *H. calycinum*) are not only used for low hedges; they also are valuable as single specimens and for grouping in heath, prairie, and steppe gardens, between evergreen shrubs and conifers, or in herbaceous borders. All are frequented by bees for their ample pollen.

All of the species discussed are not absolutely frost hardy. During cold winters with no snow cover, leaves or shoot tips can freeze. Frost damaged tops should be pruned back each year. For this reason, yearly pruning should be considered, although it is not essential.

Hypericum calycinum, Hypericaceae

H. calycinum (Zones 5–6) can be found from southeastern Europe to northwestern Asia Minor. It grows as a ground cover in *Fagus orientalis* forests or under *Rhododendron ponticum.*

This evergreen, 20–30 cm tall shrub spreads by way of underground stolons. Its 5 to 10 cm long leaves are leathery, oblong-elliptic. They are almost sessile and borne in pairs along the square stem. Leaves are deep green on top and bluish beneath. In shady locations, however, leaves are lighter green. Above the foliage, golden-yellow, 7 cm wide, single blossoms appear from midsummer to fall. The stamens with reddish anthers resemble a golden powder puff.

Hypericum androsaemum

H. calycinum will grow in any garden soil, as long as it is not too dry. It grows equally well in sunny or very shady locations. It grows well as a ground cover planting under trees, where hardly anything else will grow. In exposed plantings during snowless but cold winters, *H. calycinum* foliage becomes freeze-dried; the leaves turn brown and die. In spring it is necessary, therefore, to cut back the plants to the ground. This will rejuvenate the plants and is best done while the plants are still dormant.

Hypericum forrestii, Hypericaceae

H. forrestii (Zone 6–7) was known earlier as *H. patulum* var. *forrestii*. It is now assigned species rank. *H. forrestii* is found in the broad-leaved evergreen forests of West China, Burma, and Assam. Growing 1–1.5 m tall, it is a spreading, bushy shrub with horizontal or pendulous branches. It is substantially more frost hardy than *H. patulum*, which should not be cultivated in colder climates as it is hardy only to Zone 8. *H. forrestii*'s 2.5 to 4.5 cm long, lanceolate or ovate leaves often become reddish in autumn. This small shrub produces 5 to 7 cm wide, golden-yellow, plate-shaped, flat blossoms continuously from midsummer to fall, borne 3 to 5, in cymes on its branch tips. Its fruits color red before they fully ripen, increasing the ornamental value of this species.

For landscape uses and cultural requirements see *H. androsaemum.*

Hypericum 'Hidcote', Hypericaceae

The origin of this hybrid, which was earlier attributed to *H. hookeranum* is now known to have originated at Hidcote Estate prior to 1948 from a planting of *H. patulum.* Except in semi-tropical regions it freezes to the ground each winter but recovers with new shoots to bloom in late summer (Zone 6).

It is a broadly spreading, partly evergreen cultivar which reaches a maximum height of 1.5 m when unpruned. Its blossoms are golden-yellow, 5 to 7 cm wide and plate-shaped. They are borne 1 to 3 in a group, blooming continuously from midsummer to late fall. The ovate or lanceolate leaves are 4 to 5 cm long, dark green above and light bluish-green below.

H. 'Hidcote' is the most valuable of the woody cultivars. It was awarded 3 stars in test in Holland; *H. calycinum* is the only other so highly regarded.

Its cultural requirements and landscape uses are the same as *H. androsaemum.*

Hypericum kouytchense, Hypericaceae

This 0.5 to 1 m tall, mostly deciduous, loosely branched shrub comes from the Chinese province of Kweichow (Zone 6). Ovate, 4 to 6 cm long, short-petioled leaves with transparent dots are bluish below and grow on reddish brown branches. A fine, dense display of 6 cm wide, light golden-yellow blossoms appear on the shoot tips from late spring through late fall. Petals are either flat or reflexed. After the petals fall, the fruit capsules turn bright red.

Its cultural requirements and landscape uses are the same as *H. androsaemum.*

Hypericum kouytchense

Hypericum × moserianum, Hypericaceae

This hybrid of *H. calycinum* and *H. patulum* is a valuable and beautiful bushy, evergreen shrub (Zones 7–8). It was awarded 2 stars in Holland. It grows with somewhat pendulous branches; 60 cm tall and 90 cm wide. Ovate leaves 4 to 5 cm long, are matte green above and somewhat paler below. From midsummer through fall it blooms with 5 to 6 cm wide, golden yellow flowers. The red anthers are similar to those of *H. calycinum.*

H. × *moserianum* has vigorous stolons and accordingly is chiefly planted as a ground cover. It thrives in shady locations sheltered from the wind. It occasionally freezes in winter, but always comes back. However, it is best to prune it to the ground in autumn and cover the bed with dry leaves over winter.

Iberis saxatilis, Cruciferae

I. saxatilis (Zone 5) is found in Spain, southern and southeastern France, the Swiss Jura and in Italy and Crimea in stony sites, rock fissures, and shady slopes. This evergreen, many branched subshrub reaches a height of only 5 to 10 cm. The woody, nearly prostrate branches are nubby due to the leaf scars left from past seasons. Leaves are rather fleshy, linear-pointed, about 1–2 cm long and bunched into rosettes. White flowers appear in midspring in 2 to 2.5 cm wide cymes.

I. saxatilis is a very important garden species. It remains smaller and has a more open habit than its more frequently cultivated relatives. It is a good choice for small containers, rock gardens and dry walls. It thrives in all soils, even limy soil, in sunny and partly shady locations.

Iberis sempervirens, Cruciferae

I. sempervirens (Zone 5) is found in southern Europe, Crete and Asia Minor. It colonizes in mountain forests, subalpine hillsides covered with rocky debris, in rocky areas and moraines. Frequently, *I. sempervirens* grows with *Geranium sub-caulscens, Anthyllis montana, Myosotis alpestris, Dryas octopetala, Dianthus integer, Lilium albanicum, Fritillaria macedonica, Crocus nivalis, Tulipa grisebachiana* and *Corydalis densiflora* in the alpine meadows of southern European mountain ranges.

I. sempervirens grows to be a dense, 30 cm tall, luxuriant, evergreen cushion. Its green, low spreading branches are glabrous at the base and turn upward toward the tips. Branches are leafier on the upper part. Leaves are 1.5–3 cm long, glossy dark green above and surprisingly yellowish green below. In mid-spring, somewhat later than *I. saxatilis*, many white flowers develop above the leaves in 2 to 3 cm wide, flat inflorescences. Gradually the blossom cluster lengthens into an elongated head.

Choice cultivars and natural varieties of *Iberis sempervirens* include: *I. s.* 'Compacta'; *I. s.* 'Nana'; *I. s.* 'Supurba'; and var. *curreifolia*. Dwarf forms are: *I. s.* 'Cemlaensis', *I. s.* 'Climax'; *I. s.* 'Little Gem'; and *I. s.* 'Snowflake'.

I. sempervirens and its cultivars are valuable and widely used springflowering ornamentals. They do best in sunny locations and in fertile, well limed soil. Planting in very sandy soils leads to stunted growth. Pruning away half the length of the shoots after flowers fade promotes denser growth and a richer flower display. In rock gardens and dry walls, brightly colored shrubs and bulbs such as *Anbrieta, Alyssum,* lilies and tulips make excellent companion plants, as do roses and dwarf conifers.

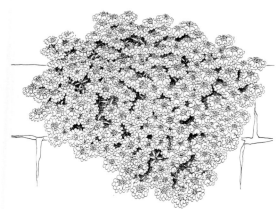

Iberis sempervirens

Ilex crenata, Aquifoliaceae

I. crenata (Zone 6), a Japanese species, grows wild in both evergreen and deciduous forests.

This densely branched, evergreen shrub has oblong-lanceolate, 2 to 3 cm long, glossy, dark green leaves. Black, 6 mm thick fruit develop from insignificant blossoms. This variable species can grow to be 2 to 3 m tall, and almost as wide. For this reason, only a few of the slower growing cultivars will be discussed.

I. c. Convexa' is considered one of the most valuable hardy cultivars. It grows rather slowly with a broad to conical, upright habit and reaches 2 m only in its maturity. The 1 to 2 cm long, stiff, leathery, compact leaves are fresh green, glossy and curved upwards on the edges like a spoon.

I. c. Golden Gem' is a dwarf cultivar with a low and spreading habit. It grows wider than tall, and its leaves are smaller than most cultivars. When the leaves first unfold, they are golden-yellow; later, they turn more or less green. It is a beautiful small shrub for protected, partly shady locations. It was awarded 2 stars in Holland.

I. c. 'Helleri, very dwarf and compact, originated in Newport, R.I. in 1925. Probably the smallest *I. convexa* cultivar; plants appear to be sheared. Leaves are less than 1 cm long, crowded.

I. c. 'Hetzii' is similar to 'Convexa' in growth habit. It has bright green leaves, which are about 2 cm long and 1–1.3 cm wide. It loses its leaves early under continental conditions and accordingly, in Dutch tests, is described as "dispensable."

I. c. 'Kingsvale', very dwarf clone, flattened globose shape, introduced by the Kingsville Nurseries, Kingsville, Md., in

161

1926. Leaves are less than 1 cm long; the original plant today is about 4 ft. high and 7 ft. across.

I. c. 'Mariesii' grows with short, more or less upright, dark gray branches, stiff and broadly columnar in habit. Its almost round, glossy leaves are only 5 to 12 mm wide and shallowly concave. Its dense, rigid growth makes it a favorite dwarfing and topiary plant in Japan. Its yearly growth only amounts to 3 cm.

I. c. 'Microphylla' is just as beautiful as 'Mariesii'. Its leaves are 7 to 13 mm long, somewhat concave and dark green. They are arranged very thickly on the branches. This cultivar remains quite low and dense.

I. c. 'Stokes' is one of the most important winter hardy cultivars. It was developed in the U.S., remains dwarf, and grows stiffly and densely compact. It has small, notched, dull green leaves. It is especially winter hardy.

Ilex crenata 'Stokes'

I. c. 'Tiny Tim' is a slow-growing, compact, winter hardy dwarf shrub also developed in the U.S. Its closely crowded leaves are small, dull green.

Other U.S. dwarf cultivars include *I. c.*

'Green Island', *I. c.* 'Kingwood Green Cushion' and *I. c.* 'Mariessii'.

All *I. crenata* cultivars have many landscape uses in the garden—slow growing ones do well in small containers. They make their best growth in partly shady locations, but often tolerate full shade well. They make few demands of soil, so they thrive in all good garden soils, even to pH levels of 7.75. Except for the tender 'Golden Gem', current cultivars are all frost hardy.

Kalmia angustifolia, Ericaceae

In the eastern half North America, mostly north of Zone 6, and in the boreal coniferous forests, *K. angustifolia* (Zone 2) is a typical inhabitant of the marshes and peaty meadows. It also appears in dry, acid and sterile soils. In Germany this kalmia has naturalized in churchyards and thickets and in warm, low-lying moors with beautiful effect.

This evergreen shrub with tightly erect branches grows to be 1 m tall. Its opposite leaves are oblong-lanceolate, and 3 to 6 cm long. They are bright green above and somewhat lighter beneath. In early summer many purple-red blossoms develop in axillary clusters just below the shoot tips. Until anthesis, the stamens lie in concavities of the lobes of the broadly companulate corolla.

K. a. 'Rubra' is the most widely propagated cultivar. It has dark purple blossoms and is considered to be more decorative than the species.

K. angustifolia, and the taller growing *K. latifolia,* are among the most beautiful, broad-leaved evergreen shrubs in cultivation. They compare favorably with their close relatives, the rhododendrons.

Kalmia angustifolia

This loose-growing, evergreen shrub only reaches a height of 50 cm. Its narrow, lanceolate, leathery, 2 to 3 cm long leaves are bluish green, nearly white beneath and rolled in on the edges. Narrowly bell-shaped, 10 to 15 mm wide, rose-purple blossoms borne in clusters open on the shoot tips in late spring.

This beautiful, plant-lover's shrub has the same cultural requirements and uses as *Kalmia angustifolia.*

K. polifolia var. *microphylla,* is a natural, well-known form like the above but only about 8″ high.

K. angustifolia is an ideal companion plant for dwarf rhododendrons, azaleas, *Ledum* species and Japanese maples. Other good companion plants are ferns, *Calluna* cultivars, *Erica cinerea* and *E. tetralix.*

K. angustifolia does very well in moist, raw humus soil or nutrient-poor, calcium deficient soils which have been amended with humus. Typically ericaceous, it grows well only in sharply acid soils. It will tolerate sunny locations if the climate is humid and the soil is damp. In continental climates it requires shady to partly shady locations.

Note: This plant is very poisonous, a fact not mentioned in the Ger. text.

Kalmia polifolia, Ericaceae

Together with *Ledum groenlandicum, K. polifolia* (Zone 2) colonizes cold peat moors in boreal North America, from Newfoundland to British Columbia south to Pennsylvania, Minnesota and the Pacific Northwest.

Lavandula angustifolia, Labiatae

From the western Mediterranean regions to Dalmatia and Greece, *L. angustifolia* (Zone 6) is a typical companion plant of *Salvia officinalis* on dry and warm slopes.

L. angustifolia is an evergreen, drought resistant, 20–60 cm tall, strongly aromatic dwarf shrub with dense gray branches. Its leaves are narrow and lanceolate. They are somewhat rolled at the edges and with fine silver-gray hair on both sides. Plants are covered with many, 15 to 20 cm long inflorescences made up of light blue to violet labiate flowers which are white-tomentose outside. Blossoms appear from midsummer through early fall.

In gardens, a few cultivars are better than the species. Some are a cross between *L. angustifolia* and *L. latifolia,* Mediterranean species. These are referred to as *L. × intermedia.* Others are simply cultivars of *L. angustifolia.*

These cultivars were critically rated in 1975 in Weihenstephan as to their value in continental conditions (see table on page 160).

In spite of its Mediterranean origin, *Lavandula angustifolia* is sufficiently frost

Lavandula angustifolia

Eriophorum vaginatum and *Drosera rotundifolia.*

L. palustre is a 1 m tall, erect, open, evergreen shrub with ascending branches. Its 2 to 4 cm long leaves, often rolled under at the edges, are linear-lanceolate and rusty-woolly beneath. The midrib is clearly distinguishable. Spring blossoms are numerous, 10 to 15 mm wide, white, with 7–10 exserted stamens. The aromatic flowers are borne in dense, round terminal clusters.

The essential oil in its aromatic leaves has a bitter taste. Years ago, fresh plants were used in making beer (to make the beer more intoxicating) and as a substitute for tea (Labrador Tea). *L. groenlandicum,* which is classified as a subspecies of *L. palustre* by some botanists, is differentiated by its elliptic-oblong leaves and only 5–8 stamens. The stamen's midrib is not discernible, and under the red-brown tomentum leaf undersides are dark green. This plant is native to Greenland and boreal North America, in marshes and cold peat moors.

hardy for continental climates. Its blossom color and blooming period make it a desirable dwarf shrub for steppe, rock, scree and heath gardens.

Roses and light-tolerant dwarf conifers make particularly attractive companion plants. Lavender is also well suited for growing in containers on patios and terraces.

L. angustifolia thrives in a warm, sunny location in well drained, alkaline soil, as well as in heavy clay soils. One of the most important things in caring for *L. angustifolia* is to prune it immediately after blooming.

Ledum palustre, Ericaceae

This plant's natural habitat is in the high and transitional sphagnum moors from northern and central Europe to the Urals and northern Asia (Zone 2). It is often found growing on hillocks in sphagnum moors with *Andromeda polifolia, Vaccinium myrtillus, V. oxycoccos, Calluna vulgaris,*

Ledum palustre

Ledum palustre var. *yedoense*

L. *palustre* does not tolerate dry or alkaline soils. It thrives in moist to damp, moorland soil in sunny locations. Both species are decorative dwarf shrubs which do well in damp moor beds, though L. *groenlandicum* is sometimes difficult to obtain.

Leiophyllum buxifolium, Ericaceae

L. *buxifolium* (Zone 6) is found in North America, from New Jersey to Florida. It covers large, granite rocks with thick, spreading carpets in the highlands and mountains, such as Grandfather Mountain in the Appalachians.

L. *buxifolium* is a 5 to 30 cm tall, mostly prostrate, myrtle-like, evergreen dwarf shrub with dark green, 3 to 8 mm long leaves. Out of red buds, numerous, small, white blossoms develop in terminal clusters from late spring into early summer.

This charming collector's shrub requires a sunny to partly shady location in well drained, sandy-loamy, lime-free soil.

Leucothoe fontanesiana, Ericaceae

L. fontanesiana (Zone 5) is native to the deciduous forests of southestern North America. It often grows in open highlands with other ericaceous species, in shallow, rocky locations.

This evergreen shrub rarely grows more than 1 m tall in cultivation. It increases by underground stolons and has wide spreading, pendulous branches which are reddish when the plant is young. The branches in direct sunlight are bronzed dark red. Its ovate-lanceolate, 6 to 15 cm long, acuminate leaves are glossy dark green on top and assume a magnificent red tinge in late autumn. White, 8 mm long, almost cylindrical, blossoms appear in spring in axillary, nodding clusters mostly toward the cane tips.

L. fontanesiana requires acid, moist, partly peat and partly gritty mineral soil. In locations with high humidity it tolerates an open planting site; beyond that, it needs partly shady sites. It tolerates very heavy shade as well as the competition of full-sized trees and shrubs. It can be used as a specimen or in clumps as a ground cover in the woodland garden.

L. f. 'Rainbow' is perfect for gardeners who love unusual cultivars. It has pink and white marbled and spotted leaves, which are coppercolored and yellow when they first appear.

L. f. 'Rolissonii' is not easy to find. It is differentiated from the species by narrower leaves.

L. f. axillaris, from southeastern North America, is not especially useful in most gardens but is more for collectors. It is similar to *L. fontanesiana* but the leaves are sharply pointed and have shorter stalks.

Ligustrum vulgare 'Lodense', Oleaceae

The species, native to Europe, North Africa and Asia Minor, will not be discussed. It is a deciduous shrub which reaches 5 m tall.

L. v. 'Lodense' (Zone 4) on the other hand, is a very compact shrub, hardly more than 50 cm tall, with dark green, narrow-elliptic, 3 to 5 cm long leaves. They change to bronze-brown in late autumn and persist for quite sometime into winter before falling.

This cultivar grows in any garden soil. Its most appropriate use is as a low hedge or ground cover. It is disease-prone in hot climates.

Linnaea borealis, Caprifoliaceae

L. borealis (Zone 2), the heraldic plant of the Swedish botanist Carolus Linnaeus, is

Leucothoe fontanesiana

Linnaea borealis

Lithospermum purpureocaeruleum

a typical inhabitant of northern moss-rich coniferous forests. It appears in the open landscape in dwarf shrub heaths, tundra in arctic regions and on high mountains (as in the U.S. and Canadian Rockies, and even in Northern Minnesota). From the middle of its natural range of distribution in northern Europe, it spreads out circumpolar in boreal regions. It is also found in larch, spruce, and *Pinus cembra* forests in the Alps, together with *Rhododendron ferrugineum, Empetrum nigrum, Calluna vulgaris, Vaccinium uliginosum, V. myrtillus* and *V. vitis-ideae.*

This dwarf evergreen shrub spreads widely with creeping branches which may grow to be meters long. Leaves are 6 to 25 mm long, shallowly toothed and fringed, ovate, dark green, and opposite. Terminal, upright flower stems develop on branch tips throughout summer. Apple-blossom pink, bell-shaped, intensely fragrant flowers are 6 to 9 mm long, borne in pairs on each stem.

L. borealis thrives only in acid, high humus content, moist soils in cool, shady locations. In moor beds this plant weaves

its thin branches between dwarf rhododendrons and over any rocks.

Lithospermum purpureocoeruleum, Boraginaceae

L. purpureocoeruleum (Zone 6) is representative of flora on the lower Alpine slopes on the Mediterranean side from the Pontic Alps westward. It is also found in rock heaths in the valleys of the upper Rhine and the Swiss Juras and in the British Isles. Its habitat is the mixed oak forests which are dry in summer. It is characteristically a member of the forest floor in the chestnut forests of the southern Alps and the Horse Chestnut forests in southern Albania, northern and central Greece. It is often accompanied by *Mercurialis perennis, Lamium maculatum, Anemone nemorosa, Euphorbia amygdaloides, Pulmonaria tuberosa* and *Cardamine bulbifera.*

This deciduous subshrub spreads quickly with long, arching branches which take root on the tips. Its leaves are 3 to 4 cm

167

long, lanceolate, acuminate on both ends, thickly pilose, and rolled under at the edges. Blossom shoots are erect, growing to about 30 cm tall. In late spring, the blossoms appear in few-flowered terminal clusters. At first they are red but later turn azure-blue. This change in blossom color is fairly common in members of the Boraginaceae.

L. purpureocoeruleum is a beautiful plant for rock gardens, as well as a very good ground cover for sunny to partly shady locations in neutral to alkaline soil. It is so robust, it tolerates conditions beneath thickly branched standard trees and shrubs.

Lithospermum purpureocaeruleum

Lonicera albertii, Caprifoliaceae

The central Asiatic high steppes and deciduous forests of Tibet and Turkestan are home to *L. albertii* (Zone 5).

This deciduous, widespreading shrub hardly reaches 50 cm tall. It has decumbent or arching branches. Its 2 to 3 cm long, sessile, linear leaves are blue-green on top and whitish beneath. In spring, small, lilac-pink, fragrant blossoms open in short stalked, axillary pairs.

It grows in any well drained soil that is not too cold. It is best planted where its pendulous branches are allowed to hang over walls or large rocks. Older plants can develop into meter-wide, dense bushes with long, trailing branches.

This species has recently been reclassified as *Lonicera spinosa* var. *Albertii*.

Lonicera nitida, Caprifoliaceae

L. nitida (Zone 7) is found in western China, from the evergreen lowland forests into the deciduous forests of higher elevations.

In its natural habitat this more or less evergreen shrub grows up to 2 m tall. In nurseries, under favorable conditions, it seldom exceeds 1 m tall, but grows substantially wider.

Leaves are borne in pairs at the nodes, each pair at right angles to the pairs above and below it; the young foliage has a purplish tinge. Its myrtle-like leaves are 6 to 12 mm long, ovate, lanceolate and dark green on top. Creamy-white, hardly noticeable blossoms appear in spring in short stalked pairs on small lateral branches. The 5 to 6 mm diameter, glossy purple fruits are hidden beneath the foliage.

Cultivars are grown almost exclusively, as they are much hardier than the species.

L. n. 'Elegant' is the most popularly grown cultivar. It is differentiated from the species by a looser, and therefore more

168

attractive, habit characterized by almost horizontally spreading or pendulous branches. Its two rows of leaves are dull green on top and, at 15 mm long, are somewhat larger than those of the species.

L. n. 'Hohenheimer Findling' received the highest rating possible in a judging in Holland. This broadly erect, up to 1.25 m tall shrub has arching branches with erect, lateral twigs. Its leaves are 10 to 18 mm long and narrowly ovate. It is similar to 'Elegant', but is more frost hardy.

L. n. 'Maigruen' is characterized by a more compact habit and very glossy leaves, which do not change color in winter.

L. nitida thrives in any soil in sunny to partly shady locations. It is not very handsome planted as a single specimen, but is well suited for pruned or loose hedges as well as ground cover.

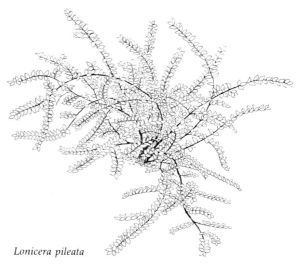
Lonicera pileata

Lonicera pileata, Caprifoliaceae

L. pileata (Zone 6) is found in the same regions of western China as L. nitida.

This well branched, evergreen shrub is smaller than L. nitida, reaching a height of only 30 cm.

With its flat, widespreading habit, it is similar to Cotoneaster horizontalis. Its pilose branches are thickly covered with two rows of oblong, lanceolate, 12 to 25 mm long, leathery leaves which are glossy green on top. In spring, pale yellow, delicately fragrant, inconspicuous blossoms with funnel-shaped perianth tubes are produced in pairs. The fruit, red at first, turns purple-violet as it matures. The fruit on this species is much more noticeable than that of L. nitida.

L. pileata has the same cultural requirements and landscape uses as L. nitida. It is, however, much hardier.

Mahonia aquifolium, Berberidaceae

M. aquifolium (Zone 5) is found along the west coast of North America from southern Alaska to northern California, in moist, coniferous forests.

This variable, usually upright evergreen shrub can be somewhat taller than 1 m when planted in favorable locations. It does not have stolons. The 5 to 11 leaflets of the pinnate leaves are glossy green on top, but bronze-red when they first appear and again in winter. They are ovate to elliptic and serrated on the edges. Blossoms are yellow, occasionally marked with red, and are borne in erect clusters above the foliage in early spring. Its blackish purple, blue-frosted fruits are very attractive.

The variability of this species, together with its proclivity for hybridizing, has led to a great number of vegetatively propagated cultivars.

M. a. 'Apollo' has a short, wide habit reaching 60 cm tall. Its leaves are large, dark green and moderately glossy. Deep golden-yellow blossoms develop in early spring in large, pyramidal, more or less erect inflorescences. Because of the large number of blossoms, branches can become bare after flowering; however, they are usually quickly covered by new shoots originating from the crown. This cultivar received the highest possible rating in a judging in The Netherlands.

M. a. 'Atropurpurea' received the same high rating as 'Apollo' in The Netherlands. It too, grows short and wide, in well branched, hardy and salt resistant. Its leaves are medium-sized, dark green, moderately glossy and deep bronze in winter. Yellow blossoms appear in small, numerous inflorescences in late winter to early spring. One of its better attributes is that after losing its leaves in severe winters, it quickly recovers and leafs out in spring.

Mahonia aquifolium

M. a. 'Jupiter' is an erect, 1 m tall cultivar which has intense red foliage in autumn and winter. Summer foliage is dark green. Leaves with 7 to 9 leaflets are 15 to 20 cm long; the 5 to 8 cm long leaflets are boat-shaped, wavy and thorny serrate. In early spring pale yellow blossoms appear, in 6 to 8 cm long inflorescences on the branch tips and in clusters along the branches. The flower petals are deeply cut and curled.

M. a. 'Smaragd', a newer cultivar from Holland, is a wide, bushy shrub with 15 to 20 cm long pinnately compound leaves. The 5 to 9 leaflets are 6 to 9 cm long and have 6 to 11 thorny notches on the edges. When the leaves first emerge they are glossy bronze-colored. As they mature, they become glossy green to blue-green and do not change color again. From the end of April to the beginning of May, golden-yellow blossoms appear in numerous, large, thick clusters on the branch ends and in the leaf axils along the branches.

M. aquifolium grows in any good garden soil as long as it is not compacted. It will not tolerate drought. It grows best in partly shady locations, but also thrives in sunny or very shady sites. It can be used in many ways—as a small hedge plant, in narrow strips between buildings and walkways, as a long-living, indestructible ground cover or as an understory planting with evergreen trees and shrubs and conifers. It can also be used with *Bergenia* and *Iberis,* which blossom at the same time.

Usually *M. aquifolium* is not pruned, although it tolerates pruning very well, even into the older wood. Pruning should be done immediately after the plant blossoms.

Mahonia repens, Berberidaceae

M. repens (Zone 5) is found in the same area of Pacific North America as *M. aquifolium,* but extends its range to the inland mountains.

In its native habitat this shrub often grows only 10–20 cm high. In cultivation *M. repens* is a 30 to 60 cm tall evergreen shrub with sprawling branches and vigorous stolons. Its 10 to 20 cm long compound leaves have 5 wide ovate, matte green, dentate leaflets, with 8 to 20 notches on either side. Golden-yellow blossoms cluster on the shoot tips in late spring. Bluish black fruits with a frosty bloom develop later. This plant is sometime confused with *M. aquifolium.*

Nurseries carry many different cultivars in the *M. aquifolium* group which have stolons. The gardener can recognize these cultivars as *M. repens* if the leaves are matte green and do not change color in autumn.

M. repens has the same cultural requirements as *M. aquifolium,* but is slightly more frost tender and therefore requires a protected planting site. In partial shade under trees it is a decorative, slow spreading ground cover. It does not tolerate excessive soil cultivation.

Moltkia petraea, Boraginaceae

M. petraea (Zone 6–7) is an endemic plant of subalpine to alpine lime meadows in the mountain ranges of Greece, Yugoslavia and northern Albania. It also appears in secondary mountain ranges along the Mediterranean coastline.

M. petraea is a bushy, thickly branched, 15 to 30 cm tall subshrub. Branches are woody at the base. Its leaves are narrow-linear to oblong-lanceolate, up to 3 cm long, tough and light green. Numerous, violet-blue, funnel-shaped, nodding blossoms appear above the foliage in early summer.

With its blue blossoms, *M. petraea* is a decorative, summer blooming dwarf shrub for dry walls and rock or container gardens. It requires sunny locations and a well drained, neutral to lime humus soil. It is quite hardy.

Muehlenbeckia axillaris,
Polygonaceae

M. axillaris (Zone 6) is native to the mountains of New Zealand, Tasmania and Australia.

This deciduous, mat-like, tangled dwarf shrub proliferates through stolons and rarely grows more than 3 to 5 cm tall in its natural habitat. In cultivation, the wire-like, slender branches grow to be 20 to 25 cm long. The 3 to 8 mm long, almost circular, leaves are brownish green. The yellowish blossoms and pale wax-colored capsules are hardly noticeable.

In protected, sunny locations with well drained soil, this dwarf shrub will cover rock garden soil and stones very densely. It is especially good in mid-size border areas that are often disturbed, such as along walking paths. Grow it with other New Zealand plants such as *Berberis buxifolia* 'Nana' or *Hebe* ssp.

Ononis fruticosa, Leguminosae

O. fruticosa (Zone 8) is found on rocky slopes and dry moraines from south-western Europe to Algeria.

O. fruticosa is an erect, thornless,

Moltkia petraea

densely branched, 0.3 to 1 m tall evergreen shrub. Young twigs are finely pilose but lose their hairs and turn gray as they mature. Compound leaves with 7 leaflets are borne in axillary clusters. Leaflets are 2 to 3 cm long, oblong-lanceolate, gray-green, tough and smooth. Pale pink, white or pink flowers with red veins appear from late spring through summer in loose, terminal panicles.

O. fruticosa is a Mediterranean region shrub with great garden appeal, well suited for rock gardens and raised rockery beds. In naturalized gardens it blends well with lavender, flax, gray-leaved perennials, and ornamental grasses. Its planting site must be sunny, warm and protected from wind. The soil should be mildly alkaline, well drained and rocky. As a rule, *O. fruticosa* should be pruned to the ground every spring.

Pachysandra procumbens, Buxaceae

Pachysandra procumbens (Zone 4–6) is an evergreen subshrub in the south, deciduous perennial in the north. Flower spikes to 12 cm appear in late winter–early spring, with tiny pink, fragrant flowers. Leaves are elliptic to ovate, toothed, slightly hairy, dark green. This is an exceptionally handsome ground cover plant for shady beds.

Pachysandra terminalis, Buxaceae

P. terminalis (Zone 5) is native to the moist, deciduous forests of Japan.

This evergreen subshrub of spreading habit forms a dense, broad carpet of 20 cm high, fleshy shoots with 5 to 10 cm long leaves; its underground, vigorous stolons grow throughout spring and summer. The close-growing leaves borne at the shoot tips are olive-green and glossy above, notched on the tips, wedge-shaped at the base. Fragrant flower spikes emerge from the shoot tips with female flowers below and male flowers atop the spike. The white flowers are closely inserted in unbranched inflorescences.

P. t. 'Green Carpet', the slowest growing, most ornamental cultivar, has small foliage and a compact habit. It reaches only 15 cm tall and does not, therefore, compete visually with taller shrubs under which it may be planted. It is very sensitive to direct sun and thus requires day-long shade from high-crowned trees.

As a ground cover, *P. t.* 'Variegata' will brighten up very shady locations and make them more pleasant with its white variegated leaves.

P. terminalis is not usually planted singly. In appropriate locations (all partly shady to shady sites with moist, humus-rich, open soil) it is one of the most useful ground covers for medium-sized areas. Its spreading surface roots do not compete with those of larger trees and shrubs. As a matter of fact, its roots protect the roots of larger plants from direct sun and dangerously low temperatures. The thick foliage of *P. terminalis* swallows up fallen tree leaves and therefore not only saves the gardener work, but also improves the soil. It can grow to be decades old and will remain beautiful with very little care. Before planting, it is absolutely essential to prepare the site properly if *P. terminalis* is to thrive. Spade or till the soil and at the same time enrich it with organic material.

Paxistima canbyi, Celastraceae

A native of eastern North America on steep, rocky slopes mainly in the mountains of Virginia, westward toward southeastern Ohio and northeastern Kentucky (Zone 3). It grows exclusively in acid soil.

This genus is represented by *P. myrsinites* in western North America. It grows in very shady as well as open locations in rocky, well drained soil in Pacific Northwest coniferous forests and Rocky Mountain valleys. It grows somewhat faster than *P. canbyi* and has wide, ovate to elliptic leaves. This species is not commonly found in cultivation.

P. canbyi is a 25 cm tall evergreen shrub and spreads by prostrate, rooting branches. It has very fine, leathery, narrow-elliptic, light green leaves; 1 to 2 cm long, finely serrated and rolled under at the edges. The axillary brownish red blossoms are insignificant.

P. canbyi is not only a beautiful dwarf shrub, but is also a wonderfully dense ground cover for small areas. It can even be used between slow growing dwarf trees and shrubs. However, it cannot compete with large trees and shrubs. It thrives in partly shady to shady locations in humus-rich, well drained, moist, lime-free soil. It survives only briefly in sun-drenched locations or in heavy soil. This species fails where summers are hot.

Penstemon davidsonii,
Scrophulariaceae

Western North America is the natural habitat of *P. davidsonii* (Zone 6), where it grows at medium to high elevations from the southern tip of the Sierra Nevadas to southern British Columbia, often on open, rocky slopes. It is also found in the lava beds of McKenzie Pass in Oregon.

    P. davidsonii makes a dense ground cover. It is a mat-forming, 5 to 15 cm tall dwarf shrub with underground runners. Its opposite, almost entire-margined leaves are only 5 mm long. This cushion plant is thickly covered with lilac-purple blossoms in summer.

Penstemon davidsonii

Penstemon newberryi,
Scophulariaceae

P. newberryi (Zone 6) occurs naturally in the high mountain ranges in western North America, from southwestern Oregon to the southern Sierra Nevadas in California. It is found thriving in small cracks and crevices in granite rock.

    P. newberryi develops into a loose, 15 to 25 cm tall, bushy cushion with vigorous shoots. The shoots are reddish tinged and are finely pilose. Leaves are elliptic to ovate, 12 to 25 mm long, opposite, glossy, and finely crenate. Numerous flower spikes develop above the foliage in early summer. Blossoms are 3 to 3.5 cm long, single, tubular, and bright pink to ruby-red.

    All *Penstemon* species require a protected, sunny location and well drained soil which is more dry than moist and not too rich. Neither *P. davidsonii* nor *P. newberryi* can be outdone in beauty of color while in flower. The shrubby penstemens are intolerant of hot, humid weather as well as harsh winter conditions.

Pernettya mucronata, Ericaceae

P. mucronata (Zone 6–7) is found growing on the eastern edge of the South American

174

Penstemon newberryi

P. mucronata exhibits an advanced form of self-sterility. Consequently, in garden culture, both female and male must be present in a ratio of 10:1 for abundant fruiting. Plants of both sexes are available in good nurseries, as is a good selection of fruit colors.

P. m. 'Alba' has white fruit.

P. m. 'Bell's Seedling' is a hermaphroditic form considered one of the best cultivars with large, deep red, and persistent fruit.

P. m. 'Purpurea' has purple-violet fruit.

As is the case with many Southern Hemisphere plants, *P. mucronata* is not very hardy. It requires a protected, sunny location and winter mulching. It thrives in cool, moist to damp, acid soil containing a high percentage of organic material. It also tolerates partly shady locations and is, therefore, a good companion for evergreen rhododendron species.

Andes, from Patagonia to Tierra del Fuego. Its habitat is the Patagonian laurel forests, composed principally of *Nothofagus* species.

This 0.5–1.5 m tall, broad and densely branched evergreen shrub has vigorous stolons. The glossy, dark green leaves are narrow-elliptic, cuspidate, nearly 2 cm long, hard and leathery. Following the small, urn-shaped, axillary blossoms, which appear in late spring, 8 to 12 mm thick, round to flat fruit develop by late summer. Fruit colors are very striking. Though fruits are generally red on wild plants, cultivars, which are not always named, have white, pink, carmine or violet colored fruits.

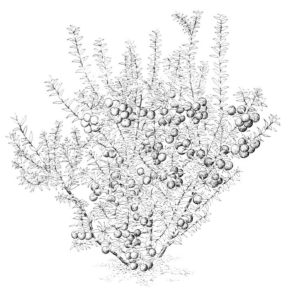

Pernettya mucronata

175

Perovskia abrotanoides, Labiatae

P. abrotanoides (Zone 6) is native to the steppes and dry deciduous forests of the botanically rich Near Eastern region, extending as far east as the western Himalayas.

P. abrotanoides reaches a height of 50 cm with numerous, erect branches. If not pruned its branches are prostrate-ascending when mature. Its 3 to 6 cm long, aromatic, gray-white leaves are serrate to double-serrate, cut in an attractive, feathery manner. Lilac-colored blossoms develop in late summer in false spikes at the tips of the current year's shoots.

This attractive, hardy, summerflowering, deciduous shrub spreads moderately with rhizome-like runners. As with all drought resistant steppe shrubs, *Perovskia* ssp. thrive in open, sunny locations in well drained, mildly alkaline, mineral soil. They do well in rock gardens, heath gardens, raised beds and roof gardens. The gray foliage harmonizes well with drought resistant, silver-needled dwarf conifers, red-leaved trees, and native perennials and grasses. Especially recommended companion plants include clumps of feathery grasses, *Linum flavum* and *Inula ensifolia,* or a carpet of *Sedum floriferum* 'Weihenstephaner Gold', which has red foliage while *P. abrotanoides* is blooming; or *Sedum middendorffiana* 'Diffusum', which blossoms at the same time as *P. abrotanoides.* Tulips and early spring crocus thrive under the protection which *Perovskia*'s roots offer them.

As is true with most summer-blooming shrubs, *Perovskia* should be pruned back to the crown in spring. This annual pruning maintains the erect growth habit and encourages blossoms.

Perovskia atriplicifolia, Labiatae

P. atriplicifolia (Zone 5) is found in steppes and dry deciduous forests. It covers relatively large areas from Afghanistan to western Tibet.

In its natural habitat it grows to 1.5 m tall. In gardens it stays much shorter either due to a colder winter or yearly pruning. Its white-tomentose twigs are round and minimally branched. Leaves are 3 to 6 cm long, unevenly and coarsely serrate, and both sides are gray-tomentose. Terminal flower panicles are 30 to 50 cm long with blue blossoms in late summer, which are much more attractive than those of *P. abrotanoides.*

P. atriplicifolia has the same general cultural requirements as *P. abrotonoides* and is used similarly in the landscape, but is more frost sensitive in cool coastal climates and hardier where summers are hot and dry. It therefore requires a deep mulch of leaves or conifer branches. Its broadly spreading habit is best displayed on the rim of walls, over which its branches can drape.

Perovskia × 'Hybrida', Labiatae

This hybrid, of unknown origin, was introduced about 1937 by Hillier in England. In 1955, botanical taxonomists assigned it the binomial *P.* × *superba,* and under this name the plant was used for years. However, further research and review produced the binomial *P.* × 'Hybrida' which may be questionable for obvious reasons, but which is in common use today.

P. × 'Hybrida' is a much better ornamental plant than either of the above two species. It seems strange that both species are more often cultivated than is

Perovskia atriplicifolia

the hybrid. 'Hybrida' grows 60 to 80 cm tall, has blue-violet blossoms and 4 to 7 cm long, simple to double pinnatisected leaves which are ovate in form and gray-green in color.

Phyllodoce coerulea, Ericaceae

P. coerulea (Zone 2) is found only in the Arctic alpine region of Europe, Scottish Highlands and the central Pyrenees in western Europe. As a relic of the last glacial period, its main range is the boreal regions of Europe to the arctic and subarctic regions of North America and north-eastern Asia.

P. coerulea is a spreading-trailing, evergreen dwarf shrub 10–15 cm tall. It has *Empetrum*-like, linear revolute leaves. Large, purple blossoms appear in late spring in terminal false spikes.

This heath-like dwarf shrub thrives in cool, partly shaded locations in moist, nutrient-poor, raw humus soil. It is an ideal companion plant for dwarf rhododendrons and other shrub-like Ericaceae having similar cultural requirements.

Other exceptionally choice *Phyllodoce* species native to North America or northern Japan are occasionally grown in botanical gardens. Normally, they are much more difficult to cultivate than *P. coerulea*. Specialty nurseries carry rarer species such as *P. breweri* and *P. empetriformis*, both native to the mountain ranges of western North America, or *P. tsugifolia*, native to northern Japan.

Pieris japonica, Ericaceae

Although all *Pieris* species (Zone 6) and cultivars grow relatively slowly, most become too large to be considered dwarf shrubs. Only *P.* 'Pygmaea', *P.* 'Valley Rose' and *P.* 'Variegata' can be classifed as dwarf shrubs.

P.j. 'Pygmaea' is a cultivar of Japanese origin. This evergreen, bushy shrub remains much smaller than the type species which is native to the Japanese evergreen laurel forests and warm, moist deciduous forests. Leaves of the cultivar are only 1.5 to 2.5 cm long, linear-lanceolate and crenate on the margins. Flower buds begin forming in autumn and are in full bloom from late winter to mid-spring. Urn-shaped white flowers are borne in simple, pendant, white clusters.

P. j. 'Valley Rose' is a slow growing cultivar developed in America. In ten years time, it may reach only 70 to 80 cm. It is one of the exquisite pink-blooming cultivars. The flower buds are dark brown in winter and the leaves emerge reddish-green.

Phyllodoce caerulea

P. j. 'Variegata' is slow growing and does not bloom well. Its small, lively-hued leaves which have a small, white rim are the most noticeable and prized part of the shrub. Of the cultivars listed here, P. 'Variegata' is the easiest to acquire, though specialty nurseries can often supply the others.

In keeping with the species' natural habitat, P. *japonica* cultivars require sheltered locations under high-crowned trees such as oaks, birches and pines. They thrive in humusy, lime-free, moist soil; do not tolerate mineral fertilizers well, but need leaf mold and peat dressings from time to time. They make excellent companion plants for rhododendrons.

Potentilla fruticosa, Rosaceae

P. *fruticosa* (Zone 2), the most commonly cultivated shrub species in this sizeable genus, is native to the boreal coniferous forests, tundra and alpine areas throughout the Northern Hemisphere. This species develops into a 1.5 m tall, slender

Pieris japonica 'Variegata'

steppe characteristics. In larger areas, they may also be used as ground covers. Their yellow blossoms go exceptionally well with blue-blooming companions such as *Nepeta* × *faassenii*, *Salvia* × *superba*, *Aster amellus* and *A. tongolensis*. *Festuca glauca* and *Helictotrichon sempervirens* also make striking companions plants.

Although potentillas do not require pruning, they tolerate it very well. As a matter of fact, it improves the plant's flowers (there are fewer of them, but they are much larger after the plant has been pruned). It is hard to rejuvenate older shrubs with pruning, though they benefit if transplanted to damp, well fertilized soil.

twigged, densely branched, deciduous shrub. Its cultivars are generally shorter. Normally, leaves are ternate. The leaflets are 1 to 3 cm long, somewhat rolled under at the edges and more or less pilose.

Pure yellow, 2 to 3 cm blossoms appear singly or in clusters borne in terminal panicles or cymes from spring through early autumn.

The type species is no longer favored by gardeners as its cultivars are richer, live longer, are more colorful and have flowers which last longer. At present, numerous cultivars are available.

P. fruticosa cultivars require full sun. When planted in partly shady locations they begin to sprawl and flower poorly. They thrive in any garden soil and tolerate dry locations well. Only the gray-leaved cultivars, however, are drought resistant; the others require a moderately watered site. These cultivars are extremely ornamental, blossoming shrubs. They should be planted in small groups in heath gardens or in gardens with dry prairie or

Potentilla fruticosa 'Goldteppich'

Prunus laurocerasus 'Otto Luyken', Rosaceae

Of the numerous *Prunus laurocerasus* (Zone 6) cultivars, only this one is currently acceptable for dwarf classification. This cultivar was introduced in 1953 by H. A. Hesse & Co., and named after the man who owned the nursery which distributed the plant at the time.

179

Potentilla fruticosa 'Abbotswood'

Potentilla fruticosa **Cultivars**

Cultivar	Habit	Height (cm)	Leaf Color	Flower Color	Flowering Period	European Rating
'Abbottswood'	Erect, at present the best white cultivar	60–80	blue-green	white	beg. May/ beg. Oct	***
'Elizabeth' (= Arbuscula) (= 'Sutters Gold')	Low spreading with age, broadly upright, long and rich blooming period	100	white beneath	dark yellow	mid June/ beg. Oct	***

Potentilla fruticosa Cultivars (cont.)

Cultivar	Habit	Height (cm)	Leaf Color	Flower Color	Flowering Period	European Rating
'Farreri' (= 'Gold Drop')	Broadly erect, bushy	60	green	intense yellow	end May/ end Oct	**
'Goldfinger'	Upright, heavy bloomer, large blossoms	80–100	green	bright yellow	mid June/ beg. Sept	
'Goldstar'	Upright to wide-spreading, large blossoms	80	green	gold-yellow	end June/ beg. Oct	
'Goldteppich'	Low growing, flatter than 'Elizabeth'	50–60	dark green	intense gold-yellow	beg. June/ beg. Oct	
'Hachmanns Gigant'	Similar to 'Elizabeth', heavy bloomer, large blossoms	60–80	green	deep gold-yellow	end June/ beg. Oct	
'Klondyke'	Similar to 'Farreri, but blossoms are larger with better color	70–90	green	dark yellow	mid June/ end Sept	***
'Longacre'	Cushion-like, numerous flowers	50–60	blue-green	soft yellow	mid June/ end Sept	*
'Maanelys'	Upright, fast growing, heavy bloomer, small flowers	120	green	medium yellow	end June/ end Sept	
var. *mandschurica*	Slow growing, low-growing, very hardy, a few, small flowers	30–40	silky gray on both sides	pure white	end June/ end Sept	
'Primrose Beauty'	Broad and elegant, pleasing flower color	100–130	gray pilose	pale yellow	end June/ beg. Sept	**
'Pyrenaica' (= 'Farreri Prostata')	Short and wide, moderate bloomer	20	bluish-green underneath	deep yellow	end June/ beg. Sept	
'Red Ace'	Upright, slender shoots, elegant leaves, blossom color not very attractive	50–60	green	red inside, yellow outside in cool climates; dirty yellow where summers are hot	end June/ beg. Sept	

Potentilla fruticosa Cultivars (cont.)

Cultivar	Habit	Height (cm)	Leaf Color	Flower Color	Flowering Period	European Rating
'Snowflake'	Stiffly erect, large leaves	60–80	deep green	white, single to double	End June/ beg. Sept	**
'Sommerflor'	Similar to 'Klondyke', but healthier in the garden	70–90	green	gold-yellow	mid June/ beg. Oct	
'Tangerine'	Short and open, only blooms in cool weather, good blossom color, fine foliage	60–80	green	copper-gold to yellow-gold; orange in cool weather	mid June/ mid Sept	*

P. l. 'Otto Luyken' is an ev-green, very dense, broadly upright, compact shrub rarely more than 1 m tall. It can, however, grow up to 2 m wide. Leaves are oblong-lanceolate and acuminate. When they first emerge, they are fresh green, but as they mature, they turn a glossy, dark green. This shrub blossoms in late spring with 20 cm long, white, very fragrant clusters. As is the case with other *P. laurocerasus* cultivars, it has a second, equally rich blooming period; in September in most climates.

P. laurocerasus does not have special soil requirements. It thrives in any well prepared garden soil, and even tolerates a mildly alkaline pH. In harsh and sunny regions it needs partly shady locations and shelter from wind. On the other hand, it tolerates open locations in warmer regions having mild winters. Thanks to its extraordinary tolerance for shade and its insensitivity to tree line drip and root competition, it also does very well when planted under large trees and shrubs. It thrives even in shade when planted against a wall exposed to the north or the northwest. It can be used as a specimen or in groups. *P.* 'Otto Luyken' is especially valuable for low hedges. It is the hardiest of the *P. laurocerasus* cultivars.

Prunus prostrata, Rosaceae

As a decidedly south Mediterranean-Oriental species, *P. prostrata* (Zone 5) is native to a wide region from Spain to Asia Minor, Northern Iran and the Himalayas, growing on rocky hillsides and spreading flat over the face of sloping boulders. It is found at elevations between 1800 and 3000 m.

This deciduous, mostly prostrate, wide-spreading and knotty, 50 to 100 cm shrub has many landscape uses. Its ovate, 1.5 cm long, finely serrated leaves are mostly white-tomentose underneath. At the same time the leaves appear in spring, 1.2 cm wide, pink flowers with a tubular-bell-shaped calyx open.

This drought resistant shrub is very hardy and unassuming. It grows in any dry garden soil in open, sunny locations and is well suited for natural rock and steppe gardens.

Prunus pumila var. depressa, Rosaceae

P. pumila (Zone 4), native to northeastern North America, has only a special place in gardens. It is erect, not very attractive, and has a sparse branching habit. However, its flat-growing variation can be a dramatic element in the landscape design.

P. p. var. *depressa* is a twiggy, low, spreading shrub which often lies flat to the ground, just a few centimeters high. Its 3 to 5 cm long leaves are narrowly ovate. They are matte-green on top and bluish white underneath, but in autumn, change color to bluish- or scarlet-red with a silvery shimmer. In mid-spring, the previous year's shoots are covered with countless, small, simple, flat-petalled white blossoms. In the fall, it produces round-elliptical, 1 cm diameter, blackish-purple, edible fruits.

This drought resistant plant is well suited to container gardens and raised beds. It also makes a good ground cover in rock and heath gardens. It thrives in open, sunny locations and is adapted to any good garden soil.

Prunus pumila var. *depressa*

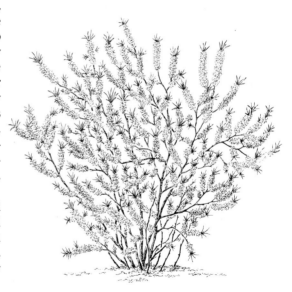

Prunus tenella

Prunus tenella, Rosaceae

P. tenella (Zone 2) is a characteristic plant of the so-called Sibljak-Faxies ecosystem; a dense, shrubby woody plant complex which follows the cutting over of oak and pine forests. This species is found from eastern Siberia to the central Asian and southern Russian steppes to Hungary and lower Austria.

P. tenella is a 50 to 150 cm tall, densely branched, deciduous shrub with quite vigorous slender twigs. Its bare, green-to-glossy-brown branches turn silver-gray

Prunus tenella

when two years old. The compact, 3 to 7 cm long, narrow elliptic to ovate or lanceolate leaves are sharply serrate. With the leaves, 2 cm wide, rose-pink blossoms appear in mid-spring. They are borne singly but thickly on the previous year's growth.

P. t. 'Fire Hill' is distinguished from the species by its darker colored and more numerous blossoms. This and other cultivars are very beautiful in spring when in full bloom; the type species is less attractive than the cultivar.

P. tenella and its cultivars quickly form large, dense thickets due to vigorous root sprouts (but only when on their own roots, not grafted). They all require large, open areas free of other plants in order to grow true to form. As steppe garden plants, they need an open, sunny location that is sparsely planted. They may be used with conifers and dwarf trees and shrubs in heath gardens, container gardens, or larger rock gardens. Thanks to their drought resistance, they are excellently suited for roof gardens, raised beds and dry walls. *P. tenella* looks well planted with narcissus, low growing tulips and and spring blooming herbaceous perennials such as *Doronicum, Aubrieta, Alyssum, Iberis* and *Phlox subulata*.

In addition to its drought resistance, *P. tenella* is relatively indifferent to its soil. This means that the plant grows as well in limy soil as it does in moderately heavy loamy soil or in light sandy soil. It is quite frost hardy, but deteriorates in hot, dry summers.

Ptilotrichum spinosum, Cruciferae

P. spinosum (= *Alyssum spinosum* L.), Zone 5, is native to the Mediterranean region (Algeria, Spain, southwestern France and elsewhere) in *Abies pinsapo* forests. Together with other thorny shrubs it is found in limy soils up to subalpine levels.

P. spinosum (= *Alyssum spinosum*) when mature, is a broad spreading, well branched, thorny dwarf shrub 20 cm tall. Its rigid, close-growing branches are covered with gray-white, stellate hairs. The leaves are silvery, 2 to 4 cm long and narrow lanceolate. Countless white flowers appear in late spring in flat, terminal and axillary clusters.

This is a hardy, heavy blooming dwarf shrub for sunny, dry sites in well drained soil containing a large quantity of fine gravel. It is also well suited for growing in rock fissures, dry walls, and rock gardens.

Rhododendron, Ericaceae

Of the numerous species and cultivars of this genus, only the dwarf forms will be discussed here. In addition to a few species, we will discuss hybrids belonging to the dwarfs deriving from *R. forrestii* var. *repens, R. impeditum, R. williamsianum* and *R. yakusimanum*. In addition, the evergreen cultivars of azalea referred to as "Japanese Azaleas" are included here.

Rhododendron cultural requirements, their landscape use in rock gardens and beds and suitable companion plants will be found in previous sections.

Following the plant description is an assessment of each plant's garden-worthiness.

"Garden Worthiness Ratings", based on the British system, have been noted after each rhododendron heading when possible.

****	= Excellent
***	= Good
**	= Fair
*	= Poor

Rhododendron 'Anna Baldsiefen'; Zone 6, not rated

This hybrid is a cross between *R.* 'Pioneer' × *R.* 'Pioneer'.

It is a 45 cm tall, 75 cm wide, compact cultivar. Its evergreen leaves are fleshy, elongate-ovate, 1.6 to 1.9 cm long. Flowers are star-shaped, 3.8 cm diameter, slightly ruffled, light rose, darker midribbed and rimmed. This is a prolific bloomer.

Rhododendron anthopogon;
Zone ?, not rated

R. anthopogon is native to Nepal and south Tibet.

This is a low, broad and compact plant, 30 to 60 cm tall and wide (usually broader than tall). Leaves are obovate-elliptic, densely scaly below, 2.5 to 3.8 cm long and 2.5 cm wide. Deep pink to cream flowers are 1.3 to 1.9 cm long and narrowly tubular.

R. a. 'Betty Graham' is a good pink cultivar.

Rhododendron calostrotum;
Zone 6,****

This plant is native to northeastern upper Burma, in Yunnan Province of China and in southeastern Tibet. It grows at elevations of 3000 to 4500 m, in groups or large mats, in damp mountain moors, on rocks and cliffs or along streams.

R. calostrotum is a 30 cm tall, stiffly erect, sparsely branched, evergreen species. Its young shoots are thickly covered with scales as are its leaves. The leaves are oval-elliptic and fringed on the rims. They are thickly covered with greenish scales on the upper surface and dry, red scales underneath. In early spring 3 cm long, bright purple-violet, broadly funnel-form flowers open which are also soft-hairy.

R. calostrotum prefers damp, shady sites in an alpine rockery.

Rhododendron camtschaticum;
Zone 6,**

This plant grows wild in mountain ranges from Kamtschatka, northern Japan and Alaska, on both sides of the Bering Strait; often in rock fissures or rocky soil.

A deciduous, 20 to 30 cm tall, low-spreading species, *R. camtschaticum* is very valuable because it is extremely frost hardy. From early summer to early fall, single, relatively large, simple, turbinate, dark purple-violet blossoms with reddish brown markings appear on the shoot tips above thin, ciliate leaves.

R. camtschaticum requires a moist, cool site in well drained soil. It tolerates sunny locations only in humid areas.

Rhododendron camtschaticum

Rhododendron carolinianum;
Zone 4,**/*

R. carolinianum is native to the open highlands and sparse coniferous forests of Tennessee, the Carolinas and Georgia; in the southern Appalachians of North America.

This is a 1 to 1.5 m tall, evergreen shrub with elliptic, 6 to 10 cm long leaves. The leaves are smooth on top with reticulate venation, and thickly covered with scurfy scales underneath. In May–June, narrow, funnel-shaped, 3 cm long, light purple-pink blossoms appear.

R. carolinianum is very frost hardy and tolerates a variety of garden soils. Unlike other Rhododendron, it does not transplant well when it is older.

One hybrid of note is R. 'Pequot'. (R. minus 'Compactum' × R. carolinianum). This plant has a low, dense habit; at 10 years it is 45 cm tall and 91 cm wide. Its evergreen leaves are 3.75 cm long and almost elliptic. Light pink flowers open bell-shaped, about 2.5 cm across.

Rhododendron 'Chikor';
Zone ?, not rated

R. 'Chikor' is a cross between R. chryseum × R. ludlowii.

It is a compact, spreading, cushion-shaped plant, 30 to 91 cm tall and broader than wide. Leaves are evergreen, 1.2 to 4 cm long and 8 to 10 mm wide; they are obovate to ovate-elliptic. Starry flowers are yellow.

Rhododendron dauricum;
Zone 5,**

A native species of Korea, Manchuria and northern Japan.

This mostly deciduous, 1 to 1.5 m shrub has pilose shoots and 2 to 4 cm long elliptic leaves. These are dark green and barely scaly above, but densely covered with scales below. In late winter to early spring, 4 cm wide, purple-pink blossoms appear. The var. sempervirens is distinguished from the species by its stiff, erect habit, darker blossoms and evergreen leaves.

R. dauricum is rather surprising because of its very early blossoms. It is often used in forcing for the florist trade. The early blooming cultivar R. 'Praecox', developed from a cross between this species and R. ciliatum, is a familiar garden plant.

Rhododendron fastigiatum;
Zone 7,**

The high mountain ranges and alpine moors of Yunnan Province in China bordering Tibet, at elevations of 3300 to 4800 m are the natural habitat of this species.

This evergreen shrub has slender twigs and a stiffly upright, open-growing habit, to 80 cm tall. Its elliptic-oblanceolate, gray-green leaves are 1 cm long and thickly covered with scales on both sides. Small, wide, funnel-shaped, purple-violet to deep purple-blue blossoms appear in spring.

Some gardeners recommend that the climbers Codonopsis vinciflora or Clematis macropetala be allowed to intertwine through the branches of R. fastigiatum to provide a particularly stunning landscape effect.

Rhododendron ferrugineum;
Zone 5,*

R. ferrugineum occurs throughout the entire length of the Alps, on primitive rock soils at altitudes of 1500 to 2300 m. It grows as an understory shrub in thin, larch, Swiss Stone Pine, spruce and Mountain Pine forests, or alder thickets. It thrives in lush communities in damp, but well drained, humus soils which overlie soft shale or sandstone. Its plant community associates are: Juniperus communis

Rhododendron fastigiatum

var. *montana, Arctostaphylos uva-ursi, Vaccinium uliginosum, Loiseleuria procumbens, Linnaea borealis* and various high alpine willows, as well as alpine perennials such as *Gentiana acaulis, Athyrium distentifolium, Genum montanum, Sibbaldia procumbens, Campanula barbata, Chrysanthemum alpinum, Saussurea alpina* and *Homogyne alpina.*

R. ferrugineum is an evergreen, 1 m tall, bushy shrub with vigorous, flexible branches. Hard leathery leaves are borne on the branch tips. The leaves are 3–5 cm long, dark green on top, thickly covered with reddish brown scales beneath, and have a prominent yellow midrib. Numerous purple-pink, funnel-shaped, bell-like blossom clusters cover the plant in early summer.

R. ferrugineum is a long-living, easily cultivated species.

Rhododendron forrestii; Zone 8,****

R. forrestii was discovered in 1905 by the English botanist J. F. Forrest, for whom it was named, in Yunnan Province, China. It is found there, as well as in southwestern Tibet, at elevations of 4000 to 5000 m, growing in moors and damp mountain meadows.

R. forrestii is an evergreen, creeping and carpet-forming shrub, 10 to 15 cm tall. Its leaves are broad-oval to round, 1.5 to 3 cm long and reddish underneath. The leaf veins on top are very prominent. In spring, single, narrow bell-shaped, 3 cm long and wide, dark carmine-red blossoms appear.

Var. *repens* is distinguished from the species by the bluish-green leaf undersides, a scarlet-red flower color, and styles and pistils which are less glandular.

In the mid 1930's, Lord Aberconway in Wales initiated, and Dietrich Hobbie continued, numerous crosses with this variable species which resulted in the Repens Hybrids. Unlike the species, these hybrids are frost hardy in continental climates.

Rhododendron repens 'Scarlet Wonder'

These hybrids tolerate sunny sites in a cool, humid climate. All are low growing and compact, with bright or scarlet-red flowers. Their early blooming period makes them susceptible to late frosts. They all do very well in containers. Suitable companion plants include humus soil and partial shade-loving plants such as *Polystichum setiferum* 'Plumosum Densum', *Galax urceolata*, *Shortia glacifolia* and *S. uniflora*, *Omphalodes verna* 'Alba' and *Crocus tommasinianus*.

Rhododendron hippophaeoides; Zone 5,***

This species is native to Yunnan and Sichuan Provinces in China at elevations of 2700 to 4200 m in moors, damp meadows, along streams and on forest edges.

This aromatic, erect, evergreen shrub grows to scarcely 1 m. The entire length of its slender branches bear narrow, ovate to lanceolate, 3 to 4 cm long leaves. The leaves gently curve under along the edges, are gray-green on top and pale green beneath. In early spring, lilac-pink blossoms with short, funnel-shaped corollas are borne in 6 to 8 clusters.

This is the hardiest, slow growing, small-leaved rhododendron species. It thrives in an evenly damp soil in sunny locations. It can even be planted directly along the bank of a body of water. If soil is kept dry it becomes sickly.

Rhododendron hirsutum; Zone 5,*

R. hirsutum is found in the Bavarian, Swiss and Austrian Alps, especially in the coniferous levels at elevations of 1200 to

189

R. repens Hybrids

Cultivar	Flower color	Blooming period[1]	Height (cm)	Winter hardiness	Observations
'Bad Eilsen'	scarlet-red	Middle	60–70	Zone 6	Flat-growing; fresh green foliage
'Baden-Baden'	scarlet-red	Early	60	Zone 6	One of the best cultivars. Flat habit; dark green foliage
'Bengal'	scarlet-red	Early	60	Zone 6	Broad and upright habit
Carmen'	dark red		30–91	Zone 6	Low-growing, compact; leaves broadly obovate, flowers campanulate
'Dr. Ernst Schäle'	bright scarlet-red	Early	80	Zone 6	Half-globed habit; heavy bloomer, large flowers
'Frühling-szauber'	bright scarlet-red	Early	60	Zone 6	Up to 1.4 m wide
'Friedrich Deus'	scarlet-red	Middle	60	Zone 6	Broad and dense
'Gertrude Schäle'	scarlet-red	Early	60	Zone 7–8	Flowers susceptible to late frosts
'Gräfin Kirchbach'	bright fire-red	Early-middle	80	Zone 6–7	Small leaved, beautiful cultivar; brownish red flower buds and large, single blossoms
'Juwel'	dark scarlet-red	Middle	50	Zone 6	Wider than tall; dark green leaves
'Mannheim'	dark red w/ light markings	Middle	80–100	Zone 6	Widely erect; dense
'Nodding Bells'	cherry red		60	Zone 6	Leaves slightly twisted; flowers open, bell-shaped; truss is flat and rather loose
'Red Carpet'	brilliant red	Early	30	Zone 6	Carpet-forming habit
'Satin'	aniline-red	Early	60	Zone 6	Dwarf habit, broad and compact
'Scarlet Wonder'	scarlet-red	Early	50–80	Zone 6	Superb cultivar. Completely flat; very heavy bloomer, brown-red flower buds

[1] Very early = Early to mid-April; Early = end of April to early May; Middle = mid-May; Late = end of May to early June; Very Late = mid- to end of June.

Rhododendron repens 'Satin'

2000 m. It is a lime-tolerant inhabitant of thin and knee-high communities on rocky slopes. It occurs in limestone soil as an understory shrub in thin pine forests with *Salix hastata, S. glabra* and *S. retusa, Rubus saxatilis, Daphne striata, Arctostaphylos uva-ursi* and *A. alpina, Vaccinium vitis-idea* and *V. myrtillus, Erica herbacea, Pyrola minor, Globularia nudicaulis, Valeriana montana, Aster bellidiastrum, Carex baldensis, Primula auricula* and *Veratrum nigrum*.

R. hirsutum is a 1 m tall, evergreen stubby-branched, twiggy, densely-leaved shrub with hard, leathery, elliptic, and 3 cm long leaves. Leaf edges are finely crenate to bristly ciliate. In late spring, it produces numerous, purple-pink, funnel-shaped, bell-like flowers arranged in terminal clusters.

Unlike other dwarf rhododendrons, *R. hirsutum* thrives in relatively dry locations, though it still requires a porous humus soil. It will seed itself in the garden when growing conditions are ideal. It easily lends itself to growing in beds and rock gardens but is very salt sensitive. The following are good companion plants: *Erica herbaceae, Digitalis grandiflora, Gentiana dinarica, Globularia cordifolia, Primula aurica* and *Dryas octopetala*.

Rhododendron impeditum;
Zone 5,****

R. impeditum is found at elevations of 2700 to 4900 m in the Lichian mountain ranges of Yunnan and Sichuan Provinces, China in open, moist locations.

This densely twiggy, evergreen shrub grows wider than tall with a cushion-forming habit. It reaches only 15 to 40 cm tall. Short twigs, especially on the branch ends, are closely covered with elliptic-ovate leaves. The 1.5 cm long leaves are thickly covered with scales on both sides and turn gray-green in winter. Slightly fragrant, 2.5 cm wide, purple-violet to lilac flowers expand from brownish buds in mid-spring.

R. impeditum, and especially its more robust hybrids, are among the most valuable dwarf rhododendrons for the rock garden. They thrive in sunny, humus-rich locations with moist to damp soil.

R. impeditum hybrids include cultivars with "blue" blossoms and very small leaves. Their height makes them ideal plants for small alpine gardens. Their miniature habit does not blend well with the large flowered rhododendrons, but rather with the small-leaved species of the Japanese azalea and other small-leaved rhododendrons.

Rhododendron keleticum; Zone 6,**

R. keleticum is native to southeastern Tibet, Yunnan Province, China and northern Burma, at elevations of 3300 to 4500 m, especially in damp, rocky heath moors, rocky slopes and cliffs.

This is a carpet-forming, evergreen shrub 15 cm tall. Its prostrate branches have 1.5 cm long, elliptic leaves. The leaves

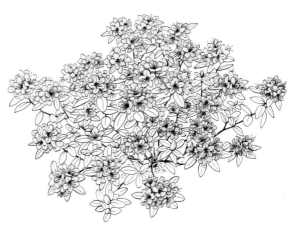

Rhododendron impeditum 'Gristede'

taper to small sharp points and are very scaly below. In June, 2.5 cm wide, rotate or wide funnel-shaped blossoms appear in terminal panicles. The flowers are purple-violet with carmine-red markings.

R. keleticum belongs in a rock garden in a sunny location in partly peat, partly mineral soil which is not too dry.

Rhododendron 'Lavendula';
Zone 6,**

This hybrid is a cross between (*R. russatum* × *R. saluense*) × *R. rubiginosum*.

It is an 80 to 100 cm tall, broad upright, slow growing and compact, evergreen cultivar. The foliage is scaly brown underneath, has a pleasant fragrance, and turns bronze in winter. Beginning in mid-spring, lavender-pink, 5 to 6 cm wide flowers appear with green to brownish-green or reddish-green blotches. The flowers are borne 3 to 5 in a loose raceme. This is a highly recommended, winter hardy cultivar. It was developed in 1952 by D. Hobbie, Linswege. 'Lavendula' grows only 15 cm tall in shady locations. It will, however, grow in sunny sites as well.

Rhododendron metternichi 'Sir Lancelot'; Zone 6, not rated

R. m. 'Sir Lancelot' is a selection of *R. m.* var. *tsukuchianum.*

At 10 years it is a low globe about 45 cm tall and 75 cm wide. Leaves are evergreen; densely felted cinnamon-red beneath; 10 cm long and 2.5 cm wide; and lanceolate oblong. Flowers are a clear rose-pink and have 7 lobes in broadly pyramidal trusses.

Rhododendron 'Praecox'; Zone 6,****

This is a hybrid between *R. ciliatum* × *R. dauricum.* It was developed by I. Davies in England and introduced in 1860.

R. 'Praecox' is a very open, upright growing, 1 to 1.5 m tall, evergreen shrub with very glossy leaves. It is considered semi-evergreen since many of its leaves fall in late autumn. In late winter to early

Rhododendron impeditum 'Violetta'

spring, wide, funnel-shaped, 4 cm wide, lilac-pink flowers appear on the shoot tips.

R. 'Praecox', with its extraordinarily heavy bloom, is one of the most valuable of the early blooming rhododendrons. A protected location is recommended to protect the flowers against late frost.

Rhododendron radicans; Zone 6,***

Open areas on rocky moors in the highlands of southeastern Tibet (4200 to 4600 m) are the habitat of this species.

This evergreen, carpet-forming shrub scarcely reaches 10 cm tall. Its narrow lanceolate leaves are 1.5 cm long, very pointed, lightly fringed, loosely scaled on top and more thickly scaled beneath. Single, terminal, purple blossoms with rotate corollas appear in May.

R. radicans is one of the most worthy dwarf rhododendrons. It should be planted in protected, partly shady locations in rock gardens; in evenly moist, partly peat, partly mineral soil.

Rhododendron 'Radistrotum'

This is a hybrid between R. radicans, from southeastern Tibet, and R. calostrotum, from northeastern Burma. It was developed by G. Arends in Ronsdorf, and introduced in 1940.

It is a small-leaved, evergreen hybrid, which does not exceed 30 cm tall. It blooms in early spring with purple-red flowers. It is less valuable as an ornamental than its parent species.

Rhododendron 'Ramapo'; Zone 4

This rhododendron is a hybrid resulting from a cross between the American species R. carolinianum and the Chinese species R. fastigiatum.

This American bred evergreen flowers in mid-spring with small, pastel-lilac blossoms. They are borne 3 to 5 in loose clusters. The plant is wide and compact, only reaching a height of 60 cm and a width of 91 cm in 10 years. It has 2 to 3 cm long aromatic leaves. When they first emerge they are a striking pale violet (often miscalled "blue"), but later turn gray-green. R. 'Ramapo' requires very little of the soil and has proved to be completely frost hardy in southern Canada. It is considered to be one of the most valuable dwarf cultivars available.

Rhododendron russatum; Zone 6,****

The natural habitat of this species is the open highlands (3300 to 4300 m) and fringes of the pine forests of northwestern Yunnan Province, China.

This upright, 50 to 80 cm tall, evergreen shrub has very scaly branches. Its leaves are oblong-lanceolate, up to 3 cm long, and very scaly on both sides. On the lower surface the scales are rust-brown. It blooms heavily in mid-spring with open-funnel-shaped, 2.5 cm wide, dark violet flowers with a white throat. The flowers are borne 4 to 5 on the branch tips.

R. russatum, with its dark violet, very impressive blossoms, is one of the most important garden species. In rhododendron beds, it requires partly shady locations in moist, partly peat, partly mineral soil. Primula sikkimensis, which produces pure yellow flowers at the same time, makes a fine companion plant.

J. Hachmann developed two fine cultivars from *R. russatum*. They have a better habit and more intense flower color than the species:

'Azurwolke' bright, pure blue flowers.
'Gletschernacht' grows vigorously erect. It also has bright blue blossoms.

Rhododendron 'Watchung'; Zone 6, not rated

This selection is a clone taken from a sport branch of *R.* 'Ramapo'.

R. 'Watchung' is a small, flattened, very dwarf plant, at 10 years only 30 cm tall and 45 cm wide. Its evergreen leaves are bluish, and similar to fir tree needles. The clustered flowers are violet-blue, about 1.25 cm across.

R. 'Watchung' resembles a miniature *R.* 'Ramapo'.

Rhododendron williamsianum; Zone 6,****

R. williamsianum is native to southwestern China. It grows in the highland evergreen laurel forests, as well as in the higher coniferous forests. It was discovered in 1908 by Wilson, on Omei mountain in the southwestern Chinese province of Sichuan. It thrives at elevations of 2500 to 3000 m in rocky soil originating from lime-bearing stone.

R. williamsianum is a slow growing, rounded, stubby-branched, evergreen shrub, which only reaches 1 m when fully mature. The leaves are round and 2–4 cm long (a characteristic of the species), apple green on top and lighter and silvery beneath. When the leaves emerge, they are bronze to chocolate in color. In early spring bell-shaped, pink blossoms appear, clustered in threes.

R. williamsianum thrives in alpine gardens in mineral rich soil with high pH levels. The new shoots and flowers of this species are quite susceptible to damage by late frosts.

R. williamsianum hybrids are distinctive due to their round, attractive leaves, colorful shoots, compact habit and bell-shaped flowers. The Williamsianum hybrids are much hardier. Over the past 40 years more than 60 cultivars incorporating this splendid species have been developed and deserve a prime place in every garden.

Williamsianum Hybrids grow best in protected sites, as both flowers and new shoots are subject to late frost injury. As is the case with most rhododendrons, the soil should be moist and made up of partly peat, partly mineral materials. The species tolerates lime, and its hybrids have inherited this tolerance. Even though *R. williamsianum* hybrids can exceed 1 m in height, they are included in this book because they grow very slowly and only reach such heights in very favorable locations after many years.

Rhododendron yakusimanum; Zone 5,***

R. yakusimanum is native to a small area on the southern Japanese island of Yaku Shima; often found there in wind-swept locations at elevations of 1200 to 1800 m.

In the last few years, this evergreen species has become very important. Its compact, 50 to 100 cm tall habit, striking

R. williamsianum Hybrids

Cultivar	Flower color	Blooming period*	Height (m)	Winter hardiness	Observations
'April Glow'	carmine-pink	Very early	1.5	Zone 6–7	Blooms earlier than most other cultivars; somewhat open habit
'August Lamken'	purple-pink, dark red markings	Middle	1.5–2	Zone 6	Broad, upright, vigorous; beautiful, dark green foliage
'Bremen'	glowing bright red	Early	.8	Zone 7	Weak growing; a difficult sort
'Dr. Schlapper'	pink	Middle	1	Zone 6–7	Broad, compact habit; striking red shoots and dark buds
'Gartendirektor Glocker'	pink-red at first, later pink	Early	1.3	Zone 6	Compact and spherical, very winter hardy; perhaps the most commonly used cultivar in Europe
'Gartendirektor Rieger'	cream colored with dark red markings	Early	1.5	Zone 6–7	Broadly upright; large blossoms, relatively long blooming period
'Görlitz'	intense pink	Early	1.5	Zone 6–7	Rather vigorous growth; a valuable cultivar
'Humming Bird'	pink	Early	1	Zone 6	Broad and compact; very few blossoms when the plant is young
'Jackwill'	soft pink	Early	1	Zone 6	Dense and wide
'Karin'	dark pink	Early	1.5	Zone 6	One of the most beautiful cultivars; large, fringed blooms
'Linda'	pinkish red	Middle	1.5	Zone 7	Late breaking, bronze-colored new growth
'Lissabon'	carmine-red	Early	1.5	Zone 6	Rich bloom, thick, ball-shaped habit, dark green foliage, new growth
'Oudijk's Sensation'	dark pink	Early to middle	1.5–2	Zone 6	Vigorous growth; more open habit than other cultivars
'Rödhätte'	blood-red	Late	1	Zone 6	Low growing, spreading
'Rothenburg'	lemon-yellow at first, later cream	Early	2.5	Zone 6–7	Upright and vigorous growth; very large blossoms, handsome brown buds

Cultivar	Flower color	Blooming period*	Height (m)	Winter hardiness	Observations
'Stadt Essen'	pink, light colored throat	Early to middle	1.5	Zone 6	Broadly upright
'Vater Böhlje'	Delicate lilac-pink	Early	1	Zone 6	Vigorous, round, bushy habit

* Very early = early to mid-April; Early = late April to early May; Middle = mid-May; Late = late May to early June; Very late = mid- to late June.

and decorative, white pilose shoots, 5 to 10 cm long, narrow, leaves with typically down-rolled edges, which are light brown-tomentose underneath; early, large, blossoms in huge heads; and its winter hardiness have all contributed to its increased popularity. This species flowers abundantly in mid-spring. Carmine-pink buds open to produce flowers which at first are a delicate pink, but later, usually when all the buds have opened, turn white.

This is a most attractive, large flowered species for small gardens. It tolerates cramped growing conditions.

'Koichiro Wada' is an especially beautiful, natural variety now propagated as a cultivar. It has white-tomentose branches and its pink buds open to white blossoms. It was awarded a First Class Certificate (F.C.C.) in 1947 by the Royal Horticulture Society.

Rhododendron yakusimanum Hybrids

R. yakusimanum has been much used as a parent in the hybridization of a large number of cultivars. Among the many cultivars resulting from these crosses are the pink-white 'Doc', the deep red, lightly marked 'Dopey', Sweet Sue', and 'Pheasant Tail'; the soft pink 'Caroline Allbrook' and 'Pink Cherub'. All are notable for their heavy blossoming, even when very young. The hardiness of many of the *R. yakusimanum* hybrids has not yet been fully established.

One of the earliest Rhododendron breeders to realize the potential of *R. yakusimanum* was David G. Leach. His selection *R. y.* 'Mist Maiden' is still regarded as one of the best cultivars from this species. The plant is hardy through Zone 5 and grows slowly; at 10 years it is 45 cm tall and 75 cm wide. Leaves are 7–10 cm long with a fern colored indumentum. Flowers, 5 cm across in trusses of 12, are apple blossom-pink fading to white; buds are carmine. This is a hardy, outstanding dwarf rhododendron.

German breeders (foremost among them J. Hachmann) have worked with *R. yakusimanum* hybridizing, producing cultivars of exceptional winter hardiness with outstanding ornamental value; these will be appearing on the market in the next few years. Some of them include *R.* 'Rosita', with beautifully ruffled pink flowers which are a delicate yellow inside with green spots; *R.* 'Fantastica', with exceptionally large flower heads, deep red buds, and pink-red flowers which are almost white inside; and *R.* 'Festival', with orange-tinted buds and golden-yellow flowers spotted orange.

R. 'André', developed by de Belder of Kalmthout, received an award from the Boskoop Growers in 1978. It is densely compact with dark green foliage, which is white-tomentose underneath. Its flowers, borne in clusters of 11 to 14, open pink and fade to white.

R. 'Bad Zwischenahn' has a flat, compact habit. Its leaves are oblong, pointed and wavy. They emerge silvery-tomentose. Flowers are pink at first, and later turn pale pink with greenish yellow markings. It blooms quite heavily, fairly early in the season.

R. 'Belona' has reddish buds and blossoms which are salmon-pink inside. This shrub grows quite wide.

R. 'Emden' grows flat and compact. Its leaves are light bronze-tomentose when they first appear. It blooms rather early

Rhododendron yakusimanum

and very heavily. Its flowers are similar to those of *R*. 'Bad Zwischenahn'.

R. 'Esveld Select' was developed in the C. Esveld nursery in Boskoop. It was awarded a Silver Medal in 1976 at the Flora Nova. It grows broadly erect and has foliage similar to that of the species. Blossoms are borne in large, full, apple blossom-pink flower heads.

R. 'Flava' is a beautiful cultivar with a globe-shaped and rather compact form. When mature, it reaches 1.5 m tall; blossoms are light yellow in late spring.

R. 'Julischka' is a heavy blooming cultivar with bright red buds which open pink inside.

R. 'Morgenrot' grows broadly, compact, and remains low. It blossoms in mid-spring. Its flowers are light red, lighter at the base, have brownish-red spots and are wavy on the edges.

R. 'Polaris' has a mounding habit and remains compact and low. Flowers appear in mid-spring. They are pink with yellowish brown to yellowish green spots. It is especially winter hardy.

R. 'Silberwolke' grows broad and compact. Delicate pink buds develop into showy flowers which are white with pale yellow-green spots and ruffled edges.

Rhododendron yakusimanum 'Flava'

Rhododendron yakusimanum

Rhododendron yakusimanum 'Polaris'

Rhododendron 'Diamant Purpur'

Japanese Azaleas

The Japanese Hybrid Azalea group is a
mixed bag at best. The cultivars in this
group have been derived from such a
variety of crosses, of so many different
parents, that even a trained botanist cannot
sort out the sources from which they were
derived. Of the numerous hybrids available, the following groups, together with a
few new cultivars, are recommended for
the small garden, but the gardener will
want to become thoroughly familiar with
all the dwarf azaleas to select others which
might better realize his other landscape
objectives.

Arendsii Hybrid Group
G. Arends, of Ronsdorf, West Germany,
crossed *R.* × 'Noordtiana', a relatively
winter hardy Japanese Azalea cultivar,
with *R. kaempferi* and other Japanese
Azalea species to create the hardiest
cultivar possible. In 1950, after 15 years of
careful breeding, the first crosses were

selected and named after various rivers in the mountainous region of Northern Rhein-Westphalia. Arendsii Hybrids are evergreen, grow to medium height with mid-sized flowers.

Diamant Azalea Group

These cultivars originated as crosses between *R.* 'Multiflorum' (an Arendsii Hybrid) and *R. kiusianum.* They were developed by C. Fleischmann of Wiesmoor, West Germany. They are exceptionally colorful, have a compact, flat habit, small blossoms and an abundance of flowers.

Rhododendron Japanese Azalea 'Diamant'

Gable Hybrids

These hardy evergreen azaleas were created by J. B. Gable of Stewartstown, Pennsylvania, U.S.A. Many originated from *R. kaempferi* × *R. poukhanense* crosses, although numerous other species and cultivars have been used as well.

Kaempferi Hybrids

This group basically was developed about 1920 by P. M. Koster, Boskoop, Holland. They are a cross between *R. kaempferi* × *R.* 'Malvatica'. Later, other cultivars were crossed with second and third generation Kaempferi Hybrids. Over the course of time, a very heterogeneous group has evolved.

Kurume Hybrids

Kurume Hybrids originate from cultivars of *R. obtusum* and crosses between *R. kiusianum* and *R. kaempferi* which occurred in wild populations. Selection of the wild crosses began in the early part of the last century in Japan. Early in this century, a number were distributed in the U.S.A., England and Holland from the collection of the best Japanese cultivars imported into the U.S.A. in 1917 by E. H. Wilson.

Kurume Azaleas grow very compactly, with almost "table-like" form, 60 to 80 cm tall. They are mostly evergreen with small flowers produced in prodigious quantity. The cultivars listed on pages 194–195 are commonly available. The gardener should, however, be alert to new cultivars appearing on the market as well as the occasional reappearance of any of the famous "Wilson Fifty".

Vuykiana Hybrids

This is a Dutch (A. Vuyk, 1921) and later Belgian breeding line between *R.* 'J. C. van Tol' (Mollis hybrid) and cultivars of *R. kaempferi.*

New cultivars (*R.* 'Vuyk's Scarlet', *R.* 'Vuyk's Rosyred') arose through further crossings with *R. simsii.* These cultivars have much better flower colors, but unfortunately, are more sensitive to frost.

Vuykiana Hybrids generally grow rather low, open, and have large, often bright blossoms.

Japanese Azaleas seldom grow taller than 1 m in cooler climates. They are very bushy, often of a mat-forming habit and evergreen in continental climates. They bloom very, very heavily. In order to develop well, they require a site which protects them from both wind and sun. Partly shady locations prevent the flowers from fading prematurely, which many tend to do. In less favorable locations, a winter covering (mid-December to early-April) of coniferous branches is absolutely necessary. In addition, azaleas need to be protected from late spring frosts (April, May) and early fall frosts (September, October).

Japanese Azaleas

Cultivar	Flowers	Blooming period*	Habit	Origin
'Agger'	light lilac	Middle	compact	Arendsii Hybrid
'Aladdin'	scarlet-red	Early	upright	Kurume Hybrid
'Allotria'	light red; large	Late	medium height	R. 'Rubinetta' × R. 'Vuyk's Scarlet
'Anne Frank'	intense wine-red	Late	broad, compact, low growing	R. 'Muttertag' × R. 'Multiflora'
'Beethoven'	purple, red-brown spots	Middle	broad, upright	Vuykiana Hybrid
'Blaauw's Pink'	salmon-pink	Early	upright and dense	Kurume Hybrid
'Campfire'	dark red, darker striped	Middle	broad, upright	Gable Hybrid
Diamond (series named by color)	salmon, purple, pink, red-white and sky blue	Middle	very low growing, broad and compact	R. 'Multiflorum' × R. kiusianum-hybrids
'Favorite'	ruby, scarlet-red spot	Early	upright	Kaempferi Hybrid
'Fedora'	vibrant pink, brown spot	Early	upright	Kaempferi Hybrid
'Gabriele'	carmine-red; mid-sized	Late	globose; somewhat open, medium height	R. 'Muttertag' × R. 'Kermesina'
'Georg Arends'	bright red, brown spots; very large	Late	upright to broad upright; open	Origin unknown
'Granada'	dark purple-pink, semidouble; small	Late	mounded-compact; bronze foliage in winter	R. 'Rubenstein' × ('Kermesina' × R. 'Red Pimponek')
'Hatsugiri'	carmine-pink	Early	low, broad, dense and compact	Kurume Hybrid
'Hino-crimson'	red	Middle	broad, relatively dense	Kurume Hybrid
'Hinodegiri'	carmine-red; small	Early	low growing, broad, compact	Kurume Hybrid

Cultivar	Flowers	Blooming period*	Habit	Origin
'Hinomayo'	delicate pink, light pink spots	Early	spreading to upright	Kurume Hybrid
'John Cairns'	scarlet-red, darker spots	Early to middle	broad, compact	Kaempferi Hybrid
'Joseph Haydn'	delicate lilac, red-brown spots	Early	upright	Vuykiana Hybrid
'Kathleen'	dark pink, light reddish-brown spots	Middle	upright	Kaempferi Hybrid
'Kermesina'	intense pink, light spots; small	Late	broad, compact; very hardy	Kurume Hybrid
'Lister'	carmine-salmon	Middle	compact	Arendsii Hybrid
'Lysande'	red with orange tones, brown markings	Late	broad and flat; foliage brown-red in winter	Unknown
'Multiflorum'	light purple; small	Middle	low growing	Arendsii Hybrid
'Muttertag'	glowing dark red	Middle	low growing, compact	Kurume Hybrid
'Nordlight'	orange-red light brown markings, large	Early	broad, compact; color constant in partly shady sites	R. 'Vuyk's Scarlet' × R. 'Aladdin'
'Orange Beauty'	Light red, light brown spots	Early	Compact; flower color washed out by sun and rain	Kaempferi Hybrid
'Palestrina'	white, light green markings	Middle	upright	Vuykiana Hybrid.
'P. W. Hardijzer'	ruby-red	Middle	broad	Vuykiana Hybrid
'Rosalind'	pure pink, light reddish spots; mid-sized	Middle	broad, bushy to upright; hardy	R. 'Kermesina' × R. 'Jeanette'
'Rubinetta'	glowing dark red, light reddish markings; small to mid-sized	Late	Flat, broad and compact; bronze-colored foliage in winter; hardy	R. 'Muttertag' × R. 'Kermesina'
'Schneeglanz'	pure white with green spot	Middle	Broad, upright, mid-sized, open	R. 'Kermesina' × R. 'Jeanette' (the only white-blooming cultivar.)
'Schubert'	light pink	Middle	broad	Vuykiana Hybrid

Japanese Azaleas (cont.)

Cultivar	Flowers	Blooming period*	Habit	Origin
'Signalgluehen'	hot-orange to orange-red; mid-sized	Late	broad, compact	'Vuyk's Scarlet' × 'Mattertag'
'Vuyk's Rosyred'	bright rose; large	Late	Broad, low growing; hardy	Vuykiana Hybrid
'Vuyk's Scarlet'	dark red; large	Late	Broad, low growing requires protected site	Vuykiana Hybrid

* Early = late April to early May; Middle = mid-May; Late = late May to early June.

Ribes alpinum 'Pumilum',
Saxifragaceae

R. alpinum (Zone 2) is found in mountain forests from Europe to Siberia. This 1 to 2 m tall, deciduous shrub is lime tolerant, but is also found growing in slightly acidic soils.

R. a. 'Pumilum' is a densely branched shrub to 1 m high with slender branches which leaf out early each year. It has small, rounded leaves which appear early each year and turn yellow or yellowish white in autumn.

This is an undistinguished shrub to be used as a ground cover, or low hedge.

Rosa, Dwarf Bengal Roses

Cultivars of Rosa chinensis 'Minima' are included in this category. A few dwarf cultivars with Polyantha characteristics are included here as well, as are the 'Compacta Roses' (Alberich and Degenhardt).

These cultivars have a healthy-looking, deep green foliage and close-set, panicle-like sprays of flowers. They all grow 20 to 40 cm tall and are, therefore, well suited for heath and rock gardens. They are normally planted in small clumps or open drifts between dwarf trees and shrubs. They also are well suited for bedding or for planting along walkways, and, if well watered, for container gardens. In the spring, all cultivars in this group should be pruned back to just above the soil line. On an average 15 plants will occupy each square meter.

Rosa nitida, Rosaceae

R. nitida (Zone 4) grows in the damp, cool, coniferous forests of eastern North America in open areas and at woods' edge in deciduous forests in boreal regions.

This twiggy, vigorous, suckering shrub reaches 50 to 70 cm tall. The branches are densely covered with short, reddish thorns and bristles. The very glossy, seven- to nine-leaflet, pinnate, dark green leaves turn bright brownish red in autumn. 4 to 5 cm wide, single, fragrant pink flowers appear singly, or 2 to 5 in clusters, in early summer. In autumn,

Dwarf Roses

Cultivar	Flowers	Remarks
'Alberich'	bright red; semidouble	vigorous grower, winter hardy; blooms tirelessly until the first signs of frost
'Baby Maskerade'	yellow-red	older cultivar with yellow flowers from red buds turn fire-red before petal fall; heavy bloomer, bushy
'Bit O'Sunshine'	light yellow; double	one of the best yellow cultivars
'Brilliant Meillandiana'	bright orange-red	30–40 cm tall; semi-double; large flowers; glossy foliage
'Colibri 79'	yellow with copper-red; double	30–40 cm tall; bushy, compact habit
'Coralin'	coral-red; double	small flowers; heavy bloomer
'Degenhardt'	pink	especially large flowers; resists disease well
'Eleanor'	pink; double	small bush with glossy foliage
'Fresh Pink'	salmon-pink	many canes, loose habit; heavy bloomer with true "rose buds"; glossy, dark green foliage
'Guletta'	lemon-yellow; double	bushy, compact plant with rich, handsome foliage; heavy bloomer, reblooms quickly
'Lillian'	light-red; double	low growing, compact and thrifty; dense foliage
'Minuetto'	mandarin-red, yellow center; double	40–50 cm tall; heavy bloomer; vigorous, bushy habit
'Orange Mellandina'	orange-red	30–40 cm tall; heavy bloomer, long-lasting flowers
'Red Dot'	scarlet-red	broad, bushy with many canes; heavy bloomer and quickly reblooms; healthy, dark green foliage
'Rosmarin'	silvery pink; double	blossoms change to a pale pink from light red buds
'Scarlet Meillandiana'	dark red with yellow stamens	30–40 cm tall; semi-double, very large blossoms
'Starina'	salmon-cherry-red; double	30–40 cm tall; compact, bushy habit; numerous small buds develop into sturdy flowers
'Sunmaid'	gold-yellow at first, later red	bushy, well-branched; dense, glossy, dark green foliage
'White Gem'	white; double	30–40 cm tall; compact habit
'Zwergenfee'	orange to blood-red	bushy and dense; reblooms quickly; dark green foliage
'Zwergkoenig 78'	bright blood-red	well-formed buds; flowers long lasting and star-shaped; plant is compact, bushy with thick canes; dark green foliage
'Zwergkonigin'	pink	related to above cultivar; blossoms borne in large clusters

Dwarf Rose 'Baby Maskerade'

Rosa 'Guletta'

round, scarlet-red fruit decorates the shrub. It spreads by vigorous root sprouts.

R. nitida thrives as well in moist sites as it does in dry spots. It is used as a specimen or as a group plant in rock gardens and heath gardens, but is especially well suited as a ground cover.

Rosa pimpinellifolia, Rosaceae

R. pimpinellifolia (Zone 5) is found from Europe to Asia. It appears on the sand dunes of the North Sea, as well as in limestone ridges and open meadows in the Alps.

R. pimpinellifolia is a variable, scarcely 1 m tall shrub with slender, very thorny or bristly branches, and vigorous root suckering habit. Its five- to nine-leaflet pinnate leaves are glandular biserrate, dark green above and lighter below. Most plants are white-flowering, but some plants produce yellow or pink flowers. Blossoms appear singly on side twigs in late spring. The fruit is flat-ball-shaped, glossy and brownish black.

R. pimpinellifolia is a lime-tolerant, drought resistant, undistinguished species, well suited for large heath gardens and for planting on garden slopes.

In the spring, all cultivars in this group should be pruned back to just above the soil line. On an average 15 plants will occupy each square meter.

Rosa, Roses as Ground Covers

Roses used as ground covers are particularly suitable for small, intimate gardens. Robust cultivars which grow either dense and bushy with upright branches, or cover the ground with semi-weeping or prostrate branches, are being used as flowering ground cover plants. Roses are used in this fashion in parks, and especially between sidewalks and roadways.

Dwarf Rose 'Fresh Pink'

Dwarf Rose 'Guletta'

The cultivars listed on page 205 are slow growing and well suited for home gardens. They do very well in containers situated in sunny locations, and are especially attractive when planted on top of walls where their branches can lie prostrate or drape over the edge. When planting roses as ground covers, space them 4 to 6 plants for each square meter. Set plants about 30 cm apart, but allow more room for larger cultivars such as 'Dagmar Hastrup' and 'The Fairy'.

Rubus calycinoides, Rosaceae

The natural habitat of this species is Taiwan.

R. calycinoides (Zones 7–8) is a slow growing, thick-leaved, evergreen shrub with prostrate, rooting branches. Canes are shaggy pilose when young and covered with small, single prickles. The broad-ovate, three-lobed, short stalked leaves are heart-shaped at the base, 2 to 4 cm long, with wavy, scalloped edges. The upper surface of the leaf is glabrous, dark green and somewhat puckered. The underside is thickly white to brownish tomentose. Only a few, white, insignificant blossoms appear on curved, erect, short shoots in May–June. The fruit is bright red.

R. calycinoides is not entirely frost hardy, but does well in winter as long as there is a snow covering or if protected with evergreen branches. In partly shady locations, this plant enlivens most gardens with its decorative leaves. It is well suited as a ground cover under dwarf trees and shrubs, and grows tightly over boulders or logs.

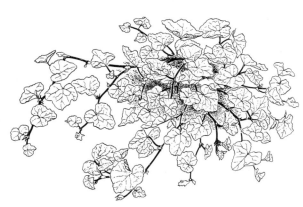

Rubus calycinoides

Rubus irenaeus, Rosaceae

Natural habitat: the Nan Shan mountain range in the western Chinese Province of Hubei.

R. irenaeus (Zone 7) is a prostrate, evergreen shrub with 1 to 2 m long branches. They may be armed with small stickers, or thornless. The 10 to 15 cm wide leaves are almost completely round but are abruptly pointed at the ends and heart-shaped at the base. Leaves are colored dark green above, with a light metallic sheen, and whitish or brownish tomentose below. Color changes to a very striking brownish red in autumn. In early summer, 2 cm wide, white blossoms appear in the leaf axils or in terminal clusters. The large fruits are red.

Neither of these *Rubus* species are entirely winter hardy. They make decorative but very slow growing ground covers and tolerate partly shady to shady locations beneath large trees and shrubs.

Salix, Salicaceae

Of the aproximately 300 willow species presently known, many occur in alpine or arctic regions.

In unfavorable sites or climate conditions, many of these species develop prostrate or bushy habits. In the arctic-alpine regions alone, approximately 30 dwarf *Salix* species can be found.

With a few notable exceptions, *Salix* species are unfortunately not generally planted in gardens. This is a great pity as in heath, rock and container gardens, most species, have no reasonable substitutes, are very attractive and some are almost indispensable. Others have proved to be excellent ground covers. Gardeners who have not yet recognized their desirable qualities tend to limit their use.

Most *Salix* species adapt to their surroundings remarkably well. As a group, they possess substantial ecological latitude. For example, even though many *Salix* species grow in more or less damp sites in their natural habitat, they are capable of withstanding the inevitably dry periods which occur in container gardens.

All *Salix* are decidedly light plants, and may fail in even partial shade. In choosing a planting site, therefore, pay special attention to overstory because *Salix* suffers from lack of full sunlight and the foliage becomes sparse.

Salix species native to the high mountain ranges of central and southern Europe or the arctic regions are especially well suited for rock gardens because they grow prostrate; branches pressed closely to ground in a mat-like habit. They are ideal companions for alpine perennials. Larger-growing species from the subalpine or subarctic regions fit well into the scale of larger rock gardens. Both quite dwarf forms and the somewhat larger *Salix* adapt very well to container culture. They grow naturally and easily with *Pinus mugo, Betula nana, Calluna vulgaris, Chamaedaphne calyculata, Ledum palustre, Empetrum nigrum* and various *Vaccinium* species, so they make suitable companion plants in the garden.

The prostrate growing species make very good ground covers especially in confined locations. Because they all lose their foliage relatively early, they do not suppress weeds as do the evergreen cotoneasters or the fast growing *Potentilla, Symphoricarpos* and *Stephanadra* species.

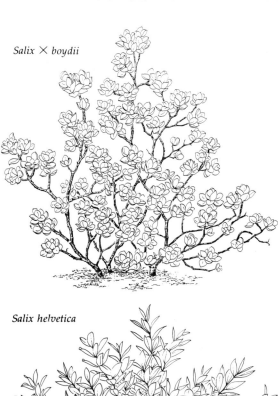

Salix × boydii

Salix helvetica

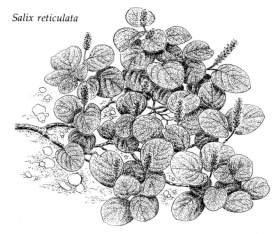

Salix reticulata

209

Salix Species Useful as Ornamental Specimens

Species	Habit	Leaves
1. Cushion-like form		
S. herbacea	With underground, mostly non-woody runners, slender, short twigs; 5 cm tall.	Few, almost round, 8 to 20 mm wide; both sides are glossy green.
S. reticulata	Branches are prostrate, rooting down, thick and glabrous, with large buds.	Decorative large, round, leathery; rugose above, deep green, prominent veining and silvery beneath
S. retusa	Prostrate shrub with long, glabrous branches and twigs; growing flat on the ground.	Small, 8–35 mm long, obovate to spathulate; turn yellow in winter.
S. serpyllifolia	Short, prostrate branches, twigs very slender and glabrous, makes an almost grass-like mat.	Especially small, obovate.
S. × *simulatrix* (*S. arbuscula* × *S. herbacea*)	Trailing, thickly-branched shrub with stout shoots and large buds in winter.	Relatively small (25 mm), nearly circular; both sides are glossy dark green.
2. *Salix* species with prostrate branches and ascending twigs.		
S. alpina	Low shrub with branches on the ground and upright twigs.	1–2 cm long, elliptic, margin almost entire; both sides green.
S. × *ambigua* (*S. aurita* × *S. repens*)	Small shrub (30–50 cm), low-spreading branches, vigorous; ascending, pilose twigs.	Small (approx. 1 cm), obovate, abruptly pointed; both sides hairy.
S. × *grahamii* (*S. herbacea* × *S. phylicifolia*)	Decumbent, 30 cm high; forms flat clumps and covers areas very quickly.	2.5–4 cm long, elliptic to oval, fresh green and holding into early winter.
S. × *moorei* (*S. herbacea* × *S. phylicifolia*)	Grows in communities; broadly prostrate, numerous slender twigs.	Small, glossy green.

Flowers	Natural Range	Landscape Use
Only a few ball-shaped catkins on leafy twig tips. Appear with or after leaves emerge.	High mountain ranges in Europe, north Asia and arctic North America. Grows on snow-covered soils where cold water runs under or through the stand of plants.	For dry locations in containers and through gardens, and rock gardens.
Long, narrow catkins at the end of leafy twigs.	High mountain ranges in Europe, the Iberian Peninsula; arctic Europe, Asia and North America. Grows mostly above timber line in nutrient-poor, lime soil, in sod, damp hillsides, rocky and graveled areas.	In moist locations in rock gardens and containers. With decorative leaves, a reliable, ornamental dwarf shrub.
Borne with the leaves, elongated; catkins about 2 cm long.	The Pyrenees, Alps, Carpathian, Balkans; in gravel, rock, rocky pastures and nutrient-poor meadows above timber line. Found in lime in the Alps, in primitive rock in the Tatras.	Plant as a specimen or in groups as ground cover in rock and heath gardens. Also for containers. Grows easily and quickly.
Small, stalked catkins with only 4 to 5 flowers; appear at the same time as the leaves.	The Alps above the timber line in rocky and gravelly soil of limestone, dolomite, or serpentine.	Considered to be the most ornamental of all dwarf *Salix*. Used in boulder fissures, in alpine gardens, and containers.
Numerous, long, cylindrical, erect catkins on leafy twigs.	The hybrid appears occasionally in Switzerland where both parent species mingle.	Attractive both as a specimen plant and as a ground cover in groups. Grows quickly, covering ground well.
Long, violet catkins appear at the same time as the leaves.	Central and southeastern European mountain ranges; in limy, dry sod, gravel and rocks above the timberline.	For rock and container gardens in dry, gravelly soil.
Numerous large, yellow flowers appear before leaves; borne upright on the horizontal twigs.	Often appears in the natural habitat of its parents. Many forms of this hybrid.	For ground cover and as a specimen plant in containers, rock and heath gardens. Grows quickly.
Erect catkins appear at the same time or after the leaves.	Natural hybrid from Scotland.	Used most often as a ground cover. Good in mid-sized areas in open sites.
Before the leaves.	Female only; a natural hybrid from Scotland.	Fast-growing, dense ground cover.

Salix Species Useful as Ornamental Specimens (cont.)

Species	Habit	Leaves
3. Shrub-like, to hip-high forms		
S. arbuscula	Well branched, thick-leaved shrub; 30–50 cm tall; various shapes, erect, bushy or prostrate.	Small, elliptic, margin almost entire; deep green and glossy on top, blue-green beneath.
S. arenaria	Creeping branches with upright twigs; previous year's branches are thick, woolly, and dark.	Obovate, with sharp, glandular teeth; both sides are thick and silky pilose, later turn matte gray-green.
S. × *boydii* (*S. lanata* × *S. reticulata*)	Small, stiffly erect shrub with short, spreading branches; 50–70 cm tall.	1–1.5 cm long, almost round; at first both sides are white pilose, later, the top is dark green and rugose.
S. glabra	30–150 cm tall, knotty, well branched shrub with short, thick, red-brown twigs.	Relatively large (4–6 cm long), elliptic; dark green on top with an oily luster, light gray-green underneath.
S. glauca	Erect; 30–100 cm tall, wide-spreading branches with brown twigs and glabrous buds.	Oblong-elliptic, margin entire; at first thickly pilose underneath and dull green on top; eventually glossy dark green on top and gray-green or bluish underneath.
S. hastata	Up to 1 m tall (often to 2 m); well branched shrub with dark gray twigs and large buds.	2–8 cm long, variable, finely and sharply serrate on the edges.
S. hastata 'Wehrhahnii'	Same as above, except twigs are yellowish brown, later very dark; buds are reddish.	Ovate, short acuminate; both sides are green, at first pilose, later glabrous.
S. helvetica	Shrub up to 1 m tall with crooked, thick limbs. Twigs are densely white tomentose at first, later glabrous and slightly glossy.	Up to 4 cm long, elliptic; underside mealy pilose, glabrous and dark gray-green on top.
S. lanata	Small, compact, wide spreading shrub; densely woolly yellow branches; large woolly flower buds.	3–7 cm long, broad-elliptic; both sides of leaves thickly pilose when young.

Flowers	Natural Range	Landscape Use
Elliptic, short stalked catkins appear with the leaves.	The mountains of Scotland and Scandinavia to the northern Urals. On banks, gravel soil and tundra. Also in sand and on rocky hillsides in limestone or unweathered rock.	Planted singly in rock and heath gardens in damp to dry locations. Requires rich soil.
Ovate catkins with short, round stigmas.	In the dunes on the Atlantic coast of Europe.	Drought resistant; good as a ground cover on dry slopes; a good massing shrub for elevated levels.
Ovate 2 cm long, silky pilose catkins with gold-yellow anthers.	Discovered in 1900 in Scotland; natural hybrid between *S. lanata* and *S. reticulata*.	Curious, somewhat stiff dwarf willow for specimen planting in rock gardens and containers.
Large, elliptic catkins; appear just before the leaves.	In high mountainous locations in the Julian Alps and the Dinaric Mountains; grows in limestone and dolomite moraines.	A very attractive species with its glossy leaves and red-brown shoots. Well suited for rock, heath and container gardens. Tolerates drought.
Large, cylindrical, stalked petiolate catkins; appear before or at the same time as leaves.	The arctic regions of Europe in a variety of plant communities. Found in acid soil in tall shrub communities, and in dry grass and dwarf shrub heaths.	Use as single specimen in heath, rock and container gardens in acid, moist to dry soil.
Very large, ball-shaped to elliptic catkins. Appear just before leaves; scales reverse with long, white hairs.	Circumpolar mountain and forest tundra in swampy meadows. Often along running streams in southern mountain ranges, also in sand dunes, lime and slate.	Very attractive willow, single specimens in rock and heath gardens; in damp to moist sites; in acid or lime soil.
Male cultivar; catkins are a pretty white at first, later turning yellow.	Reportedly found in Scandinavia. Noted for its attractive catkins.	Landscape use as above.
Large, broad-cylindrical, thick woolly catkins appear just before leaves.	Above the timber line in the Alps, Carpathian and Dinaric mountains; along creeks, on hil!sides covered with rock debris, and moraines, overlying weathered stone.	Very attractive and unusual gray foliage. Use as a specimen plant in rock, heath and large container gardens. Tolerates drought, does better in containers than *S. lanata*.
Large, elliptic, sessile, thick, gold-yellow woolly catkins; appear before the leaves.	High mountains of southern Scandinavia to north of the polar circle and northern Asia. Found in moist pastures, along streams and in gravelly soil.	Its striking catkins and gray foliage make *S. lanata* a beautiful shrub for damp to moist locations in rock and heath gardens.

Salix Species Useful as Ornamental Specimens (cont.)

Species	Habit	Leaves
S. myrsinites	Short, erect, 40 cm tall shrub; short, red-brown, glossy branches.	Small, ovate, sharply serrate; both sides green. Remain on the branches part of the winter.
S. purpurea 'Gracilis'	1 m tall, with many slender branches. Forms an almost round bush.	Silver-gray; narrow lanceolate.
S. rosmarinifolia (= S. repens var. rosmarinifolia)	Mostly prostrate, spring shoots are erect; many slender, short branches at the base.	Thin, linear lanceolate, 2 to 5 cm long, narrow at both ends; dark green above, silky-gray below.
S. waldsteiniana	Short, well branched, flat growing shrub with gray bark and yellow-green glabrous twigs.	3–5 long, elliptic, many veined; yellowish-brown in fall.

Flowers	Natural Range	Landscape
Small, cylindrical stalked catkins with violet anthers; appear before the leaves.	In swampy to wet locations in forest tundra and grassy moors. Often appear in lime soil in the high mountain of Scandinavia to the northern Urals.	Very decorative *Salix* (especially the var. *jacquiniana*) with striking blossoms for rock and container gardens.
Small, not very attractive.	Garden cultivar.	Non-descript, salt and drought resistant; for container gardens, low hedges and ground cover.
Catkins are round, subtending bracts and capsules are pilose.	Central and eastern Europe, western to northern Italy and Belgium, as far North as Sweden.	Drought resistant shrub for rock and heath gardens.
Long, elliptic, golden-yellow catkins; appear at the same time as the leaves.	High mountain ranges in the Eastern Alps and the Northern Iberian Peninsula; above timber line, especially on limestone and dolomite.	Heavy blooming; attractive, flat; rapid growth in rock and heath gardens. Also makes a good ground cover.

Salix lanata

Salix hastata 'Wehrhanii'

Santolina chamaecyparissus, Compositae

S. chamaecyparissus (Zone 6) grows in plant communities on the boulder-strewn coastlines from the western Mediterranean to Dalmatia. In exposed south-facing locations, it grows with *Genista aspalathoides*, *Helichrysum italicum*, *Narcissus serotinus*, *Bupleurum fruticosum* and *Pancratium illyricum*.

This fragrant, 30–50 cm tall, evergreen subshrub has squarish stems crowded with soft, brittle branches. The small, linear, somewhat thickened leaves are densely gray tomentose, incised and feather-like. In late summer, yellow flower heads appear on long, sparsely-leaved stems.

S. chamaecyparissus is an uncommon and unique dwarf shrub for well-drained soil and dry locations in sunny sites on dry walls or in rock beds. Good companion plants are both garden type and species gladiolas, *Centranthus ruber* and *Euphorbia myrsinites*. Because *S. chamaecyparissus* is only moderately frost hardy, a winter covering of evergreen boughs should be provided. Cultivars of *S. chamaecyparissus* include *S. c.* 'Nana'—dwarf—about one-half species dimensions; *S. c.* 'Plumosus', with silvery gray, lacy foliage.

Santolina ✕ *lindavica*, a hybrid between *S. chamaecyparissus* and the Italian *S. pinnata*, grows into a dense, 20 to 40 cm tall bush with gray-green leaves. It flowers very heavily with yellowish flower-heads.

Sarcococca humilis, Buxaceae

S. humilis (Zone 6) is widespread in western China and broadleaf evergreen forests and moist deciduous forests.

This evergreen shrub grows to be 50 cm tall. It spreads slowly via non-agressive underground runners. Its 4 to 8 cm long leaves are tapering-elliptic, smooth and glossy. In mid- to late winter, small, white, very fragrant flowers appear in spikelets in the leaf axils.

S. humilis grows best in a humus-rich soil and a warm, wind-protected, reasonably dry location. It tolerates shade, but does not do well when forced to compete with other plants. In mild climates it is a very good, if tall, ground cover.

Sasa pumila, Gramineae

S. pumila (Zone 6) is a bamboo found in Japan in moist deciduous forests. With slender, hollow stems, it reaches 30 to 60 cm tall. It spreads rapidly with vigorous rhizomes to form dense beds. Its leaves are

Santolina ✕ *lindavica*

Sasa pumila

217

7 to 15 cm long, 0.8 to 2 cm wide, long and pointed, finely serrate, rounded at the base, and light green on both sides.

S. pumila thrives in humus-rich, loamy soil in partly shady to shady locations. Close attention must be paid to this plant in small gardens or narrow strips as its rhizomes roam so widely, and are so tenacious, that it is difficult to control. It is, however, an excellent ground cover under high crowned trees.

Skimmia × foremanii, Rutaceae

This is an evergreen hybrid of S. japonica × S. reevesiana.

S. × foremanii (Zone 7) is about 50 cm tall and has closely-growing, leathery, 5 to 10 cm long, oblong to lanceolate, evergreen, yellowish-green leaves with reddish petioles. Its flowers (small, white, in terminal panicles) are normally female, although bisexual flowers are not unusual. The showy fruits are scarlet-red and remain on the plant until spring. Within one cluster of fruit, some individual fruits are round, while others are pear-shaped (characteristics of both parents).

Skimmia is one of the most important evergreen dwarf genera, with laurel-like leaves, flower buds which form in autumn, decorative flower panicles (male flowers are fragrant) and long-lasting, colorful fruit. They make excellent companion and massing plants, and are well suited as undershrubs or ground covers. They thrive in humus-rich, moist, fertile loamy soil in partly shady to shady locations (even under a dense tree canopy), which offer protection from winter sun. In exposed areas, and when there is no snow covering, a protective cover of evergreen boughs is recommended.

Skimmia japonica, Rutaceae

S. japonica (Zone 7) occurs as an understory shrub at higher elevations in the damp deciduous forests and evergreen laurel forests of Japan.

This dioecious, evergreen shrub only grows to 1.5 m in very mild climates. It is dense and compact, with gray shoots and leathery leaves in whorls. The narrow oblong to narrow obovate leaves are 6 to 12 cm long with entire margins. On top, they are glossy green and below, yellowish green. In early spring, small, white, four-petalled, fragrant flowers appear in 4 to 8 cm wide panicles above the foliage. Female plants produce round to oblate, 8 mm diameter, red berries.

Cultural requirements for S. japonica are similar to those of Skimmia × foremanii.

Skimmia reevesiana, Rutaceae

S. reevesiana (Zone 9) is native to the damp deciduous forests and evergreen laurel forests of China and Taiwan.

This species grows to 50 cm tall; a dense, compact, evergreen shrub with olive-green branches. Leaves are 5–10 cm long, lanceolate, tapering to a point, dark green above and light green below. Mostly bisexual, white, fragrant, five petal flowers appear in mid-spring in large loose panicles. S. reevesiana normally bears more fruit than other Skimmia species. The fruit is 8 mm long, dull red and pear-shaped. It remains on the plant until spring.

S. r. 'Rubella' is differentiated from the species by its red-tinged buds, petioles and flower pedicels, and increased hardiness. Male flower panicles are reddish through winter and expand to 15 cm, with white flowers, in late winter or early spring. They are grouped in especially large inflorescences.

For cultural and site requirements, see *Skimmia* × *foremanii.*

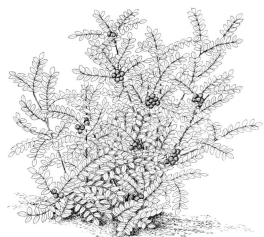

Sorbus reducta

Skimmia reevesiana 'Rubella'

Sorbus reducta, Rosaceae

High elevations in Burma and western China are the natural habitat of this Mountaine-Ash.

Of the numerous *Sorbus* species, this dwarf (Zone 6) reaches 15–40 cm high. With its underground root suckering habit, it forms small thickets. Its 9 to 15 featherly leaflets are 7 to 10 cm long and turn a striking carmine-red in autumn. This color is also displayed by the round, 6 mm thick, fall fruits. A few white flowers open in spring in terminal clusters and are 1.2 cm wide.

S. reducta is not outstanding, but is an attractive and different dwarf shrub for open locations in rock and heath gardens.

Spiraea albiflora, Rosaceae

S. albiflora (Zone 5) is a Japanese garden shrub of unknown origin.

This is a 30–60 cm tall, much-branched shrub with brown, angular canes similar in habit to the *S.* × *bumalda* cultivars. Its 6 to 7 cm long, narrow-elliptic to lanceolate leaves are light green. In summer, small, white flowers develop in numerous, terminal clusters.

S. albiflora is a beautiful, modest dwarf shrub for rock gardens, low hedges and ground covers. Its white flowers make a nice contrast to the red-flowered *S.* × *bumalda* cultivars, which blossom at the same time. This spiraea should be pruned back severely each year.

Spiraea bullata, Rosaceae

As is true of *S. albiflora*, *S. bullata* (Zone 6) originated in Japan but the wild type has disappeared.

This 35 to 40 cm shrub grows stiff, densely and compactly with rust-brown pilose canes. The small, scarcely 3 cm long, thick, leathery leaves are very rugose. On top, they are dark green; below, lighter. In early summer, the flowers are dark pink, but later, turn a smudgy pale red. They are borne in 4 to 9 cm wide, compound, flattish clusters on the branch tips.

S. bullata is more unusual looking than it is attractive. It tolerates dry locations in rock gardens very well.

Spiraea bullata

Spiraea × bumalda hybrids, Rosaceae

S. × *bumalda* (Zone 3) originated from a cross between *S. albiflora* × *S. japonica*; numerous cultivars have been selected from this hybrid population.

S. × *bumalda* hybrids grow with bunched, striped, erect branches to a height of 60 to 100 cm. Free-standing, the plant is hemispherical, a dense shrub with flat, terminal flower clusters in mid-summer.

All of the cultivars flower heavily. They may be used as specimens or in masses, in low hedges, or as ground covers. They thrive in full sun and do well in any good garden soil. For neat plants and best flowers, prune these plants to the ground in early spring every year.

S. 'Anthony Waterer' is the most commonly planted cultivar. It grows to approximately 80 cm. Narrow, sharply serrate, dark green leaves are borne along square, striped branches. New growth is red with occasional green and white variegated leaves. From early summer to early fall, carmine-red, 5 to 8 cm wide, flat flower heads are constantly produced.

S. 'Crispa' is differentiated by slower, more compact growth. Its curled, deeply incised leaves are wavy on the margins and red when they appear. The purplish-red flowers are borne in 5 to 7 cm wide flat clusters.

S. 'Dart's Red' received an award of merit in Holland. This mutation of *S.* 'Anthony Waterer' has deeper carmine-red flowers.

S. 'Froebelii' grows somewhat taller than does *S.* 'Anthony Waterer', to about 1 m high. Its elliptic to narrowly ovate leaves are brownish red when they first appear. They turn green later and are never white variegated. Its glowing cherry-red flowers are arranged in large, well branched, flat clusters.

S. 'Goldflame' is a 60 to 80 cm tall, slow-growing, very bushy shrub. Its elliptic, 7 cm long leaves are bronze-orange when they first appear, turning golden-yellow, to change again in summer to a greenish-yellow, and are copper-orange in autumn. The small, carmine-pink flowers are just barely visible above the foliage. Obviously, the main attraction of this cultivar is its colorful foliage.

220

Spiraea × *bumalda* cultivar 'Froebeli'

Spiraea decumbens, Rosaceae

S. decumbens (Zone 6) is found scattered over rocky slopes, among boulders and rock debris, in the mountains of the southern Alps, predominantly in mildly alkaline soil.

Although only 25 cm tall, it is capable of covering an area very rapidly and thickly with numerous underground runners. It is not evergreen, but does have a noteworthy inflorescence. Its many, wiry branches are covered thickly, even in winter, with blossoms. When covered with hoarfrost, they are exquisite. The leaves are 1 to 3 cm long, elongated-elliptic, single or double serrate. In early summer, small, white blossoms develop on the branch tips in 3 to 5 cm wide, flat, clusters of up to 50 blossoms.

S. decumbens is well suited for containers, rock gardens and as an underplanting in sunny locations. It is rather modest and, when pruned yearly, forms an even carpet of crowded, twiggy branches.

This dwarf shrub makes an outstanding ground cover and adds variation in gardens planted exclusively with cotoneaster species and cultivars.

Spiraea japonica cultivars, Rosaceae

S. japonica (Zones 3–8), native to Japan, grows to be 1.5 m tall and therefore, cannot be considered a dwarf plant. The two cultivars described below grow much smaller than the species. There is much confusion surrounding these Japanese Spirea and their names. Probably 'Nyewoods' and 'Little Princess' are cultivars from *S. alpina,* not *S. japonica* 'Alpina', but no taxonomist has positively said so.

S. 'Alpina' (= 'Nyewoods') is a very short, compact shrub. It reaches 30 cm tall and wide in 5 years' time. Its leaves are very small, 1 to 2 cm long and dark green. They remain on the plant until late fall. In midsummer, pink flowers develop on the tips of young shoots in dense, roundish clusters.

S. 'Little Princess' differs from *S.* 'Alpina' in that it grows much faster and it has paler flowers. It is very twiggy, with a compact habit, and grows to 60 cm tall. In midsummer, within a matter of weeks, the shrub is covered with 4 cm wide, flat flower clusters. It begins blooming as a young plant.

Both cultivars may be used as specimens in containers and rock gardens. Otherwise, they are planted usually in drifts and as ground covers in sunny locations in any good garden soil.

221

Spiraea japonica 'Little Princess'

Syringa meyeri, Oleaceae

Syringa meyeri (Zone 5) was discovered in northern Chinese horticulture. There is confusion about the wild type and its habitat, as it is no longer found in the wild.

It is a small, dense, handsome, shrub which only exceeds 1 m tall when fully mature. Its light, rectangular, pilose branches are furnished with 2 to 4 cm long, elliptic to ovate leaves which are green on both sides. In late spring, fragrant, pink-violet flowers appear in 8 cm long, dense, pilose panicles. It begins blooming as a young plant.

Syringa patula, erroneously called "palibiniana". This lilac is native to Korea and adjacent China; leaves are elliptic to ovate-oblong, about 10 cm long, pubescent on both surfaces. Flowers are lilac, in panicles to 15 cm, and appear with or just after the french hybrid lilacs.

Both plants are treasures for rock

gardens and containers (their resistance to drought allows them to thrive well in containers). They need sunlight, and are undemanding in their soil requirements.

Syringa microphylla, Oleaceae

Northern and western China (Zone 4) is the natural habitat of this species. This is a 1 to 1.5 m tall, bushy, erect shrub with slender, lightly pilose branches. Its leaves are 1 to 4 cm long, round-ovate to elliptic and gray-green below. Fragrant lilac colored flowers appear in 4 to 7 cm long, finely pilose panicles in late spring.

A cultivar S. 'Superba' has a particularly long flowering period, with flowers produced intermittently from May to October. The blossoms are pinkish-red. They become paler as the season progresses.

Teucrium chamaedrys, Labiatae

T. chamaedrys (Zone 6) is native to central and southern Europe (also to the east as far as the southern Caucasus Mountains and Iran, and to the south as far as the Atlas Mountains) on dry, rocky hillsides, in rock debris and usually in alkaline soil. It is a typical plant of the southern Alps, especially in the Graubünden, around Wallis and Konstanz. It often grows together with *Anthericum liliago, Laserpitum latifolium, L. siler* and *Buphthalmum salicifolium.*

T. chamaedrys is distinctly rhozomatous (Bailey) =stoloniferous. See Bean, R.H.S. Dictionary, etc. and garden plants. This deciduous subshrub forms low carpets from vigorous stolons. It is 15–25 cm high with dense branches and green leaves.

Flowers are purplish to light pink with red and white spots. These blossoms are in whorls of 2–6 and are carried in apical racemes from May to September.

Another garden species is *T. massiliense,* a 10–15 cm, evergreen subshrub with many, upright branches. *T. massiliense* does not have stolons. Its leaves are gray-tomentose, ovate, crenate, but lanceolate with entire margins on the upper part. Pink flowers appear in long, terminal false spikes above the foliage in June–July.

These plants are beautiful late summer-bloomers for dry, sunny sites on well drained soil in rock and heath gardens. They are also well suited for very low hedges and as a ground cover. Plants should be sheared each year to encourage compact growth.

Ulex europaeus, Leguminosae

U. europaeus (Zone 6) is native to Portugal but is now found on the Iberian Peninsula, and the coastlines of France, Belgium and England. For the most part, plants found in central and southern Europe are naturalized, having escaped from cultivation. It is an understory shrub in sparse oak and pine forests in regions with mild, damp climates.

U. europaeus generally does not exceed 1 m in height. It is an evergreen shrub with wide-spreading, stiff, thorny branches and green, grooved twigs. Its leaves are modified into 6 to 12 cm long thorns. Huge quantities of solitary, golden-yellow, butterfly-shaped flowers are produced on the ends of lateral, thornless short shoots. Following the main flowering period, a constant sputtering of single flowers appears throughout the summer growing season.

223

U. europaeus is well suited for large heath gardens. It thrives only in very well drained, somewhat warm, strongly acid, nutrient-poor soil in sunny to partly shady locations. It tolerates drought well, but does poorly in continental climates with cold winters.

Ulmus glabra 'Nana', Ulmaceae

Of the several forms of Ulmus glabra (Zone 5) found in northern and central Europe and in Asia Minor, only U. 'Nana' grows as a dwarf shrub.

This shrub is wider than tall, and when mature is often up to 2 m in height. It is dense and usually hemispherical, its branches bearing horizontal and drooping twigs along their length. The leaves are attractive, large, glossy, deep green and have distinct venation. It is a handsome, yet unusual shrub for large rock gardens.

Vaccinium macrocarpon, Ericaceae

V. macrocarpon (Zone 2) is found in North America from Newfoundland to North Carolina, Indiana and Ohio. It grows in open coniferous forests and in the glades of cool, damp deciduous forests.

This evergreen shrub grows into large, flat mats with prostrate, trailing, branches and rooting stolons. Its beautiful leaves are narrowly elliptic, 1 to 2 cm long, lightly rolled under along the margins, dark green on top and whitish underneath. Long stalked, pale purple flowers with a four-part reflexed corolla, are sparsely borne in the leaf axils in early to midsummer. The 1 to 2 cm thick, red berries are edible.

Selections of V. macrocarpon are cultivated in bogs for commercial cranberry production. In gardens, this ground cover plant thrives only in wet, acid, nutrient-poor, raw humus soil, in full sun. This is a lovely ornamental plant but difficult to grow under average garden conditons. It is the cranberry of American cuisine.

Vaccinium oxycoccos, Ericaceae

V. oxycoccos (Zone 2) is a typical plant of the high transitional moors in boreal Europe, Siberia, northern and central Japan and North America. In the few southerly distributions (the Alps up to 1800 m), it is found almost exclusively in sphagnum moors.

This is an evergreen, nearly prostrate dwarf shrub with sprawling, 80 cm long, brownish red branches and short, erect flowering twigs. Its leaves are only 3 to 7 mm long. They are firm, leathery, glossy dark green on top and have a persistent, blue-green waxy bloom below. Axillary, nodding flowers, in clusters of 1 to 4, are 6 to 7 mm wide, with turban-like corolla. They appear from spring to midsummer, depending on the altitude and exposure. The round, succulent, deep red berries remain on the plant throughout the winter.

V. oxycoccos readily scrambles over flat rocks and root stumps in a heath garden (in light, sandy, sharply acid, moist soil) forming a carpet of handsome leaves. In suitable locatons this is an almost indispensable plant for heath gardens.

Vaccinium uliginosum, Ericaceae

V. uliginosum (Zone 2) is found in the boreal regions of Europe, Asia and North America. It grows in forest and transi-

Vaccinium macrocarpon

tional moors, often to considerable elevations. It also occurs in dry, nutrient-poor,
raw humus soil in subalpine and alpine
meadows. In northern Europe it is often
found growing with other *Vaccinium*
species, *Ledum palustre, Andromeda polifolia,
Trientalis europaea* and *Eriophorum vaginatum*. In mountainous ecosystems it is the
dominant plant on the forest floor in thin,
dry pine forests.

This is a deciduous, thickly branched,
stiffly upright shrub 50 cm tall. Its hard,
sessile leaves are 1 to 3 cm long, elliptic to

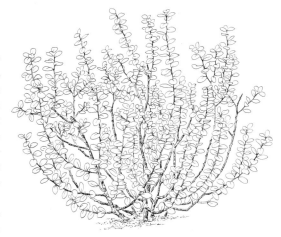

Vaccinium uliginosum

225

obovate and bluish green on both sides. Urn-shaped blossoms are borne 1 to 4 at the tips of short, lateral branches in spring. The 7 to 9 mm diameter fruits are bluish black and pubescent.

V. uliginosum is a widely distributed species. It thrives in damp or dry locations and tolerates sun or light shade. It makes an excellent companion plant for rhododendrons and is a fine addition to heath gardens.

Vaccinium vitis-idaea, Ericaceae

V. vitis-idaea (Zone 5), like other members of this genus, is widely distributed in central and northern Europe, Asia and North America. It is a woodland floor shrub in dry pine forests in sandy, nutrient-poor, acid soil. It is also found in high and transitional moors. In sphagnum-transitional moors, it is often accompanied by *Ledum palustre, Vaccinium uliginosum, V. oxycoccos, Eriphorum vaginatum, Trientalis europaea* and *Maianthemum bifolium.*

This plant develops into an evergreen, 30 cm tall shrub with a bushy, spreading mat of branchlets above ground and spreading runners below ground. Hard, leathery leaves may be opposite or alternate. They are glossy, dark green above and dull, pale green below with black punctate spots. In late spring, red tinged, white flowers appear in dense clusters on the shoot tips.

A few vegetatively propagated cultivars are available. Fruiting cultivars such as *V.* 'Erntedank', *V.* 'Erntekrone' and *V.* 'Koralle' bear more heavily and consistently than the species. *V. vitis-idaea* cultivars are often used as ground covers. They colonize in patches between dwarf pines, junipers, *Calluna, Empetrum* and *Arctostaphylos* species. They only thrive, however, in well drained, sandy-humus, acid soil. *V. vitis-idaea* tolerates lightly shady locations as well as competition from deep rooted pines. This is the Lingonnerry of Scandinavian cuisine.

Viburnum davidii, Caprifoliaceae

In its western China habitat, this evergreen shrub occurs in laurel forests and warm, damp, deciduous forests.

V. davidii (Zones 7–8) grows to 1 m only in mild climates; it usually is much lower. This very thickly branched shrub has 5 to 14 cm long, firm, leathery, dark green evergreen leaves with entire margins. Leaf venation is very striking; the curving main veins are deeply inbedded in the leafblade. In late spring, pink-white blossoms open in 8 cm wide, flat clusters. The dark blue, 6 mm long fruit are very attractive.

V. davidii is a very attractive dwarf shrub, as well as an important companion plant for rhododendrons. It grows in any moist, humus-rich soil in partly shady to shady locations. It is not completely frost hardy so requires winter protection.

Viburnum davidii

Viburnum opulus 'Nanum', Caprifoliaceae

This dwarf cultivar of the familiar snowball bush (Zone 3) originated in France in 1841.

   This scarcely 60 cm tall shrub is almost ball-shaped with witches' broom-like twigs and very small leaves. This cultivar never bloom or produce fruit and is, therefore, not as attractive in the summer as the species. In winter, bright orange-red twigs of both cultivars enliven rock and container gardens.

Vinca minor

Vinca minor, Apocynaceae

V. minor is native from southern and central Europe to Asia Minor and the Caucasus Mountains. It occurs in mild, humid climates as a ground cover in oak, beech and hornbeam forests. It grows from the plains into the montane levels, and not infrequently runs wild in the garden.

   This evergreen shrub trails long, low-arching, rooting leafy stems which form dense, 15 cm high mats. Its single, entire margined, opposite flat-lying leaves are leathery and glossy. Disc-shaped flowers are lilac-blue, 2 to 3 cm wide; they appear on the tips of erect shoots from spring through early fall.

   Of its numerous cultivars, the following are very popular:

   V.m. 'Alba' has pure white single flowers and leaves which are smaller than those of the species.

   V.m. 'Bowles' flowers abundantly with large deep blue flowers.

   V.m. 'Rubra' is distinctive for its striking purple-red flowers.

   V. minor and its cultivars are some of the most ornamental ground-covering, shade tolerant plants available. They tolerate competition from larger trees very well. *V. minor* thrives in moist, high humus, loose soil, generally preferring partly shady locations. It grows luxuriantly in warm climates.

   V. major (Zones 6–7), native to southern Europe and Asia Minor, differs from *V. minor* in its taller, more luxuriant habit, larger leaves and larger, charming bright blue flowers. Unfortunately, it is not as frost hardy as *V. Minor,* but usually recovers from deeply buried rhizomes.

Xanthorhizza simplicissima, Ranunculaceae

X. simplicissima (Zone 3) is native to the damp, deciduous forests of eastern North America.

   This 50 to 60 cm tall, thinly branched, deciduous shrub proliferates by underground runners. Its alternate, mostly 5-leaflet pinnate leaves are denser towards the tips of twigs. Reddish brown, unattractive blooms appear in early

227

spring, before the leaves emerge. They are arranged in 5 to 10 cm long, terminal clusters.

X. *simplicissima* thrives in loose, loamy soil and tolerates shade and competition from large trees. It makes a good ground cover and is often used among or around the edges of deciduous tree plantings. It may spread very quickly. In the right cultural conditions, a single plant can spread approximately 2 m in 4 years' time.

Yucca filamentosa, Liliaceae

Y. filamentosa (Zone 5) is found in North America from Florida to Texas north to Kansas and New Jersey. It grows on the edge of deciduous forests bordered by prairies. It thrives in coarse calcium-poor, sandy or stony soil.

This evergreen, stemless shrub develops short lateral shoots at the base and stiffly erect, up to 70 cm long, sword-shaped, glaucous blue-green leaves arranged in a rosette. In late summer, the flower stalk emerges up to 1 m or more. It bears a tapering cluster of cream-white, green spotted, pendulous blossoms.

Y. filamentosa thrives in any (even limy) well drained, deep soil. The plant is very sensitive to excessive winter dampness. In sunny locations, it goes beautifully with sedum species, wild grasses, gray-green wild dianthus species and lavender.

Zenobia pulverulenta, Ericaceae

Z. pulverulenta (Zone 6) is native to the damp deciduous forests of southeastern North America. It is a semi-evergreen shrub which is deciduous in colder climates.

This 50 to 100 cm tall shrub develops curving, upright, more or less sturdy bluish frosted canes. The ovate-oblong to elliptic, 2–7 cm long leaves with entire margins are uniformly and lightly blue frosted on both sides. In late spring, pure white, bell-shaped pendent blossoms are borne in drooping axillary clusters on the upper part of the previous year's twigs.

This shrub is a good addition to heath gardens and moor beds, growing in sandy-humusy, moist, acid soil in partly shady locations. Its greatest value lies in the unusual red foliage. If plants overgrow, they respond well to pruning, especially in early summer.

Encyclopedia of Conifers

Abies amabilis 'Spreading Star', Pinaceae

A. amabilis (Zone 6) is native to the Cascade Mountain Range in western North America. 'Spreading Star' was developed in Pinetum Blijdenstein in Hilversum, Holland.

The branches of this 1 m tall, dwarf fir grow in horizontal tiers. It develops into a spreading, almost tablelike, loose, handsome dwarf conifer. Its lower branches lay prostrate on the soil. The upright-pointed, spreading, dark green needles are 20 to 30 mm long and lighter in color when they first emerge. When rubbed, they smell like oranges.

A. a. 'Spreading Star' is a beautiful cultivar for sunny to partly shady locations in larger heath gardens.

Abies balsamea f. hudsonia, Pinaceae

This is a high mountain North American species found from Virginia to Mt. Katahdin, Maine, and in Canada, north to the timberline. f. *hudsonia* comes from the White Mountain area in New Hampshire.

Abies balsamea 'Nana'

It develops into a roundish cushion-like, short but thickly branched, 50 cm tall dwarf fir. It has spreading branches and broad, flat needles which are half-radially borne around the branchlets, black-green above and blue-green beneath.

A.b. 'Nana' is a more readily available cultivar. It is differentiated by radiate needles which are dark green on top and marked with 2 white stomatal lines beneath.

Both are very handsome dwarfs for rock and heath gardens in moist, cool soil in partly shady to sunny locations.

Abies cephalonica 'Meyer's Dwarf'

Abies cephalonica 'Meyer's Dwarf', Pinaceae

A. cephalonica (Zone 6) is native throughout Greece and on the islands of Euboea and Cephalonia at subalpine levels.

A.c. 'Meyer's Dwarf' develops without a leader into a short, flat-mounded, irregular-growing shrub. When young, it has a nest-like center. In 10 years, it grows approximately 25 to 30 cm tall, and 50 to 60 cm wide. Its 8 to 15 mm long, tapering needles are radiate and glossy dark green on top.

This is a very useful cultivar for heath, rock and container gardens. It tolerates more heat and drier conditions than most other dwarf firs.

Abies amabilis 'Spreading Star'

Abies balsamea 'Nana' (top left)

Abies concolor 'Green Globe' (top right)

Abies lasiocarpa 'Compacta' (middle left)

Abies pinsapo 'Horstmann' (middle right)

Abies procera 'Blaue Hexe' (bottom right)

Abies concolor cultivars, Pinaceae

A. concolor (Zone 4) occurs in dry locations in the southwestern states of Colorado, Arizona, New Mexico and California, U.S.A. and northern Mexico. It is often found growing with *Pinus ponderosa, Calocedrus decurrens* and *Pseudotsuga menziesii.*

A.c. 'Compacta' is an irregular-growing, shrubby, compact, yet slightly sprawling, cultivar with thick, short branches. It grows an average of 3 to 5 cm per year, to a height of 2 to 3 m when mature. Its needles are firmer than the species, 25 to 40 mm long, erect or curved to a crescent-shape, and glaucous blue.

A.c. 'Green Globe' is an especially attractive cultivar with long, apple-green needles. It grows flat-globe-shaped when young but forms a leader when mature, then develops a compact, cone shape.

'Piggelmee' was introduced in 1972 by Draijer. Unlike 'Compacta' it is a genuine dwarf cultivar which hardly ever exceeds 30 cm, propagated from a witches-broom on *A. concolor* 'Candicans'. It won a silver medal in Boskoop, Holland in 1970. Its thickly crowded, 2 to 3 cm long needles are blue-green.

These are beautiful cultivars with strikingly colored needles, especially when they first emerge. They are used in sunny to partly shady sites, are adaptable to a varieties of soils, and tolerate higher soil temperatures and are more drought resistant than most other firs.

Abies koreana 'Piccolo', Pinaceae

A. koreana (Zone 5) is native to the mountains of southern Korea.

A. k. 'Piccolo' is a shrubby cultivar with a broad, flat habit. It reaches only 30 cm tall, but grows to be 1.5 m wide. The needles spread widely, lying almost flat, glossy on top and with white stomatal bands beneath.

Other flat-growing *A. koreana* cultivars, such as 'Compact Dwarf', are available but are rare. In addition, a number of relatively unknown cultivars are recorded. These usually are propagated by grafts from lateral shoots, or may be vegetatively reproduced from very compact, selected seedling plants.

Most *A. koreana* cultivars are suited to sunny to partly shady locations. Some have dark green needles with attractive markings on the underside, and the needles grow closer together than those of 'Piccolo'. The majority also fruit while very young (the cones are showy violet-purple before they reach maturity). Prune out any vertical shoots which develop near the lateral branches to retain the plant's dwarf habit.

Abies lasiocarpa Compacta', Pinaceae

A. lasiocarpa (Zone 5) is distributed from Alaska to New Mexico at high mountain elevations in western North America. It is often found growing with *Picea engelmanii, Pinus albicaulis* and *Tsuga mertensiana*. It is also found above timberline as a flat-growing, wind-shorn specimen. The species grows poorly in eastern North America.

A. l. 'Compacta' develops with a compact, regular, narrow-to wide-globe habit, and short, very crowded, upright-reaching branches to a mature height of 1.5 to 2 m. After 10 years, however, the plant usually only reaches 60 to 80 cm tall. The needles are 15 to 25 mm long, upward

pointing, a beautiful silver-blue underneath with white stomatal bands. The plant
also has yellowish brown, resinous winter
buds.

This is a hardy dwarf conifer for moist
sand and loamy soils, which are not too
light. It becomes somewhat chlorotic in
alkaline soil.

Abies procera 'Glauca Prostrata'

Abies pinsapo 'Horstmann', Pinaceae

Abies pinsapo (Zone 6) is native to the
southern Spanish Province of Malaga, at
elevations of 1000 m.

When young, *A. p.* 'Horstmann' is
almost globe-shaped. Later, it is more
upright-growing, with spreading, well
branched, rigid shoots. Its needles grow at
right angles all round the twigs and
branches; short, rigid, borne thickly, and a
blue-gray color.

This is a choice, winter hardy cultivar
for sunny locations in dry, well drained
soil. It was developed by G. Horstmann,
Schneverdingen, West Germany.

Abies procera cultivars, Pinaceae

A. procera (Zone 5) is a rainforest tree in the
Cascade and Siskiyou Mountains of the
west coast of North America.

Some cultivars of this and other species
are simply lateral shoot grafts. Such plants
tend to maintain a horizontal growth habit
in the garden, developing into scarcely
dwarfed, sprawling specimens of little
ornamental value. Upright, staked, these
eventually develop into fair ornamentals.
It is better to choose dwarf conifers grown
from witches' brooms or naturally dwarfed

branches. Only then can the gardener be
assured of obtaining a genuine dwarf
plant.

A. p. 'Blaue Hexe' ('Blue Witch') was
grown from a witches' broom in 1972 by
G. D. Boehlje, Westerstede, Holland, 1965.
It is completely flat-growing, rather evenly
mounded and grows broader than it does
tall. An older plant is about 40 to 80 cm
wide, thickly branched with short twigs.
During its first year, *A.* 'Blaue Hexe' is 1 cm
long; needles are gray-blue and bent
backward. As they mature, they turn
green. *A. p.* 'Blaue Hexe' is a genuine dwarf
cultivar. It grows much more slowly than
the two following cultivars.

A. p. 'Glauca Prostrata' develops with
bushy, prostrate-spreading or slightly
ascending branches. Commonly, after
many years, it scarcely reaches 1 m. It may
develop a leader gradually or suddenly,
which must be removed immediately in
order to maintain the dwarf habit. The
needles are very similar to those of the
species but are uniformly blue.

A. p. 'Nobel' originated from the Nobel
Collection in Golden Gate Park, San
Francisco. It is differentiated from *A. p.*
Glauca Prostrata' by a flatter immature
habit, branches which tend to grow
downward, and relatively long blue

234

needles, crowded on the twigs brush-fashion which bend upwards.

With their blue-gray needles, all are very exceptionally attractive dwarf conifers. They do best in sunny locations in deep, sandy-humus soil. They will not tolerate lime or constant dampness. Because they resume growth late in the spring, they are not usually affected by late frosts.

Cedrus deodara cultivars, Pinaceae

C. deodara (Zone 7) is native to Afghanistan and the northwestern Himalayas at elevations of 1000 to 4000 m. It is usually found growing singly, but also occurs in dense stands.

C.d. 'Golden Horizon' grows flat and broad with pendulous branch tips. Its 15 to 28 mm long needles (they are 4 cm long on young twigs) are pale to greenish yellow on the side exposed to the sun. On the inside of the plant, the needles are gray-green. This is an unusually colorful dwarf conifer for sheltered, lightly shaded locations above low walls or in large rock

gardens. In sunny, low humidity locations, as well as in containers, the needles of this only moderately winter hardy cultivar turn brown. The plant requires well drained, acid soil.

C.d. 'Nana' is a slow growing, thick and bushy cultivar with pendulous shoot tips and relatively short, green needles. An exceptionally fine example of this cultivar can be found in the rock garden at Kew Garden, London.

Cedrus libania 'Sargentii'

Cedrus libani 'Sargentii', Pinaceae

C. libani (Zone 7) is native to Asia Minor (Taurus and Antitaurus mountains), Cyprus, Lebanon and parts of Algeria. It thrives in mountains up to 2000 m.

C. l. 'Sargentii' is a flat-growing, or creeping cultivar. Its branches lay prostrate, spreading over the soil, or hang over walls cascading down. When mature, it reaches 0.6 to 1.5 m tall, but grows as wide as 3 to 4 m. If permitted, its branches hang down on all sides. Needles are long, stout, and glaucous blue.

Cedrus deodora 'Golden Horizon'

235

This is a very attractive, hardy dwarf cultivar to be planted in elevated locations, taking advantage of its weeping habit, and fertile, loamy soil. It is very well suited for container growing.

Chamaecyparis lawsoniana cultivars, Cupressaceae

Native to the Pacific North American Coast (northwestern California and Oregon and Washington). Numerous cultivars are available, some of which are dwarf. Most grow evenly but somewhat openly, so their habit may be less pleasing to some than that of juniper, dwarf pine and cedar.

Many cultivars however, have beautifully colored needles. Often, they are blue or yellow. For this very reason, as is the case with other dwarf conifers, they should be used sparingly in gardens.

All are relatively undemanding, though not reliably hardy in continental climates or windy, exposed sites. They require sunny to lightly shaded locations and thrive in any good garden soil. They will not tolerate very dry soil, but do grow in mildly alkaline soil.

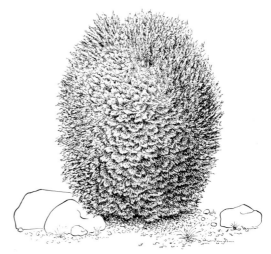

Chamaecyparis lawsoniana 'Gimbornii'

Chamaecyparis obtusa cultivars, Cupressaceae

C. obtusa (Zone 3), native to Taiwan and southern and central Japan at elevations up to 1000 m, has given rise to many cultivars which are less well known than those of *C. lawsoniana*. Almost all originated in Japan, where they have been cultivated for centuries. They are gaining in popularity in the West as they grow with a comparatively more open surface texture and at a slower rate than cultivars of *C. lawsoniana*. *C. o.* 'Nana Gracilis' is certainly one of the most widely used dwarf conifers.

C. obtusa cultivars are widely adaptable and can be used in rock and container gardens, narrow beds and other small areas. They grow best in moist soil in lightly shaded locations, in mild humid climates. This is especially true of the yellow-needled cultivars, as they scald very quickly in direct, winter sun. If cared for properly (regular irrigation and fertilization), green-needled cultivars thrive well in small containers.

Chamaecyparis lawsoniana 'Rijnhof'

236

Chamaecyparis lawsoniana 'Minima Glauca'

Chamaecyparis lawsoniana **Dwarf Cultivars**

Cultivar	Height (cm); Habit	Twigs	Needles
'Aurea Densa'	60–80; at first shrubby, later conical with a truncated top	Dense, curved slightly upward	Short and broad, densely appressed, golden-yellow
'Filiformis Compacta'	100–150; flat to broad globose; slender branches	Threadlike, dense, with pendulous tips	Small, tightly appressed, dark bluish green
'Forsteckensis'	100–150; broad globose to conical; very popular	Vigorous, short, twisted	Very small, appressed, gray-blue
'Gimbornii'	100, dense and compact, oval	Short, upright, thick and rigid, purple-blue	Blue frosted
'Gnom'	Almost ball-shaped; slow growing, fine textured foliage; dark green, light green in spring	Spread evenly on all sides	Rather compact, scale-like
'Green Globe'	Evenly globose; bluish cast; sturdy form	Almost flat, spreading on all sides	Fine, scaly
'Minima Aurea'	80; globose, spreading limbs	Spreading, pale yellow, yellow in the middle of the plant	Very short, appressed; pale yellow
'Minima Glauca'	100; at first globular, when mature broadly conical; branches are upright-spreading; one of the most popular	Curved upwards, upright-spreading	Short, blunt, dull, glaucous blue
'Nidiformis'	100; multiple-trunked, branches spreading, somewhat arching; nest in the middle, up to 2 m wide when mature	Pendulous	Short, blue to gray-green, more blue on the underside
'Pixie'	80–100; globose to broad-elliptic, with small tips; finer twigged than the similar 'Minima Glauca'	Dense	Fine, scaly, bluish green
'Pygmaea Argentea'	100; round at first, later broadly conical; erect branches	Erect, dark green, easily sunburned	Creamy white on branch tips
'Rijnhof'	30; branches spread horizontally in very flat tiers; grows 15 cm per year to 1 wide; very winter hardy	Dense, pendulous twig tips, branches almost fishbonelike	Juvenile needle-form, gray-green, underside blue-green; color constant in winter
'Tharandtensis Caesia'	150–200; globose at first, later broadly conical; few stout branches; old cultivar	Numerous, twisted	Small, very thick, loosely appressed, dull blue-gray, glaucous

238

Chamaecyparis obtusa Dwarf Cultivars

Cultivar	Height (cm); Habit	Twigs	Needles
'Caespitosa'	20–30; very dense, broad conical; very slow growing	Cupped, shell-like	Very small, blue-green
'Coralliformis'	50; flat, shrubby, branches slender growing loosely intertwined	Thin, cord-like, somewhat pendulous, coral-like, unevenly compressed	Bluish green, flecked light brown; very glossy
'Hage'	100; dense, broad conical; very slow growing	Dense and twisted	Very small, apple-green
'H.J. Draht'	150–200; upright, narrow conical; loose surface texture; new, promising cultivar	Thick, as in *C. o.* 'Lycopodioides'	Thick and short, scale-like, apple-green, maintains color during winter
'Intermedia'	30; open-conical, grows only 1 cm per year	Spreading, somewhat pendulous	Light green
'Juniperoides'	25; densely globose; grows 1 cm per year	Fan-shaped, tips nod downwards	Narrow, appressed, dark green
'Kosteri'	100–120; loose, conical with dense, ascending-pendulous, or arching branches	Thick, somewhat brown	Light green
'Lycopodioides Aurea'	100; abnormal form with uneven, ascending branches; bushy to globose	Thick, cockscomb-like at the tips	Light yellow
'Mariesii'	60; conical; slow growing	Thin, pendulous	Yellow-white, milk-white in summer; yellow-green in winter
'Nana'	60; globose; very slow growing	Short, shell-like	Blackish green
'Nana Gracilis'	200 when fully mature; broad conical; horizontal branching when young, unevenly globose to conical	Uneven; twisted or curved, shell-like	Glossy, dark green
'Pygmaea'	150; broad and globose; spreading branches; loose	Fan-shaped, attractive red-brown, tips somewhat nodding	Sparkling apple-green, green underneath, brownish in fall and winter
'Repens'	60; twice as wide as tall when mature, otherwise similar to 'Pygmaea'	More coarsely branched than *C. o.* 'Pygmaea'	Always apple-green, never with bronze tones
'Rigid Dwarf'	90; narrow conical, with stiff upright branches	Palmate-spreading	Deep, dark green
'Tetragona Aurea'	200; conical when mature, shrubby when young, ascending to spreading branches, very ornamental	Unevenly short, cockscomb-like tips; four-sided	Thickly imbricate in four rows, gold- to brownish-yellow; in shade yellow- to blue-green

Chamaecyparis obtusa 'Rigid Dwarf'

The frequently favored *C. p.* 'Filifera Aurea Nana' is not a genuine dwarf form, rather, a very slow growing cultivar propagated from selected lateral branches of *C. p.* 'Filifera Aurea'. Of the yellow-needled *C. p.* 'Filifera' cultivars, only *C. p.* 'Golden Mop' is a genuine dwarf.

Chamaecyparis pisifera 'Filifera Sungold'

Chamaecyparis pisifera cultivars, Cupressaceae

C. pisifera (Zone 3) is another native of Japan. It is found in moist soil in the valleys. It too has yielded numerous familiar cultivars. Some have feathery-curled needles, others bear cord-like, pendulous branchlets with closely compressed needles which may be yellow or blue-colored. This is a very versatile group of dwarf conifers. They can be used in many locations such as terraces, front yards and entryway gardens, rock gardens, container gardens, and trough gardens. They thrive in any moist garden soil and need a sunny to lightly shaded location sheltered from drying winds.

Some of the yellow-needled cultivars sunburn easily in locations where the air is too dry. However, they only display their best color in sunny locations, so it is important to use them only in more humid and mild climates.

Chamaecyparis pisifera 'Plumosa Rogersii'

240

Chamaecyparis pisifera Dwarf Cultivars

Cultivar	Height (cm); Habit	Twigs	Needles
'Filifera Nana'	60; flat-globose; dense; spreading when mature; handsome, ornamental form	Cord-like tips; pendulous, cascading	Deep green
'Filifera Sungold'	100–200; much flatter growing, and more coarsely branched than C. p. 'Filifera Aurea'; relatively sun-tolerant	Cord-like; ascending-arching	Yellow-green, constant color in sun
'Golden Mop'	100; grows like C. p. 'Filifera Nana'		Constant golden-yellow
'Nana'	60; 1.5 wide when mature; compact, globose to cushion-like, very slow growing, spreading branches	Very dense, fan-shaped; tips nod downwards, curled	Very small, deep green above, blue-green beneath
'Nana Aureo-variegata'	60; like C. p. 'Nana'		Creamy-white flecked needles give the entire plant a yellowish cast
'Plumosa Compressa'	60; wide and unevenly globose to cushion-like; very dense when mature, brown patches develop easily in the foliage due to sunscald	Branches and twigs very dense, moss-like and curled	Pale yellow to bluish gray or green; part juvenile-type needles, part mature
'Plumosa Nana Aurea'	80; flat-globose; slow growing, sunburns easily	Similar to those of C. 'Squarrosa'	Golden-yellow, greenish-yellow inside the plant
'Plumosa Rogersii'	100; conical	Similar to those of C. 'Squarrosa'	Golden-yellow, even in winter

Cryptomeria japonica cultivars, Taxodiaceae

C. japonica (Zone 5) forms extensive forests in Japan, from the southernmost islands, to Hondo in the north. This extremely variable species has numerous dwarf cultivars, grown in Japan for many years. Some of them are very unusual, with monstrous, fasciate (cockscomb-like) branches. Others have slender, pendulous branch-tips and are very elegant. They may be used in every sort of garden situation suitable for dwarf conifers, other than containers.

All of the dwarf forms of *Cryptomeria* grow best in mild, humid climates; in moist, humus-rich soil; in partly shady locations. Drought, low winter temperatures, winter sun and wet snow injure them.

In Japan, approximately 200 cultivars are used in culture. Only a few of these have been introduced in the West.

241

Chamaecyperis pisifera 'Nana Aureovariegata'

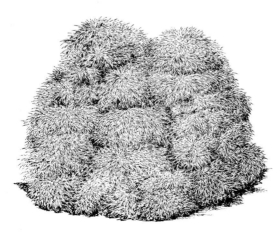

Cryptomeria japonica 'Globosa Nana'

Ephedra distachia, Ephedraceae

E. distachia (Zone 5) is distributed from the western coast of France and the Mediterranean regions of Spain and Italy, to the Russian steppes (southern USSR and Siberia). It colonizes sunny, dry and sandy locations.

This xerophilic species develops into an erect or prostrate, almost leafless, thickly branched switchy plant with bluish green or dark green, finely striated branches. Papery, scale-like leaves along the canes

Ephedra distachia

stubby, scale-like leaves, appressed closely in 4 rows and with a recessed gland on the reverse side. The other type of leaf is pointed, needle-like, borne in whorls of 3, or 2 opposite; 8 to 12 mm long; upper side with a green midrib, the lower (reverse) surface with 2 bluish white stomatal bands.

J. chinensis has a number of well-known cultivars, several of which are slow growing and included here. They are used as specimen plants, or massed in front gardens, heath and rock gardens, on top of retaining walls, in containers, and as ground covers. They all prefer open, airy, sunny to lightly shaded locations and light to somewhat loamy, well drained, dry soil.

are only 2 mm long. Round berry-like false fruits 6 to 7 mm in diameter develop from inconspicuous, dioecious blossoms.

E.d. ssp. *helvetica* differs from the species in that it has a shorter, thicker, broom-like habit. It is a part of the Walliser rock heaths from Fallaterres to Sierre in very sunny, dry locations on exposed limestone.

Both are unusual plants for sunny, dry locations in well drained soil on dry walls, and in rock, heath and container gardens.

Juniperus chinensis cultivars, Cupressaceae

In its natural habitat (China, Mongolia and Japan; Zone 3), this variable species can grow to be a 20 m tall, conical to columnar tree. It can, however, also be shrubby or prostrate. This consistently dioecious juniper bears two kinds of leaves (often, one plant has both kinds). The first are about 1.5 mm long, narrow rhombic,

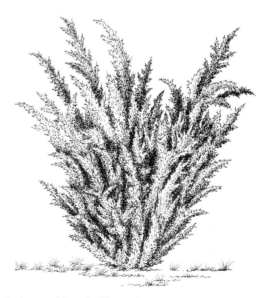

Juniperus chinensis 'Blaauw'

243

Juniperus chinensis Dwarf Cultivars

Cultivar	Height (cm); Habit	Twigs	Needles
'Dropmore'	Broad, hemispherical; particularly slow growing	Dense	3 mm long needle leaves; mature leaves paried at right angles to ones above or below
'Echiniformis'	Globose to flat-globose	Short, crowded	All leaves needle-like, small, spreading on tips
'Gold Coast'	Moderate growing, broad, low table-like cultivar in which compact habit and intense color are combined	Slightly pendulous	Golden-yellow, darker in winter; green on the inside
'Japonica'	Wide, irregularly conical to 2 m or procumbent	Short; branch tips tend to droop; very dense	Needle-like leaves in whorls of 3, prickly, 2 blue stomatal bands on top, light green beneath; scale leaves on older plants, yellow-green at branch tips
'Mordigan Aurea'	Has a looser, but still compact, habit than 'Gold Coast'; branches ascend at a slight angle	Slightly pendulous	Lively golden-yellow needles, more pleasant color than most yellow forms
'Rockery Gem'	80–100; slow growing, limbs spread horizontally prostrate when young, later tiered	Loosely branched, rigid, tips ascend slightly	Gray-green

Juniperus chinensis 'Plumosa Aurea'

Juniperus communis cultivars, Cupressaceae

J. communis (Zone 2) is found from the plains to the mountain ranges of Europe, northern Africa, northern and western Asia and North America. It grows in heaths, moors, on sterile slopes, sometimes developing miniature forests, or more commonly in sparse pine forests as an understory shrub. In the mountains and northerly latitudes, ssp. *nana* is the predominant form.

This polymorphic species often grows to be a more or less slender, many-stemmed, tree-like, 15 m tall specimen.

Juniperus chinensis 'Mordigam Aurea'

Occasionally, however, it remains shrubby or grows as a picturesque ornamental with loose or pendulous branches. Its numerous cultivars are often nothing more than cloned and vegetatively propagated wild forms.

J. communis always bears needle-like leaves arranged in whorls of 3. They are 15 mm long and 1 to 2 mm wide, mostly gray-green, shallowly grooved on top and have a wide, white margin. Flowers are mostly dioecious. The round, fleshy cones (juniper "berries") which ripen during the

Juniperus communis var. *montana*

245

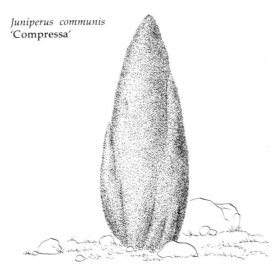

Juniperus communis
'Compressa'

second or third year are blackish-brown when fully ripe.

All these junipers can be used in landscaping as can the *J. chinensis* cultivars. They are especially useful in poor sandy soil, but also do well in limey and fertile soils. They do not tolerate constant dampness, however.

Juniperus communis 'Depressa Aurea'

Juniperus conferta, Cupressaceae

J. conferta (Zone 5) is found along the coastline in Japan and Sachalin, where it forms thick cushions on loose sand.

It is a prostrate shrub with red-brown, creeping, vigorous branches and densely crowded, upright growing twigs. The gray-green needle-like leaves are arranged in very compact whorls of three. They are straight, 10 to 15 mm long, 1 mm wide and have a long tapering point. The upper side has a white band and lacks a green midrib. Color is generally a bright green, but leaves turn a gray-green in the second year. The 8 to 12 mm thick, smooth, very dark blue fruits have a gray bloom and are very striking.

J. c. conferta can be found in some nurseries, as well as the following cultivars:

J. c. 'Blue Pacific' differs from the species due to its even flatter habit and beautiful, blue-green needles.

J. c. 'Emerald Sea' was developed in the National Arboretum in Washington, D.C., U.S.A. It is a thick, mat-forming, salt tolerant cultivar with large, emerald-green needles with a gray-green band on the upper side. Needle color changes to yellow-green in winter.

This species and its cultivars are often planted in the landscape as ground covers. They do well in open, sunny locations in well drained, infertile soil and develop into close-knit carpets with a dense display of erect branch-tips and strikingly long needles. They are valuable also as specimens or for a massed planting in the home garden combined with other junipers. These are quite handsome in containers, as their branches and shoots droop over the edges. The cultivars are relatively frost hardy.

Juniperus communis Dwarf Cultivars

Cultivar	Height (cm); Habit	Twigs	Needles
ssp. *alpina*	20–30; found at high elevations in the mountains of Europe and subalpine regions of northern Asia and North America: prostrate, crowded branches. *J.* 'Sibirica' is an especially attractive cultivar.	Short, thick, triangular, often zig-zag growing	4–8 mm, needle whorls are very dense; deeply concave above with a wide, white stomatic band
'Compressa'	80; decorative, spindle-shaped, columnar; grows 2–3 cm per year; not frost hardy	Thick, stiffly upright	4–5 mm, light green; distinct, white stomatic bands above, dark green underneath
'Depressa Aurea'	100; branches widespread and divergent; the middle of the plant is bowled or hollow	Nodding; tips yellow when they emerge, later bronze	In summer, a few needles on the upper sides of the twigs are entirely or partly yellow or bronze-ringed.
'Echiniformis'	50; irregular, flattened, densely globe-shaped; an ideal plant for small containers	Short and very dense	3–4 mm, always needle-like; blue-green above, gray-green below
'Hornibrookii'	50; up to 2 m wide; branches are low-spreading, develops into a low, mounded bush. One of the best low growing sorts, good as a ground cover and on retaining walls.	Unevenly long, tips ascend slightly, glossy dark brown	5–6 mm long, very thick; silvery-white striped above, green below, often brown in winter; prickly
'Nana Aurea'	50; branches are spreading, prostrate; unsurpassed color, especially when leaves emerge, better than 'Depressa Aurea'	Pendulous tips, twiglets are fan-shaped	Silver-white striped with green margin; underside golden-yellow from spring until late autumn, bronze-yellow in winter
'Repanda'	30–40, up to 1.5 m broad; forms a round cushion, branches spread evenly on all sides, vigorous, healthy, handsome; suitable as a ground cover	Slender, crouched; brown	5–8 mm, convex; soft, ringed densely around the twigs; silvery striped above, green beneath
'Sibirica' *J.C.*	differs from *J.C. alpina* in its more compact habit and thick, striking silver needles; an especially attractive form		
'Suecica Nana'	100–150, to 30 cm wide; columnar, narrow and dense, truncated top. More vigorous, hardier and more open than 'Compressa'.	Branches and twigs ascending	Short; blue-white striped above, underside blue-green

Juniperus conferta

Juniperus horizontalis,
Cupressaceae

J. horizontalis (Zone southward) is found in North America, especially on the dunes and sandy shores of northern interior lakes and in the Rocky Mountains.

J. horizontalis forms flatter, more spreading plants than most of the other *Juniperus* species. It has trailing, rooting branches with close-set, short, densely needled upright shoots. Leaves are needle-like, blue-green or steel-green, usually arranged in threes, 2 to 6 mm long and somewhat spreading. Scale leaves are less common on plants in cultivation but are found on the species. The scale leaf is narrow elliptic, tapering to a point, and is convex on the dorsal side with a gland. Stout, round, 7 to 9 mm diameter, blue-black, lightly bloomy fruit develop only on wild plants.

This species and its numerous cultivars (especially *J. h.* 'Glauca') are among the most popular juniper ground covers. All

Juniperus horizontalis Cultivars

Cultivar	Height (cm); Habit	Twigs	Needles
'Alpina'	60; at first the branches are nearly upright, later more prostrate	Ascending to almost upright	Needle-like, 3–4 mm long, bluish green; purple in fall and winter
'Andorra Compact'	30–40, similar to *J.* 'Plumosa' but denser	Slanting-ascending from the center of the plant	Somewhat narrower than those of 'Plumosa'
'Bar Harbor'	Forms dense mats; main branches prostrate, lateral branches ascend slanted; vigorous habit, a good ground cover	Slender; orange-brown when young, lilac tips	Very small and appressed; dark green, gray-green pruinose; purple cast in winter
'Blue Chip'	40–50; prostrate, densely twiggy, sometimes referred to as *J.* 'Blue Moon'	Ascending; in a dense stand twigs are quite upright	Very ornamental; silver-blue needles do not discolor in winter
'Douglasii'	30–40, 2–3 m wide when mature; mat-like prostrate, long branches; branches lay over each other in the center	Tips are long and straight, branchlets 5–8 cm long, ascending	Both scale- and needle-like; scale leaves, dense, gray-green, glaucous blue, light purple in autumn and winter; needle leaves
'Emerald Spreader'	Prostrate habit; valuable because of its varying needle colors; an American cultivar	Prostrate, spreading evenly in all directions	Emerald-green
'Emerson'	30; creeping; very slow growing, female clone		Both scale- and needle-like; blue-green summer and winter
'Glauca'	30; thickly mat-like; main branches lie tight against the soil and root down; branches layered only in the center of the plant; one of the most intense blue cultivars, very popular	Many angled forward, whip cord texture	Awl-shaped, densely crowded; steel-blue summer and winter
'Jade River'	Habit is similar to 'Glauca' but more vigorous and dense		Silvery gray-blue; purple cast in winter
'Plumosa'	50–60; flat, round shrub; main branches prostrate, secondary branches ascend at a 45° angle. Older cultivar. Soil should not be too dry.	Smallest twigs feather-like	Awl-shaped, dense and loosely appressed; light gray-green, striking purple in winter

Cultivar	Height (cm); Habit	Twigs	Needles
'Prostrata'	30, 3–4 m wide; mat-like, main branches long and rigid, prostrate up to the ascending tips. In cultivation more than 100 years. Similar to *J. sabina* 'Prostrata'	Thickly crowded, prostrate; blue-green with purple tips	Mostly awl-shaped; blue-green, more scale-like toward the branch tips
'Turquoise Spreader'	Branches especially prostrate; forms thick carpets	Smallest twigs feather-like, spreading	Turquoise-green; only slightly discolors in winter
'Wiltonii'	10; carpet-like, slow growing. The lowest growing cultivar, beautiful in containers and rock gardens. Often marketed incorrectly as "Blue Rug".	Dense	Mostly awl-shaped, small, silver-blue; minimal discoloration in winter

Juniperus horizontalus 'Prostrata'

thrive in situations which duplicate their natural habit. Planted above retaining walls, above or behind rocks, or in containers, their branches droop gracefully downward. They are also well suited for small planting strips or to cover long slopes. All do exceptionally well as ground covers as they form dense, unbroken carpets. In general, junipers with horizontal branches spreading out from the main trunk and then bending sharply upward are most favored.

The cultural requirements of *J. horizontalis* cultivars are more demanding than those of *J. communis*. Under the most favorable conditions, *J. horizontalis* cultivars never do as well as *J. communis* cultivars in moist, mild areas, but in harsh, inland regions *J. horizontalis* and its cultivars are the better growers.

Juniperus procumbens, Cupressaceae

The mountains of central Japan and the coast of Kyushu Island are the natural habitat of this Juniper (Zones 4–9). It was introduced into The Netherlands in 1843 and is one of the most beautiful naturally creeping species.

J. procumbens grows scarcely knee-high, but is 2 m wide when mature. It has rigid, prostrate branches with erect tips. Its rather short, needle-like, 6–8 mm long, gray-blue leaves are appressed closely to the branches, 3 to a whorl. Berry-like cones are 8 to 9 mm thick and nearly round.

J.p. 'Nana' is lower growing, and more densely branched than the species. Its limbs are stockier and shorter and its lower woody structure makes a tight cushion-like tangle with erect short shoots. Consequently, the plant has a thick, flatly arched surface. It is a very attractive dwarf for rock gardens, beds, and to plant in containers.

Juniperus sabina cultivars, Cupressaceae

J. sabina (Zone southward) is found from the mountain ranges of southern Europe, over the Carpathians, the southern Urals, the limestone mountains along the Donets River, the mountains along the Volga and to the Baltic in limey soil. It is often present on warm, sunny mountain slopes or as an understory shrub in sparse pine forests in mineral-poor soil, or even, on stony screes.

This usually low shrub sometimes develops into a small tree to 4 m high, with slanting-ascending branches. Its low growing cultivars, however, are of great value in small gardens. They are un-demanding as to their location, do well in calcium-rich soil and are used in the same manner as low growing *J. chinensis* cultivars.

Most cultivars can grow to be many meters wide when mature. They often choke out neighboring plants, but can be kept in check if pruned correctly.

Juniperus squamata cultivars, Cupressaceae

The western and eastern Himalayas, the Chinese-Tibetan mountain border and Taiwan comprise the natural range of this Juniper (Zone 4 southward).

This low-growing shrub has short, more or less ascending main branches and nodding branch tips. Densely crowded, needle-like leaves are white on the upper surface and green on the underside.

The species is usually cultivated in botanical gardens only, but its cultivars are extremely valuable in garden landscapes. Although long available and well known, and considered by some to be a dwarf conifer, *J.s.* 'Meyeri' grows to be at least 5 to 6 m tall and is, therefore, not a dwarf at all. In the last few years, however, genuine dwarf cultivars which are mutations of *J.s.* 'Meyeri' have been introduced. Where summers are hot and humid, *J. squamata* and its cultivars are subjected to foliar fungi and spider mites.

J.s. 'Blue Carpet' is reminiscent of its forebear only in its intense blue-gray, pointed, needle-like leaves on young shoots. Older twigs have green leaves. *J.s.* 'Blue Carpet' grows very flat and dense with spreading twigs. It grows 20 to 30 cm tall and is a vigorous ground cover for open, sunny locations. In such locations, it spreads as widely as 2 meters. It was awarded a Gold Medal in 1976 at the Flora Nova in Boskoop.

J.s. 'Blue Spider' is differentiated from *J.s.* 'Blue Carpet' by its more intense silvery-blue needles. It spreads broadly and is disk-shaped with pendulous branch tips. Its needles are awl-shaped; young twigs are orangish-brown.

J.s. 'Blue Star', a genuine dwarf, originated as a witches' broom of *J.s.* 'Meyeri' in 1950. It has become very popular and, as a matter of fact, no other new dwarf conifer has gained in popularity nearly as quickly. It was awarded a Gold Medal in Boskoop in 1964.

J.s. 'Blue Star' reaches 70 to 80 cm tall and 1.5 m wide. It grows into a thick, hemispherical bush, with needles shaped

251

Juniperus sabina 'Tamariscifolia'

Juniperus sabina 'Blue Moon'

and colored like those of *J. s.* 'Meyeri'. It is an ideal plant for containers and narrow strip beds.

J. × 'Holger' is a hybrid probably of *J. squamata* 'Meyeri and *J. chinensis* 'Pfitzeriana Aurea'. It develops into a spreading, 2 m wide cultivar with gently ascending branches and nodding tips. New twigs are pale yellow giving the plant a yellow cast. The plant's mature foliage is gray-green and so the plant appears bicolored in spring. This is a very unusual cultivar.

Juniperus sabina Dwarf Cultivars

Cultivar	Height (cm); Habit	Twigs	Needles
'Arcadia'	50, up to 1.25 m wide; similar to *J.* 'Tamariscifolia', but flatter, smaller and more ornamental		Preponderantly scale-like; small and light green
'Blue Danube'	Broad and low growing, branch tips bent upwards; not especially attractive but very frost hardy; also known as 'Blaue Donau' in Europe	Clustered	Mostly scale-like, needle-like inside the plant; light gray-blue
'Broadmoor'	60, up to 3.5 m wide; similar to *J.* 'Tamariscifolia'; main branches strongly horizontal; very vigorous cultivar	Short and erect	Finer than *J.* 'Tamariscifolia'; 3–4 mm; gray-green
'Buffalo'	Prostrate, wide, spreading; wider and lower than 'Tamariscifolia'; exceptionally frost hardy		Glossy apple-green
'Tamariscifolia'	100, to 2 m wide when very old; limbs spread horizontally, overlying which encourages leaf diseases	Dense, short and spreading	Mostly needle-like; very short, pointed; light bluish green

Juniperus squamata 'Blue Carpet'

All *J. squamata* cultivars should be planted in sunny locations in dry, sandy, loamy soil. They are lime tolerant. Both prostrate cultivars, 'Blue Carpet' and 'Blue Spider' are ideal ground covers for small and large areas, and also can be used as specimen plants or massed in groups wherever junipers are commonly used: front gardens, larger heath, rock and steppe gardens. The unusual foliage color of *J.* × 'Holger' only appeals to those who enjoy yellow foliage plants. *J.s.* 'Blue Star' is especially well suited for containers, where it can thrive for years if well tended.

Larix kaempferi cultivars, Pinaceae

Species habitat: Japan, volcanic slopes in the mountains of Hondo; zones 4 southward. Botanical taxonomists are not in agreement about the name of this plant. All larches are deciduous.

L.k. 'Nana' was found as a witches'-broom in W. Germany in 1976 by H. Neumann. It grows very slowly into a decorative, extremely dense bush. Needles on short twigs are 8 to 10 mm long. Young shoots have substantially longer, gray-

253

green needles which are slightly recurved. In contrast, the longest needles of *L.k.* 'Wolterdingen' are in the middle of the twigs.

L.k. 'Wolterdingen' was discovered by G. Horstmann of Schneverdingen, W. Germany in 1970. *L. k.* 'Wolterdingen' grows with almost horizontally spreading branches. In 10 years, grafted plants grow 40 cm tall and 70 cm wide. The soft needles on the tips of young shoots are only 2 cm long and recurved. Mature needles are 35 mm long, and slightly twisted. On long shoots, the needles are blue-green above and somewhat lighter on the under side. Needles on short twigs are usually green. Coloration is attractive and unusual and makes a valuable contribution to a collection of dwarf conifers.

Larix kaempferi 'Wolterdingen'

Microbiota decussata, Cupressaceae

Native habitat: ranges through the coastal mountain range near the Tatar Strait, the Satluj River in southwestern Tibet, to the upper reaches of the Angara River in south central Siberia. *M. decussata* (Zone 2) is found growing with *Pinus pumila* in southeastern Siberia, extending beyond the timber line in granite and shale dry screes.

M. decussata is a prostrate dwarf shrub. Usually, it scarcely reaches 60 cm in height, but can grow as wide as 1.5 m. The shrub normally has stout, fan-shaped branches which completely cover the ground. When planted on a raised surface, its branches hang over in a distinctive fashion. The twigs are short, four-sided, and form flattened sprays. The very small leaves are usually three-cornered and scale-like when mature; when young, they are needle-like. Leaves are green in summer. Color changes to a copper-brown in winter; a very clear, pleasant color, not washed out and soiled-looking as the needles of *Thuja occidentalis*.

Larix kaempferi 'Wolterdingen'

Microbiota decussata

It was formerly assumed that *M. decussata* was dioecious, but The Botanical Garden in Nocy Dvur, U.S.S.R., claims that the plant is monoecious.

In its natural habitat, *M. decussata* grows on stony hillsides in rocky soil. In coastal climates it tolerates dry sites well. It thrives in sunny locations as well as it does in lightly shaded ones and is not demanding as to soil. Since it is native to Siberia, it is very frost hardy. Thanks to its adaptation to harsh sites, it can be used in containers with great success. As a container plant it is very attractive with its branches drooping over the edges. Whenever possible, it should be planted above walls on stone ledges in the rockery where its branches can trail. In addition, it can be planted, as are the prostrate junipers, as a ground cover.

Microbiota decussata

Picea abies cultivars, Pinaceae

P. abies (Zone 2) is native from western Europe to central Asia in moderate to high elevations in mountains (in the Alps up to 2000 m).

P. abies is prone to deviations in habit, branches, needles and cone shape. In addition to these modifications, numerous cultivars originated from mutations, many of which are dwarfs.

Only some of the most important cultivars will be discussed here. Most do not exceed one meter in several decades, but some, although they grow incredibly slowly, eventually reach human height.

These plants can be used as specimen plants or in small masses in rock and heath gardens, or narrow strip beds. They remain healthy in containers only in high humidity and if knowingly tended. They thrive in cool, moist, fertile, limed soil in humid climates, in sunny to lightly shady sites. They do not tolerate heat and drought well.

Picea abies 'Little Gem'

Picea abies 'Pumila Nigra'

Picea abies 'Emsland'

Picea abies 'Nidiformis'

256

Picea abies Dwarf Cultivars

Cultivars	Height (cm); Habit	Branches and Twigs	Needles
'Clanbrassiliana'	150; densely compact, beeskep-like (high mound form)	Thin and flexible, grows 2–5 cm per year	Fine and thin, 5–10 mm long, closely crowded; vibrant green
'Compacta'	150; wide-conical and compact	Numerous, short; lower branches horizontal	6–9 mm; four-sided, glossy green
'Echiniformis'-'Igelfiche'	20–30; slow growing, globose; dense spikes form bumpy cushion	Light brown, rather thick and rigid; grows 15–20 mm per year	12–15 mm long, narrow, thick, rather sparse; light yellow-green
'Elegans'	150, as broad as high; conical, very dense, many main limbs; very attractive. Not a commonly used form.	Yellow-brown, short and thin	Pointed, 4–8 mm long; thickly crowded and radiate; light green
'Emsland'	100–150; similar in habit to *P. glauca* 'Conica'; dense surface texture, good replacement for *P. glauca* 'Conica' which is often attacked by red-spider	Limbs acute-angled, widely spaced; twigs thick; main branches with large winter buds; grows 5–8 cm per year	8–12 mm long; radiate on main shoots; glossy dark green
'Gregoryana'	60–80; densely globose, irregular outline; differs from 'Echiniformis' in shorter, more densely crowded needles and lack of extremely vigorous shoots	Rather thick, but flexible; grows 5–20 mm per year	Radiate on all twigs; dull gray-green with finely pointed tips
'Gregoryana Veitchii'	100, to 180 cm wide; differs from 'Gregoryana' in greater vigor, less compact habit; more often cultivated than 'Gregoryana'	12–35 mm growth per year; very flexible, often pendent in spring	Radiate only on upright leaders; when mature, half-radiate or parted along the top of the lateral twigs and branches
'Kamon'	50 cm tall in 10 years, twice as wide; unevenly broad; of interest because needles change color	Reddish brown	Mostly radiate; rigid, strikingly silvery blue-green
'Little Gem'	Very twiggy, flat-globose and cushion-like; mutation of 'Nidiformis'	Very slender, densely compact, slanting upwards from the middle of the plant; grows 2–3 cm per year	2–5 mm; very narrow and densely crowded
'Mariae-Orffiae'	Compact-globose; grows very slowly, the smallest of all *Picea* cultivars	Dense, spreading; yellowish-white, small and thin; grow 5–10 mm per year	4–8 mm; rigid and thick, light yellow-green with yellow tips

Picea abies Dwarf Cultivars (cont.)

Cultivars	Height (cm); Habit	Branches and Twigs	Needles
'Maxwellii'	Moderately slow-growing; round, cushion-like	Many, short, thick twigs clustered at the tip annual growth 20–25 mm	5–12 mm; radiate on erect shoots; thick and rigid; apple-green
'Nidiformis'-'Nestfichte'	80–100; uniformly flat-globose; has no central trunk; nest-like concavity in the center	Diagonally ascending from the center; tips bent downward; grow 3–4 cm per year	Imperfectly radiate; 7–10 mm long; appressed marginal teeth; light green
'Ohlendorffii'	Globose when young, later, broadly conical; has a central trunk; limbs ascend and spread	Uneven, not in one plane; thin, and flexible; grow 3–6 per year	4–8 mm; radiate on leaders, very slender; rigid and glossy yellow-green
'Procumbens'	Fast growing; broad, flat habit; uneven surface texture; limbs rigid, slightly ascending	Thick and rigid; grow 5–10 cm per year; twigs orange-brown	Long, 10–17 mm; closely crowded; half-radiate; rigid, thick yet flat, apple-green
'Pumila Nigra'	1 m when mature; flattened-ball habit; limbs stacked in close whorls, plate-like; young tips droop slightly; scarcely distinguished from 'Pumila Glauca'	Thin and very flexible, lateral shoots spread uniformly; annual growth	Half-radiate, very dense; rigid; 8–12 mm; dark bluish green
'Pygmaea'-'Gnomenfichte'	Usually 100; extremely slow growing, truncate-conical; very dense and compressed. The oldest known *Picea* dwarf.	Bright-to gray-yellow; glossy; thick; flexible; grow 10 to 30 mm per year	Radiate only on strong shoots; 5–8 mm long; very crowded on the twigs; apple-green
'Repens'-'Kriechfichte'	50; prostrate; branches rest upon one another; dense	Orange-brown; glabrous, thin and very flexible; grow 3–5 cm per year	Half-radiate; 8–10 mm; very crowded on twigs; bright green to yellow-green
'Tabuliformis'	Mat-like when young; later, branches rest upon one another, eventually developing a flat-globose and open habit	Light brown, glossy; very flexible; grow 2–3 cm per year	Half-radiate; 7–10 mm long, somewhat sparse; light yellowish green

Picea abies 'Elegans'

Picea glauca cultivars, Pinaceae

P. glauca (Zone 3) is found in northern North America to Labrador and Alaska, on lake, river and ocean shores in humid areas. The species is seldom seen in cultivation in western Europe and in much of the U.S., but on the other hand, one cultivar, *Picea glauca* 'Conica', is commonn. This cultivar is not an easy plant to incorporate into the design of a garden due to its severe, formal habit.

All *P. glauca* cultivars do well in moist, well drained, acid to alkaline soil, in cool, humid sites. If the environment is not suitable, they are easy prey for Red Spiders, which kill entire branches and eventually the plant. They are, for that reason, not suitable for container.

P. g. 'Alberta Globe' is a dwarf mutation of *P. glauca* 'Conica' with an open, globose form. The needles are green, 6 to 9 mm long and slender, as are the needles of *P. g.* 'Conica'. It is less susceptible to Red Spider infestations than *P. g.* 'Conica'. This

259

Picea glauca 'Alberta Globe'

Picea mariana 'Nana', Pinaceae

P. mariana (Zone 3) is another species of spruce distributed over a large part of Canada and south to Wisconsin and Michigan. Only a few gardens forms of *P. mariana* are cultivated, and of them *P. m.* 'Nana' is the only dwarf cultivar suitable for continental locations.

When mature, *P. m.* 'Nana' scarcely reaches 50 cm. It is a densely branched, open textured, globose dwarf spruce. The thin, flexible twigs have slender, closely crowded needles that are bluish green with 2–4 very pronounced stomatal lines on both sides.

This is a beautiful conifer for rock and heath gardens. It requires moist, cool, humid locations.

cultivar received a gold medal in Holland in 1968.

P. g. 'Conica' is very well known and greatly appreciated by most gardeners. It grows very slowly, reaching 1 m after 10 years. When mature, however, it can reach 4 m. It always maintains its uniform, dense, narrowly conical or domed habit. Its twigs are very slender with thin, 10 mm long, light green to bluish green needles.

P. g. 'Echiniformis' grows very slowly to about 1 m wide, and half as high. It is a dense, bushy globose to cushion form dwarf with short branches and 5 to 7 mm long, radiate, rigid, strongly colored blue-green needles—an interesting cultivar for rock and heath gardens.

P. g. 'Laurin' has a habit similar to that of *P. g.* 'Conica' but unlike it, grows even more slowly, extending its branches by only 15–25 mm per year. Its branches are very crowded bearing 5 to 10 mm long, dark green, radiate needles. This is a genuine dwarf for exposed sites in the alpine garden.

These cultivars are easily damaged by cold, drying winds or intense sunlight. All are, however, quite frost hardy.

Picea mariana 'Nana'

Picea × mariorika, Pinaceae

This is a hybrid between the North American *P. mariana* and the Yugoslavian *P. omorika*, as indicated by the specific epithet combining the name of both parents. Currently two dwarf cultivars derive from this hybrid:

P. × 'Kobold' was selected by J. P. Zu Jeddeloh in 1951. In 20 years, it will reach 1 m in both height and width. It has a roundish habit and is densely branched. The twigs are rather thick, rigid, reddish brown and furrowed. The needles are radiate, 8 to 12 mm long, with 3 to 4 stomatic lines on the upper side and a deep green color underneath.

P. × 'Machala' is a dwarf spruce with fairly stiff, horizontal to slightly ascending branches. The habit ranges from spreading to flat-globose and is comparatively open. It reaches 30–50 cm in height and 1 m or more in width. The 10 to 15 mm long needles are rigid, very pointed and dark green. They have 2 separate rows of stomata on the upper side and another 2 bands on the underside which give the conifer a silvery white to grayish blue cast.

Both P. × merlorike cultivars are decorative, attractively colored dwarf spruces. Neither is culturally demanding when compared with the cultivars of P. glauca or P. mariana. P. g. 'Machala', with its looser habit, is somewhat more attractive than P. × 'Kobold'.

cm per year. Branches are gray-yellow, slender and flexible. Its crowded, radiate needles are 10–15 mm long, glossy green beneath and with 4–5 white stomatic lines on top.

P. o. 'Minima' is another Jeddeloh introduction. Welch assigns this cultivar to P. × moriorika, originating from a witches'-broom of P. 'Nana'. It has very short branches and a loose, open surface texture. Exceptionally dwarfed, it grows with a broadly globose to flat hemispherical form, reaching 15–20 cm tall in 10 years. Its needles are similar to those of P. 'Nana'.

P. o. 'Nana' is a dwarf cultivar with a broadly conical form and very dense habit. It will eventually exceed 3 m in height. Its more or less radiate, sparsely-spaced, 7–8 mm long, still needles are twisted, clearly showing their broad, white stomatal lines which produce an attractive bicolor effect.

P. o. 'Pimoko', a recent Wuestemeyer introduction, originated from a witches'-broom. It develops into a thickly branched,

Picea omorika cultivars, Pinaceae

P. omorika (Zone 4) has a relatively small natural range of distribution. It is only found at moderate to high elevations in the Zelengora Mountains, in the middle and upper course of the Drina River and in the Viogora Mountains above the mouth of the Lim River.

P. o. 'Gnom' was developed in Oldenburg from by Jeddeloh. It is a broadly conical, densely branched spruce with an open surface. In 20 years it grows to 1.5 m tall. Mature plants grow only about 2 to 3

Picea omorika 'Nana'

Picea omorika 'Pimoco'

Picea orientalis cultivars, Pinaceae

P. orientalis (Zone 7), together with *Abies nordmanniana*, dominate forests in the Caucasus and Taurus Mountains. This species and its cultivars thrive in a variety of garden soils and sites. They are better adapted to harsh continental climates than most spruces, and also tolerate nearly continuous shade.

P. o. 'Aurea Compacta' is a very compact, broadly upright, irregularly-growing cultivar, usually lacking a main trunk. In 10 years a plant will grow to approximately 60 cm tall and wide, gaining 4–7 cm per year. The short needles on at least the upper side of the branches are lighter or darker yellow throughout the year while needles on the underside, or in shaded areas, are green.

P. o. 'Gracilis' grows 3–7 cm per year, but is 6 m tall when mature. It has an ovate habit with slender, very ornamental, thickly crowded limbs and branches. Like the species, it has beautiful, glossy green needles.

Picea pungens cultivars, Pinaceae

P. pungens (Zone 2) is found in the Rocky Mountains and eastern Cascade Mountains of western U.S.A. and Canada. It is a high mountain species found at elevations up to 3300 m.

The selected blue-needled cultivars, including dwarf forms, are becoming more widely known and planted. As conifers are increasingly incorporated into home gardens, choice, colorful cultivars, such as some of the *P. pungens* forms, take on a special significance in creating color contrasts in the landscape.

flat-globose bush lacking a central trunk (the center of the plant has a cup-like depression). It only grows to be about 30 cm tall and 40 cm wide in 10 years. Branches are short and rather thick, more or less upright on the upper part of the shrub, and spreading at the sides. Numerous buds are brownish red. Terminal buds are nearly hidden by the 4–8 mm long emerald-green needles. White stomatal bands, 1.2 cm long, appear to decorate the upper surface. This is a noteworthy and beautiful dwarf spruce.

A few dwarf cultivars have been derived from *P. omorika*. They are robust and hardy, lime tolerant, and grow in any well drained, friable garden soil. They thrive in urban areas, but may be injured by stagnant dampness, strongly acidic soil and magnesium deficiency in the soil. In the garden dwarf cultivars of Serbian Spruce are used in the landscape in the same way as other dwarf Spruces.

None of the Colorado Spruce cultivars are particularly sensitive to site or soil. They tolerate more hot sun and drought than do most other spruces, as well as smoke, soot and dust, at least up to a point. Occasionally, needles are attacked by aphids in late winter. Symptoms of infestation are yellowish puncture wounds on needles, which sooner or later discolor to reddish brown and fall. As soon as an insect attack is identified, the infested spruce as well as other susceptible evergreens growing nearby should be sprayed. Refer to the Insect Pest and Disease Section for specific recommendations.

P. p. 'Glauca Globosa' is a very slow growing dwarf cultivar. While young, its growth is somewhat open and irregular, but later, the plant develops into a very dense, flat-globose, 1m tall and 1.5 m wide bush. The whitish blue needles are 10–12 mm long, with 3–4 stomatal lines on each side. This is the most commonly cultivated dwarf spruce.

Picea pungens 'Glauca Procumbens'

P. p. 'Glauca Procumbens' is a shrubby, silvery gray dwarf cultivar, holding its color the year-round. It has a very irregular surface and is, therefore, more attractive and vibrant than *P. p.* 'Glauca Globosa'. However, it requires substantially more room in which to grow. It remains very low but can easily cover a square meter area. In alpine gardens, it conforms to the surface contours, growing around and over stones and rocks. A handsome planting combination is this silvery dwarf spreading over brown lava fragments.

It is believed that this cultivar originated as a lateral branch from *P. p.* 'Kosteri'. This explanation would account for the appearance of an occasional vigorous, upright shoot, which should be removed immediately.

P. p. 'Glauca Prostrata' grows mat-like to about 40 cm tall and 2 m wide. Its branches lie flat on the ground, covered with silver-blue needles. This is a beautiful cultivar for larger rock gardens or to plant above low walls.

Picea pungens 'Glauca Globosa'

Picea sitchensis 'Compacta', Pinaceae

P. sitchensis (Zone 6) is native to the Pacific North American coast, from southern Alaska to northwestern California, in damp soil and a very humid, cool, rainy fog belt. It is found growing with *Tsuga heterophylla*.

P. s. 'Compacta' is a 1–2 m tall, broadly conical dwarf cultivar with spreading branches and a very dense, uniform surface texture. The short needles are thickly crowded and radiate. They are dark green on top and have white or bluish stomatic bands beneath. With fine, blue tinged needles, this is an extraordinarily beautiful, yet seldom cultivated dwarf.

Picea sitchensis 'Nana'

Pinus Species and Cultivars

Dwarf cultivars of various pine species are among the most popular dwarf conifers. They are not demanding as to soil or site and are very attractive. Their generally loose, open habit is more natural than the stubby, dense, compact cultivars of other species of dwarf conifers.

The dwarf pines are quite suitable for front garden landscaping, for rock gardens and heath gardens, entryway and roof gardens, and containers of all shapes and sizes. Due to their relatively high drought resistance, they do very well in containers.

Dwarf pines grow in any good garden soil, as long as it is not too damp. Poorly-drained, level sites can be modified by building raised beds in which dwarf pines can then be planted. In their natural habitat, pines are light-loving. Dwarf cultivars require open, sunny locations if they are to develop optimally.

Dwarf pines blend well with other low growing species: for example, cushion-forming herbaceous perennials and small bulbs, ornamental grasses, and ground covers such as *Cotoneaster dammeri*, and *C. dammeri* 'Streib's Findling', *Gaultheria procumbens*, *Paxistima canbyi*, and most important, *Erica* and *Calluna* sp.

Pinus contorta 'Spaan's Dwarf', Pinaceae

This two-needled pine (Zone 5) is found in several different ecosystems on the Pacific Coast of North America from Alaska to Mexico. Four races of the species have been distinguished.

P. c. 'Spaan's Dwarf' develops into a vigorous, upright, rather loose and sparsely branched, 75 cm tall dwarf pine. The thick, ascending branches are covered with short, slender, medium-green needles. It is an interesting cultivar with a loose, tree-like habit.

Pinus densiflora cultivars, Pinaceae

P. densiflora (Zone 4) is found in Korea and central Japan, especially in northern Hondo. There it develops forests on old sand dunes and barren hills.

Numerous cultivars are available in Japan, but in the West, *P. d.* 'Umbraculifera', sometimes called 'Pumila', is the only one planted widely.

P. d. 'Alice Verkade' is only available from specialty nurseries. A very attractive, broad growing, densely twiggy dwarf pine, this cultivar bears long, light green needles which are yellowish green at the base. It eventually develops into a tight, globose form 70 cm high and wide.

P. d. 'Umbraculifera' only displays its true character when fully mature. At first, this two-needled pine grows as a globose shrub and only later develops its typical, umbrella-like, flattened crown which may be 2–4 m high and 5–6 m wide at maturity. *P. d.* 'Umbraculifera', is a very slow growing and maturing ornamental and is also noteworthy for its smooth, light brown branches, apple-green needles, and the freely produced cones.

Pinus densiflora 'Umbraculifera'

P. d. 'Umbraculifera' (according to Welch, its correct Japanese name is pronounced 'Tanyo-sho') is completely winter hardy but must be planted in dry, well drained soil. In damp sites, it unfortunately becomes susceptible to blister rust.

Pinus × hakkodensis, Pinaceae

P. × hakkodensis (Zone 6) is a natural hybrid of *P. parviflora* and *P. pumila* from northern Honshu, Japan. It resembles *P. pumila* in its shrubby, low habit reaching only 1.5 m tall. *P. × hakkodensis* differs most greatly from *P. pumila* in its longer, coarser and twisted needles. It grows more vigorously and sturdily than *P. pumila* so can be used in a wider range of sites.

Pinus koraiensis 'Winton', Pinaceae

This five-needled pine species (Zone 3) is found in Korea, Japan, Manchuria and the Amur district. Its cultivar, *P. k.* 'Compacta Glauca', is an especially attractive, relatively slow growing tree with thick, strong blue needles. *P. k.* 'Compacta Glauca' seems to be an American phenomenon—the same plant in Europe, Australia, and New Zealand is listed as 'Glauca'.

P. k. 'Winton' was discovered in the Hillier Nursery in 1964. When mature, it probably will be about 2 m tall and 4 m wide, but it grows so slowly that it can be included among dwarf conifers. It is one of the most beautiful dwarf pines with soft, distinct bluish white needles and a loose habit.

Pinus leucodermis 'Schmidtii', Pinaceae

P. leucodermis (Zone 5) is found in dry, limestone cliffs, often in exposed locations, in Yugoslavia, Albania, Bulgaria, Greece and Italy. The correct current epithet of the Bosnian Redcone Pine is Pinus *heldreichii* var. *leucodermis*.

P. h. 'Schmidtii' was found as a 100-year old, 3 m tall tree, in the Bosnian mountains near Sarajevo by E. Schmidt in 1926. The original grafted specimen of this beautiful, dense, hedgehog-like pine can still be seen in the Alpine Garden of Pruhonice Botanical Garden near Prague. It is now only 50–60 cm tall. It has thickly crowded, 4–5 cm long, light green needles. Grafted specimens grow somewhat faster and have a somewhat looser habit, but this may be a response to the position of the scion selected for propagation

P. h. 'Schmidtii' is an ideal plant for trough gardens due to its slow growth and resistance to drought.

P. h. 'Compact Gem', commonly offered by nurseries, is not a genuine dwarf conifer. Although it grows very slowly and compactly, it has a central trunk and reaches 3 m within 10 years.

Pinus mugo cultivars, Pinaceae

P. mugo (Zone 2) is found in the subalpine and alpine elevations of the Alps. It covers large areas and often makes up the upper limit of the timber line; up to, or slightly higher than, 2300 m. It is a tough plant which holds the soil against rock slides and avalanches. It is usually found growing with *Juniperus communis* var. *montana*, *Rhododendron ferrugineum* and *R. hirsutum*, *Erica herbacea*, *Arctostaphylos alpina*, *Clema-*

Pinus leucodermis 'Schmidtii'

Handsome little pillow-shaped bushes may suddenly explode into porch height and width!

In its natural habitat, *P. mugo* grows as well in acid moor soil as in dry, limy soil. It is, perhaps, the least exacting and hardiest of all pines, even doing well in poor sand soil in the lowlands. It is indispensable on coastal dunes as it deflects the wind and is not harmed by coastal storms or salty spray. In the garden *P. mugo* cultivars are used in the same way as *P. densiflora* 'Umbraculifera' and have the same cultural requirements.

They can be planted as single specimens or in mass plantings, in containers, rock and heath gardens, or even as hedges. They are full sun plants and do not tolerate competition from other trees and shrubs, but live easily in large groups by themselves.

tis alpina, various *Salix* species, *Dryas octopetala, Daphne mezereum, D. striata* and countless alpine perennials. It is also found in the Pyrenees, the central mountains of Germany, the Carpathians and the high Tatras.

This two-needled species is extremely variable in habit—from a completely prostrate, mat-forming shrub to an upright tree, and everything in between. The two geographically separate and botanically distinct varieties *P. mugo* ssp. *mugo* and *P. mugo* ssp. *pumilio,* with their cultivars are the most important dwarf forms used in gardens. When selecting a Mugo Pine which is to grow as a compact, dwarf specimen, a grafted plant should be purchased. When grown from seed, *P. mugo* often exhibits quite a different appearance and habit as a young plant than it does beyond the juvenile stages.

Pinus mugo 'Frisia'

267

Pinus mugo ssp. *pumilio*

Pinus mugo ssp. *pumilio*

Pinus mugo 'Gnom'

268

Pinus mugo 'Gnom'

Regulate their height and density by lightly pruning the shoot tips in summer, or by pinching the new candles on all branch tips in spring (providing the new shoot is at its maximum length and the short shoots have begun to develop). The lateral shoots should be left intact (see drawing).

Pinus nigra cultivars, Pinaceae

P. nigra (Zone 4) is found in Austria and the Balkans, in dry, limestone soil. It is often planted in gardens and parks, but grows too large for the average small, city garden.

Its cultivars are very undemanding. They thrive in hot, sunny sites in any well drained soil. Their cultural requirements are similar to those of *P. densiflora* 'Umbraculifera'.

Pinus parviflora cultivars, Pinaceae

P. parviflora (Zone 5), native to Japan, is an ideal pine for small gardens. It can be grown and maintained satisfactorily for years in small gardens and even in small flower beds.

In Japan, numerous cultivars are available from specialist nurseries, but the only dwarf cultivated with any regularity in the West is *P.* 'Adock's Dwarf'.

P. p. 'Adock's Dwarf' is a very compact, slow-growing, open, shrubby upright cultivar with short, almost horizontally spreading branches. The 15–25 mm long, slightly twisted, gray-green needles are crowded at the twig tips, whisk broom-fashion. This plant is truly a treasure among dwarf conifers.

P. p. 'Shirbubana' grows faster than

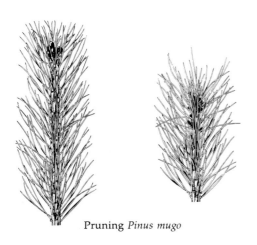

Pruning *Pinus mugo*

269

Pinus mugo Cultivars and Varieties

Name	Height (cm); Habit, Branching Habit	Needles
'Frisia'	200 cm; up to 1.4 m wide; thickly branched, rigid, upright branches	Moss-green
'Gnom'	200 cm tall and wide; dense, globose habit, numerous, well branched twigs; heart-shaped buds	Dense, radiate; 3.5–4.5 cm long, deep green
'Hesse'	150–200 cm; cushion-like, very dense; twigs short, very crowded	7–8 cm long, somewhat twisted; dark green
'Humpy'	Very slow growing, annual growth 3–4 cm; short branches, very dense; striking red buds	Deep green; 15 mm long
'Kissen'	30 cm tall and 80 cm wide, annual growth only about 5 cm; flat and dense, numerous lateral branches	10 mm long, dark green
'Knapenburg'	100, compact and dense; uneven texture	3 cm long, uniform length; deep green
'Kobold'	Broad globose; rather rigid, thick branches; distinctive brown buds	Dense, straight; 2–3.5 cm long; glossy green
'Kokarde'	Similar to var. *mughus* in growth rate and habit; rare in cultivation, but needle coloration makes it a collector's item	Two gold-yellow spots arranged radially; when viewed from the top, they appear to be 2 yellow rings
'Laurin'	Upright to globose habit; grows about 10 cm per year	Striking dark green
ssp. *mugo*	A local race from the eastern Alps and the Balkans; usually not taller than 200 cm even in lowlands; shrubby to prostrate habit; limbs angularly bent; more often cultivated than the grafted cultivars	3–4 cm; often sickle-shaped and slightly twisted
'Ophir'	Flat-globose; 60 cm wide and 30–40 cm tall in 6 years	Golden-yellow on the top and sunny side of the plant, green on the lower; 4–7 cm long
ssp. *pumilio*	Native to mountains in central and eastern Europe, the Alps, Carpathians, and Balkans; 1 m tall, 3 m wide; shrubby prostrate habit; grows with uneven, crowded, prostrate limbs and upright twigs; very popular	Variable in length; standing upward
'Rigi'	3 m tall and half as wide; broadly conical cultivar with rigidly upright limbs; very pretty but not a genuine dwarf form	

Pinus nigra **Cultivars**

Cultivar	Height (cm); Habit, Branching Habit	Needles
'Globosa'	250, somewhat taller when mature; broad conical short branches, distinctive scaffold limbs; light brown buds, slightly resinous	12–16 cm long, somewhat twisted
'Helga'	Compact and slow growing, shrubby cultivar with short, stiff branches; has striking white buds and needle sheaths; especially handsome	Dark green, rather short
'Horni-brookiana'	60 cm tall and broad in 10 years; shrubby, spreading habit; limbs thick and rigid, ascending to upright; an especially beautiful cultivar	5–6 cm long, closely crowded; straight and rigid, sharply pointed; glossy dark green
'Nana'	300, grows 4–5 cm per year; upright and broad; buds are covered with wax in fall, a splendid plant. Awarded the silver medal at Boskoop in 1968.	6–7 cm, somewhat twisted, dark green, a good color contrast to the light buds
'Pygmaea'	Grows very slowly; twigs close-set, dense; broadly globular when mature, and about 6 feet high	5–6 cm, rigid and twisted
'Spielberg'	About 2 m after 15 years; at first globe-shaped, later broadly pyramidal; branches without terminal or lateral buds in summer; this cultivar makes additional small twigs with short needles and only weakly-formed buds	Vigorous; 10 cm long; twisted; spreading at a very flat angle, umbrella-fashion

Pinus nigra 'Helga'

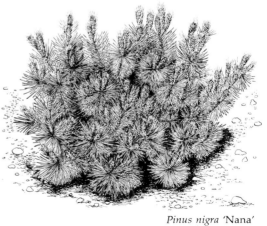

Pinus nigra 'Nana'

271

'Adock's Dwarf', but much slower than the non-grafted *P. p.* 'Glauca'. It is fine-needled, gray-blue, bushy, and grows as wide as it does tall.

P. parviflora and its cultivars do best in well drained, loamy soil. They grow well in containers only if given sufficient maintenance, especially regular watering. In the garden, they are used as are other dwarf conifers. They do, however, grow exceptionally slowly.

Pinus parviflora 'Adock's Dwarf'

Pinus pumila, Pinaceae

P. pumila (Zone 5) is found in northeastern Siberia and from Sachalin to Japan. It develops thick, impenetrable colonies at the upper edge of the timber line.

This East Asian pine, related to the European Mountain Pine, is often described as the most beautiful of all the pines. *P. pumila* is a low growing, (50 cm to 3 m tall) five-needled pine which lacks a central trunk. Branches are prostrate-ascending with erect tips. Its 4–7(10) cm long, blue-bloomy needles are densely crowded on the branches. Needles are blue-green above, with 5–6 very noticeable stomatal lines and dark green on the underside. Deep red, male flowers which appear in early spring are especially handsome. The egg-shaped female cones are 3.5–4.5 cm long, violet at first, and later turning brown; the scale tips curve backwards. The cones ripen during the summer of the second year.

Due to its broad range of distribution, the species has developed many variations in habit and height, as well as needle form, color and length. Consequently there is considerable confusion about the correct identification and naming of them. *P. pumila* is often listed in nursery catalogues as a dwarf variety of *P. cembra*. Also, the plant often described as *"P. cembra* 'Pygmaea' " is identical to *P. pumila*. The cones of this plant are shorter and narrower than those of *P. cembra*, which ripen during the third year, rather than the second year.

The blue-needled cultivars of *P. pumila* are readily available in nurseries. In addition, specialty nurseries offer a selection of cultivars which vary in height and habit. All cultivars of *P. pumila* thrive in gardens where Mugo Pines grow well. They need very good drainage, and if they receive too much moisture, the distinctive blue color in the needles is lost. If necessary, the growing site might be artificially raised.

Pinus strobus cultivars, Pinaceae

P. strobus (Zone 3) is native to eastern North America, from Canada to the Allegheny Mountains. It grows at low elevations in damp soil, but at higher

Pinus pumila Cultivars

Cultivar	Height (cm); Habit, Branching Habit	Needles
'Draijers Dwarf'	5–6 cm per year; compact, spreading	3–4 cm long; loosely arranged, very blue
'Dwarf Blue'	Very flat and spreading, much broader than tall	3–4 cm long; widely erect, white stomatic bands
'Glauca'*	Selected and grafted wild form; grows slowly; broad bushy habit; sturdy branches	Gray-blue
'Globe'	Up to 2 m wide and tall; globose and very dense; relatively vigorous growth	5–7 cm long; straight or slightly curved; beautiful blue-green
'Jeddeloh'	Grows 7–10 cm per year; flat, broad spreading habit; branches ascend slanting outward, with "bird nest" in the center; healthy and vigorous	Densely crowded on twigs; 3–5 cm long; apple-green underside, bluish white above
'Saphir'	Slow, irregular growth	Short, beautifully blue

*In some north German nurseries another 'Glauca' is marketed, with a similar strong, upright habit but with very long, twisted needles. The mother plant is in the forestry Botanical Garden at Hannoverische-Münden, supposedly grown from seed collected in Sapporo in 1928.

Pinus pumila 'Globe'

elevations in dry, rocky and gravelly soils. Europeans know this species as Weymouth's Pine, while Americans refer to it as Eastern White Pine.

P. strobus and its few dwarf cultivars grow best in moist, sandy loam. Both heavy wet and dry alkaline soil should be avoided. They tolerate more shade than any other pines. They are susceptible to blister rusts under environmental conditions which favor the disease.

P. p. 'Brevifolia' is a bushy, very slow growing dwarf cultivar reaching 1–2 m high and wide when mature. It has a flat top and thin, 2.5–3.5 cm long needles. It is a bizarre, sparsely branched plant suitable for small trough gardens.

P. s. 'Krueger's Liliput' was developed by the Krueger Nursery from a sport of *P. strobus* 'Radiata'. It differs from *P.* 'Radiata' in its weaker growth and shorter, blue-tinted needles.

P. s. 'Minima' is distinguished from *P.* 'Radiata' in substantially less thrifty growth. With a flat globose habit, it is much wider than tall. Its thin twigs bear very thin, but fairly rigid, 22 mm long, somewhat curved, dark green needles.

P. s. 'Radiata' is the most commonly cultivated *P. s.* cultivar. It is a globose

273

dwarf, reaching 1.5 m tall and wide when mature. Twigs are thickly crowded and quite slender. The 7–9 cm long needles are directed upwards, never drooping. Needle color is blue-green on top and green beneath. With its delicate, soft needles and irregular surface texture, this is a decorative cultivar (sometimes labeled 'Nana').

P. s. 'Reinshaus' has an even denser surface texture than *P.* 'Radiata'. It grows wider than tall with a flat, globose, almost disc-like, habit.

Pinus sylvestris 'Globosa Viridis'

Pinus sylvestris cultivars, Pinaceae

P. sylvestris (Zone 2) is found from central and northern Europe to Siberia and East Asia. It develops extensive, pure stands in poor sandy soils, but also thrives in dry alkaline or damp moor soils. As a tree of northern continental climates, it tolerates extremely low temperatures, has a very deep and extensive root system and requires full, day-long sunlight.

Its numerous dwarf cultivars are as undemanding as to climate and soil as their parents. As with all dwarf conifers, these may be planted as single specimens or in groups. Culturally, they are treated in the same fashion as *P. densiflora* 'Umbraculifera.'

Pinus sylvestris 'Hibernica'

Pinus wallichiana 'Nana', Pinaceae

This five-needled pine (Zone 5) with characteristic "weeping" needles, develops extensive forests in the Himalayas, with *Cedrus deodara*. The traditional epithet for this plant was *Pinus excelsa;* currently, it appears in taxonomic literature as *P. griffithii,* and *P. wallichiana.*

P. w. 'Nana' develops into a rather open, broadly funnel-shaped bush, flattened on top. As a dwarf form, it hardly reaches 60 cm tall in 10 years. Its airy, silvery, 10 cm long, slender, persistent needles are clustered horizontally in groups of five. It is a striking dwarf conifer which is much hardier than would be expected given its natural habitat.

Pinus sylvestris Cultivars

Cultivar	Height (cm); Habit, Branching Habit	Needles
'Albyns'	Original plant is 2.5 m wide and 30 cm tall, growing about 10 cm per year; prostrate, branches are horizontal to slightly ascending	Gray-green
'Argentea Compacta'	Exceeds 2 m only when very old; upright and oval when young; later, globose to broadly conical	Silvery gray; 6 cm long; dense
'Beuvronensis'	Grows only to 50 cm in 25 years; slow growing; irregular form; very branchy; green, glossy twigs; buds are reddish brown and very resinous; highly recommended	About 1.5 cm long; blue-green
'Compressa'	Annual growth 4–5 cm; broadly columnar, sometimes hemispherical when mature; numerous, upright branches, shoots ascend at an acute angle, short and rigid; an especially ornamental cultivar	1–2 cm long; clustered, occasionally twisted
'Doone Valley'	English dwarf; grows slowly into a dense, narrow conical bush; very loose, open texture	Intense blue
'Globosa Viridis'	100–150 cm; globe-shaped to ovate; branches are short and crowded, spreading, prostrate; needles differ significantly from other cultivars	To 10 cm long; coarse, very twisted, somewhat rigid; dark green; new needles appear in late summer and cover the winter buds
'Hibernica'	Mature plants grow 10 cm per year; oval, with sturdy branches; winter buds are strikingly red	Rather short, blue
'Nana'	About 50 cm high; bushy, very twiggy habit; branches very short, directed upwards. In nurseries often confused with 'Watereri'	3 cm long; widely spaced, blue-green
'Repanda'	Annual growth 10–15 cm; wide, quite flat, wide-spreading; after a few years it forms short, horizontal lateral shoots	5–8 cm long; gray-green
'Watereri'	Slow growing to 3–4 m high and wide or more, grows about 5 cm per year; upright and broadly conical at first, more globose when older; develops a 3–4 m wide crown above a rigid and twisted short trunk; one of the most commonly cultivated cultivars	2.5–4 cm; blue-gray, narrow, rigid and twisted

Podocarpus nivalis, Podocarpaceae

The mountain ranges of New Zealand (Zone 6 southward) are the nature habitat of *Podocarpus nivalis.*

P. nivalis is an evergreen, decumbent, 1–3 m tall, much branched shrub with short twigs. The spirally-borne, stiff, leathery olive-green needles are reminiscent of yew. The narrow strap-shaped needles are 5–15 mm long and 2–4 mm wide. Male plants are adorned with 5–15 mm long, violet-red, axillary flowering cones in May.

Pinus sylvestris 'Argentea Compacta'

Pinus wallichiana 'Nana'

Unlike other species of this rather large genus, *P. nivalis* is sufficiently winter hardy for continental climates. This is a very slow growing dwarf suitable for rock and heath gardens. It thrives in any good garden soil, but requires a warm, protected, sunny to partly shady location. In severe winters, additional protection should be provided.

Pseudotsuga menziesii 'Fletcheri', Pinaceae

P. menziesii (Douglas Fir, Zone 4) has a very extensive distribution in western North America, from British Columbia to central California, and north and central Mexico. The Coast Douglas Fir (var. *menziesii*) is found in the Pacific rain forests on acid, humus soil. The Rocky Mountain

Douglas Fir (var. *glauca*) grows on stony, alkaline, dry soil at the higher elevations of the Rocky Mountains and Sierra Nevadas. Only the latter is adaptable to a variety of environments.

Of its numerous local races, varieties and cultivars, only *P. m.* 'Fletcheri' is sufficiently slow-growing and small to be included in small gardens.

P. m. 'Fletcheri' grows very slowly and will only reach 1–3 m tall after many years. It forms a flattened-globose, open, bushy shrub. Its branches are of uneven lengths and are arranged in layers. Needles are 15–20 mm long, rather soft, and somewhat twisted and bowed. They are green on top and have 2 blue-green stomatal bands beneath.

P. m. 'Fletcheri' is a decorative dwarf conifer for sunny to partly shady locations, wherever dwarf conifers are commonly planted. Quite adaptable, it thrives in any good garden soil, but heavy clay, infertile sand, and wet sites should be avoided.

one of the most useful evergreen hedge plants as well as being the most shade tolerant understory shrub. It also thrives in sunny locations, grows in almost any good soil, but does not tolerate highly acid soil.

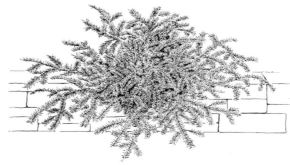

Taxus baccata 'Repandens'

Taxus baccata cultivars, Taxaceae

T. baccata (Zone 6) is found in Europe, North Africa and western Asia Minor. In central Europe, however, it occurs naturally in only a few places. It is often found as an understory shrub in more or less sparse, mature, lowland beech forests, growing on porous sedimentary soils.

Most of the many cultivars of yew are not dwarfs, but are very popular in gardens for a wide range of landscape uses. No other conifer will tolerate as much shade, or regenerate as well after pruning as *T. baccata* and its cultivars. It is

Taxus baccata 'Repandens Aurea'

Taxus baccata Cultivars

Cultivar	Height (cm); Habit, Branching Habitat	Needles
'Adpressa Aurea'	300 cm; ascending, broad bushy limbs of uneven lengths; thickly twiggy; grows much slower than 'Adpressa'	Very short, only 5–9 mm long; golden-yellow on branch tips, others yellowish
'Amersfoort'	Very slow growing, loose and open; rigid, spreading limbs and short, densely crowded twigs; a very distinctive form reminiscent of *Podocarpus* or *Buxus*	5–7 mm long, 3–4 mm wide; radiate; dark green above, lighter beneath
'Procumbens'	50 cm high, about 2 m wide; decumbent, densely and unevenly twiggy; young shoots thickly covered with needles, older branches bare	Quite variable, to 15 mm long; fairly stiff; borne almost vertically; green on top, light bronze in winter
'Repandens'-'Tafeleibe'	40–50 cm, 2–5 m wide; prostrate and broad spreading; main limbs are horizontal, lateral twigs curved down; most commonly cultivated of all slow growing cultivars; good as a ground covering understory shrub	20–30 mm long; sickle-shaped, glossy dark green on top with distinct midrib, dull green beneath
'Repandens Aurea'	Presumably not an independent variety, but a lateral shoot propagation from *I.* 'Dovastoniana Aurea'; grows very flat and can be several meters wide	

Taxus cuspidata 'Nana', Taxaceae

T. cuspidata (zone 4) is found in Japan, primarily in the mountain ranges around Yokohama. It also grows in Manchuria, Korea, and in Sachalin, always at higher elevations.

Its cultivars, as well as the 20 m tall species, have the same garden uses and landscape applications as *Taxus baccata*. They also have the same cultural requirements, but are substantially more frost hardy and, therefore, very valuable.

T. c. 'Nana' grows very slowly, seldom exceeding 1 m tall and 3 m wide; with advanced age, it may be somewhat taller, wider, and of irregular habit. Its rigid limbs spread widely. The branches and twigs are short, and needles are 20–25 mm long and dull green.

Taxus × media 'Nidiformis', Taxaceae

Of the numerous hybrids currently available which have resulted from the European *T. baccata* and the Japanese *T. cuspidata*, only *T.* 'Nidiformis' is a dwarf.

T. × m. 'Nidiformis' is a female cultivar. It grows with horizontally spreading branches resulting in a "bird's nest" depression in the center. Propagated from a cutting, it is very slow growing, about 20–25 cm in 8–9 years. Its needles are 15 mm long and deep green.

Taxus baccata 'Procumbens'

Thuja occidentalis cultivars, Cupressaceae

The occidental Arborvitee, *T. occidentalis* (Zone 2) is native to the northeastern United States and Canada. It appears in boreal spruce and fir forests, often growing in cold, swampy soil.

More than 100 cultivars (Zone 4) of this variable species are known. Of them, a few are interesting dwarf cultivars displaying variations in habit, branching and needle

Thuja occidentalis 'Danica'

279

Thuja occidentalis Dwarf Cultivars

Cultivar	Height (cm); Habit	Branches and twigs	Needles
'Danica'	Very slow-growing, 50 cm in 20 years; smoothly globose, may be somewhat broader than high; very popular	Dense, upright	Scale-like; apple-green, bluish green in winter
'Globosa'	100–200 cm; dense globose	Overlapping, dense; flat branches; spreading, ascending	Light green, gray-green in winter
'Little Champion'	Fast growing to 50 cm, slower to 100 cm; spherical, compact	Loose, upright, ascending	Dark green, somewhat brown in winter
'Little Gem'	100 cm, up to 2 m wide; slow growing; flattened-globose	Limbs in part horizontally spreading; twigs curly, flat, thin, some vertical, some horizontal	Dark green, russet brown in winter
'Mecki'	Slow growing; symmetrical; globose	Flat, all erect; dense	Apple-green, brown tips in winter
'Ohlendorffii'	100 cm; irregularly globose; unusual, somewhat bizarre cultivar	Long, upright, only twiggy on the tips; thread-like twigs overlap in a disorderly fashion	Two forms: on long shoots scale-like, small; others needle-like, 12 mm long, reddish-brown
'Recurva Nana'	100–200 cm; globose, conical with age	Upright to spreading; pendulous tips, twisted shoots	Matte-green, russet in winter
'Tiny Tim'	Very slow growing, in 12 years 30 cm tall and 60 cm wide; flattened globe-shaped	Very slender	Light green, brownish in winter
'Umbraculifera'	80 cm high, 1.5 cm wide; hemispherical to flattened umbrella-shaped	Branches nearly erect; somewhat twisted; slightly pendulous	Thin, green, blue-frosted

color. They are used effectively as specimens or in groups, but certainly are not as commonly favored as the spruces and pines. They thrive in almost any garden soil, as long as it is damp, in sunny to partly shady, humid locations. They do not tolerate dry sandy soil, or root competition and leaf drip from the canopy of large trees.

Thuja orientalis cultivars, Cupressaceae

The oriental Arborvitae, *T. orientalis* (Zone 6) is distributed from the Trans-Caucausus, to China, Manchuria, Korea and Japan.

This species and its cultivars tolerate even damper soils and higher ambient

Thuja occidentalis 'Globosa'

humidity than do its occidental relatives but are less frost hardy. *T. o.* 'Aurea Nana' is sufficiently frost hardy only for mild climates and winters, but is usually damaged in extreme winters.

T. o. 'Aurea Nana' is one of the most beautiful yellow-leaved dwarf conifers. It has a globose to oval form deriving from a dense, very twiggy habit, and seldom exceeds 60 cm in height. It grows with numerous, slender, vertically arranged twiggy branches which are nearly parallel. New needles emerge in spring and are light yellowish green. Later, needles appear more light green and are brownish yellow in winter.

T. o. 'Rosedalis' has fine, heather-like leaves. It develops into a small, densely twiggy, ovate shrub with very slender branches and twigs. It grows 3 to 9 cm per year and remains dwarf. The spring growth is yellowish, and the plant's very soft needles gradually turn light bluish green and are purple-blue in winter. Some horticulturists list this as *T. o.* 'Rosedalis Compacta'.

281

Thuja orientalis 'Aurea Nana'

Thuja orientalis 'Aurea Nana'

Thujopsis dolabrata 'Nana'
Cupressaceae

T. dolabrata (Zone 6) has two distinct geographical areas in the north and south of Japan, where it is found in damp forests. The dwarf form *T. d.* 'Nana' was introduced into Europe in 1861.

T. d. 'Nana' is a charming, dense, bushy dwarf conifer without a central trunk. It grows scarcely 50 cm tall and forms thick, spreading cushions. The flat twigs are finer than those of the species. Glossy green leaves have white markings beneath and remain a bright green summer and winter.

'Nana' is very hardy, thrives in rich soil, high humidity and a cool site. It tolerates shade but not overhanging branches of other trees and plants. It thrives in sunny locations, and makes a beautiful border or low bedding plant.

Tsuga canadensis cultivars, Pinaceae

T. canadensis (Zone 4) is found in eastern North America from Hudson Bay to the Carolinas and Georgia.

It grows in mixed forests with beech and Sugar Maples, as well as in conifer forests with white pine, from Hudson Bay to the Carolinas.

A few dwarf cultivars of *T. canadensis* are usually available in nurseries, as well as some tree forms. With their attractive needles and graceful habit, they are among the most charming of all dwarf conifers. They thrive in sheltered, partly shady locations in fertile, moist, moderately heavy loam. They do poorly in hot, dry, sunny locations or alkaline soils, and cannot compete with the root systems of other woody plants. They can only be successfully grown in containers if watered regularly.

As a rule, retail nurseries offer only a few of the more common cultivars. Extremely slow growing cultivars such as 'Horsford Dwarf', 'Hussii', 'Minuta' or 'Ruggs Washington Dwarf' can only be found in specialty nurseries.

Tsuga canadensis 'Gracilis Oldenburg'

Tsuga canadensis 'Gracilis Oldenburg'

Tsuga canadensis **Cultivars**

Cultivar	Height (cm); Habit	Branches	Needles
'Bennett'	80–100 cm, annual growth about 15 cm; compact, somewhat broader than high, flat, depression in the middle	Slightly ascending from the middle, tips bent downward; fan-shaped spreading	10 mm long, usually shorter; dense, light green
'Gracilis Oldenburg'	Very slow growing, in 10 years 25 cm tall and 40–50 cm wide; 2 m tall after 75 years; hemispherical with a bowl-like recess in the middle when young. An elegant cultivar, also known as 'Nana Gracilis'.	Pendulous tips, very short shoots	6–10 mm long; deep green
'Jeddeloh'	Remains dwarf; hemispherical; appear spirally arranged when viewed from the top with an almost funnel-shaped recess in the center; coarser and less elegant than 'Gracilis Oldenburg', but easier to propagate, and widely distributed		Stout, directed outwards; 8–16 mm; apple-green, underside lighter with gray-white stomatal bands
'Pendula'*	When mature 2–3 m tall, somewhat wider; weeping, cascading; elegant	Horizontally spreading, loose, unevenly distributed branches and down-curved, pendent twigs	Resemble the species

*Collective name; 'Brookline', 'Gable Weeping', 'Sargentii', et al. have all been referred to as 'Pendula' Check description with local nurseries for corresponding referent.

Sources

Far from every dwarf tree and shrub suitable for small gardens are dealt with in this book. Those who wish to pursue these fascinating plants in greater depth should consult the books dealing with various genera.

Garden Centers do not carry many of the plants included here, but some are willing to order from specialty growers.

Bibliography

Cox, P. A. *Dwarf Rhododendrons.* London: B. T. Batsford Ltd, 1973.

Fletcher, H. R. *The International Rhododendron Register.* London: The Royal Horticulture Society, 1958.

Foster, H. L. *Rock Gardening.* Portland, Oregon: Timber Press, 1983.

Heath, H. R. *Collectors Alpines.* Portland: Timber Press, 1983.

Heath, H. R. *Rock Plants for Small Gardens.* Portland: Timber Press, 1985.

Krüssmann, G. *Manual of Cultivated Conifers.* Portland: Timber Press, 1985.

Krüssmann, G. *Manual of Cultivated Broadleaved Trees and Shrubs, Vol. 1–3.* Portland: Timber Press, 1984–86.

Welch, H. J. *Manual of Dwarf Conifers.* New York: Theophrastus Publishers/Garland STPM Press, 1979.

Index